Just for the Summer

iUniverse, Inc.
New York   Bloomington

Just for the Summer

Memoirs from a Mental Hospital

iUniverse books may be ordered through booksellers or by contacting:

iUniverse
1663 Liberty Drive
Bloomington, IN 47403
www.iuniverse.com
1-800-Authors (1-800-288-4677)

ISBN: 978-0-595-48536-9 (pbk)
ISBN: 978-0-595-60631-3 (ebk)

Printed in the United States of America

iUniverse rev. date: 8/10/2009

Just for the Summer

by
Laurel Lorraine Lancer, PhD.

Contents

Acknowledgments

I would like to thank certain people who have been of great support to me over the years and encouraged me to write my story: my family and special friends—Anne, Joyce, Ruth, Mary, Bill, Dale, Richard, and Craig; counselors—Joe, Alan, Cal, and Jan; and my very helpful editor, Valerie Holladay.

Preface

This is a true story. All characters and events are true. It is also a memoir. The major part of the book was written some years ago while I still remembered the specifics of all that had happened and could still tell the story accurately. Because my later doctorate degree was in psychology, and I had done some writing, I felt I should write these memoirs.

When I originally wrote the story, I sent out some query letters. I started working with one publisher, but then another publishing company bought it out. The book was neglected as we both became busy with other projects. Having recently retired, I have again placed my focus on this book.

The patients' first names are real since the events happened so long ago I did not feel that anyone could be identified. Nevertheless, the family names and doctors' names have been changed.

I felt this book should be written for three reasons. First, it illustrates the consequences of poor parenting to children. Long-term damages are incurred in their personalities. Both my husband and I had families that had poor skills for rearing children. Our backgrounds made it almost impossible to adjust to our marriage. We need to be more aware of the effects of parenting and protect our children.

Second, I wanted to expose the poor treatment of the mentally ill and the insensitivity in the old "mental hospitals." In the 1950s and 1960s husbands were actually able to commit their wives for any perceived "misbehaviors." Electroshock and insulin shock were prevalent forms of treatment. I wanted to expose the way the therapies were administered. Electroshock is still used to some extent to this day although it has been refined. On the other hand, insulin shock was dangerous and barbaric and has been discontinued, much like snake pits and lobotomies. Dr. Ashford, to whom I refer, died of lung cancer that same year that I was in the hospital. The old hospital in the book has since been torn down, and the group of psychiatrists who ran it was disbanded; many are deceased. Many things have improved since those days, but we still need to give better care to those dealing with mental and/or emotional trauma.

My third reason is this: I wanted to describe thoroughly what it is to be anxiety-ridden, to face panic attacks, and deal with the resultant problem of agoraphobia that often results. There are countless individuals suffering from these symptoms, and I would like them to know they are not unique or alone. Also, they need to know that life can improve without insulin comas or electroshocks.

Other mental disorders are described in this book, and these cases and precipitating causes are accurate. I hope my book will give insight and empathy for those so suffering and provide more understanding to those who care for the mentally ill.

Dr. Laurel Lorraine Lancer

Chapter One
A Growing Anxiety

All except the very deepest puddles in the pavement had been sucked back into the muggy late summer air. The air hovered heavily over the neat row of houses, all oriented identically on their own lot, but each with its eaves and wooden trim across the kitchen window a varied shade of Montgomery Ward's "specially priced exterior matte." A few houses flaunted an added carport, a larger porch overhang, or even some rock veneer. These small differences only served to belie the sameness of each house and the similarity of the families within. The air embarrassed them all with equality and sat heavily waiting to release more rain or to be blown dry from the West. Its heaviness made the sky seem less luminous and decreased the reflections from the dwindling evening traffic. A police car moved slowly through the neighborhood displaying lights that made circles only a few feet ahead of the car and then disappeared in the black. No one observed it.

Neither did anyone appear to notice one of the doors within the tract open to permit my husband, Martin, and me to follow our walkway to the dark street. I walked behind Martin, my head lowered, partly to watch my footing, and partly in denial to myself that anyone might see although I was aware that at least two of the houses held inhabitants who "knew." I was feeling dizzy and a little confused so I let Martin carry the worn weekender. The tacky feeling of the rainy air increased the dampness that I experienced in my hands and feet when the anxiety took hold; the black night exaggerated the difficulty I had focusing my vision. I felt my way along the walk with my feet, keeping each close to the ground and setting each down haltingly, to avoid any irregularity in the cement that, combined with my weak ankle, would plunge me into unseen darkness, causing all my pent-up terror to release and alarm the entire block of residents and thus call attention to our departure.

I edged into the seat of the car, no doubt stoic and controlled to anyone watching but trembling inside. Martin placed the case next to my feet. I wished it were not in my way, although I did like to have everything within reach; I knew I would become confused and worried about how to reassemble everything upon our arrival and that would cause even more stress.

Martin had not spoken at all. I did not know if this meant displeasure, preoccupation, or concern for my feelings. He got into the driver's seat and I flinched as the car started and the headlights flashed on. If only we could shoot out of there, noiselessly and unseen, and arrive at our destination in seconds, I thought. My apprehension about this trip had gripped me all day making me coldly unresponsive to anything. I felt unreal and disconnected.

I wasn't even sure if I had said goodbye to anyone in the house. The baby was in bed, but awake, and Karen had hovered nearby, watching as Martin and I got ready. This had annoyed and upset me. Why hadn't Martin sent her across the street to the sitter's? I couldn't look at my five-year old and didn't want to speak to her. What if she started to cry? She hadn't, but her frightened, puzzled look bothered me even more. I had told Martin to explain to Karen that I would be back in a few days and that she needn't worry. I really didn't feel secure enough to speak to Karen by myself, and I didn't think Martin had done as I had asked. As I sat in the car, I didn't look back at the house for fear I might see Karen looking after us. Had I kissed her or said goodbye? I couldn't remember.

When I was a girl, my own mother had left us once, a little like this, but in an ambulance. I had been offered an ambulance for a similar trip last summer, but I had declined. I had remembered how frightened I had been as a child, seeing the flashing lights and the neighbors standing about. Maybe that was why I chose to sneak away now. When the ambulance had borne my mother away, we children had been taken to a neighbor's house and told to wait there until our father returned. The memory was as clear to me as though it were last night. I had stared at a picture of Jesus on the neighbor's wall and prayed so hard that I almost felt like exploding, "Please let everything be all right!" I had prayed over and over. But it hadn't been.

Why was I repeating this scenario for Karen and the baby? No, I told myself. I *wasn't*. *My* mother had been crazy, really crazy, screaming and tearing at her hair. I was quiet. I was controlled. True, I needed help but it was for "other things." As I sat in the car, I focused on my physical sensations—the tingling in my hands, the confusion in my head, and the tenseness in my arms and legs.

There wasn't much traffic on the streets, thank heaven. It was as late as Martin could arrange for us to come. I dug my nails into my palms and whispered "serenity" to myself several quick times even though this trick had never worked for me before and I was far too nervous now to concentrate on the word. My pulse seemed to race and I felt shaky. I could feel my toes curled tightly within my shoes but at least my shoes were still on and I hadn't pulled my knees up to my chest yet. I started to ask how many more minutes till we would arrive, but instead I clenched my jaw harder and said nothing.

Martin always seemed patient when I was "shook up," but tonight I felt a coldness in his responses that told me he was annoyed. Another red light! Oh God! How many more stops? How many more minutes? Every time the car went over even a small dip in the road, I felt as if every nerve in my body was suffering an assault. I tried to breathe deeply but this didn't work for me either. The experts had all these tricks that would supposedly help you not to panic; they probably have never even had an anxiety attack, I told myself, proud that I could even think the thought through to its conclusion. Usually when the panic hit hard, all I could do was sit frozen, legs to chest, heart racing, eyes not focusing, jaw clenched, and repeat frantic pleas in my mind. Then, if relief did not come, I would dissolve into a sobbing uncontrolled pile of insanity.

Even now the electrical charges that seemed to flow through my body had all my nerve terminals activated, and I tried to control the impulse to cry out. And yet despite the aroused sensitivity in each sensory channel, there was still a strange numbness that insulated my mental capacities. It was difficult to concentrate. I lost my sense of direction and balance. I couldn't reason effectively. The best I could do, like now, was try to maintain a normal outward appearance and wait in agony for the trip to be over.

Neither Martin nor I spoke, which was a relief to me, although I wondered if he were annoyed with me or just trying to be considerate. The muted atmosphere, caused by the earlier rain, seemed to distance the few cars from my immediate environment; the muggy air seemed to serve as a protective insulation. I could see the cars from the corners of my eyes but would not let myself focus on them as other people were upsetting to me now. The vehicles seemed less threatening after dark, and I could ignore the fact that the people inside could pass judgment or place themselves in my way, arousing frustration in me, and then anger. Cars were inanimate objects; they might sometimes be in the wrong places but were never deliberately at fault.

I kept my head lowered and focused my eyes on the familiar surroundings within the car. I had asked Martin to take back streets because of my fear of lots of people and cars. He reluctantly chose side streets to avoid traffic and traffic lights when at all possible. Taller two-story houses and mature trees with frightening shadows announced to me that I was no longer in my safe suburban blocks. Seconds stretched to minutes and minutes to eternities. Finally, Martin slowed and moved toward the curbing.

The car stopped on the dark, tree-lined, residential street. When Martin came around to open my door, I felt myself stiffen and tried to make all my body parts work. The entrance was well lit and the only lights on the street were coming from the old white three-story structure. The moon was full and had emerged from the few heavy clouds that remained in the sky. This eerie light would help me find my footing along the walkway. I remembered that my grandmother had always said that everyone in the family reacted strangely to the full moon. They all went a little crazy. Perhaps that was part of what had precipitated my need to come here.

The building wasn't exactly as I remembered it from my first visit and the strangeness of things always upset me. I grabbed Martin's arm and climbed out of the car. The dankness of the night air and the absence of life around us added to the dreamlike quality of the night. I took careful steps, trying my hardest to walk evenly up the sidewalk, so as not to seem out of control. Then, with sudden orchestration, the crickets in the heavily arbored street initiated their concert. All noises seemed exaggerated and penetrating to my ears. The rhythmic high drone of the insects made me want to cover my ears. But I was afraid the extra coordination needed to lift my arms would interfere with the concentration I needed to propel myself normally, despite my firm hold on Martin for my balance.

Oh God, I'm really here, *again,* I thought. Then I spoke hurriedly to myself, assuring myself that it was not the same. *I am different than the others who return,* I told myself. *I'll just be here for a couple of days. Just until they see how "together" I am.* Martin had even said so.

"Why, they probably won't even keep you," he had said earlier. "Maybe just a couple of days. They'll just talk to you. It's nothing like last time."

I prayed that he was right, but on some level I knew that I felt about the same, and that those feelings had been quicker in solidifying this time. Perhaps this time, I thought, they could pull me away from depression more quickly than before and the nightmare would soon be over. Caught up in my thoughts, I let my foot drag over an irregular square in the walk and I stumbled, catching myself with Martin's arm. I wanted to swear but talking would also interfere with my singleness of intent to get to the door without falling or fainting. Besides, Martin hated it when I used that kind of language, and I didn't feel strong enough to cope with his censorship. His annoyance and disapproval of me made me feel so very insecure and I needed his alliance now. I stopped anxiously at the entry and looked at him, watching for some reassurance as we made our presence known. Then Martin rang the bell.

A white-uniformed orderly answered the bell and led us to a rather nice office behind the admissions station and front desk. I didn't remember that there had been offices here but it made sense. It was good to see some logic. It helped me feel that I wasn't completely absent from reality. I dreaded trying to talk to anyone and hoped that Martin would handle everything. I didn't want to seem incompetent but I also didn't want to fall apart in front of the personnel here. Maybe I could "look" intelligent and capable and just keep my confusion and inner turmoil to myself. The muscles in my feet, legs, and arms were all tight and strained but I had learned to hold my hands and face in a relaxed position and appear as if I were okay. The music teacher in the school where I used to teach had told me, "You always seem so calm. *You* were the last one I suspected." That had been three years earlier when my panics at work got so bad that stepping out into the hall for a few deep breaths no longer provided any relief. So I had told my principal that I would have to leave. I had tried to make it to spring break, but just couldn't manage it.

I had begun crying frequently, at home (though only in the shower where Martin and little Karen couldn't hear), and in the car (making excuses to drive myself around in the evenings and making unnecessary trips to the store after dark, when I felt more comfortable). My tears were partly from sadness that I had not escaped some predisposed tendency to insanity, and partly from the fear and desperation of wanting things to get better just from sheer desire on my part. The spring break would have given me some time to "pull myself together," in my father's words. But things only seemed to get worse so I had admitted to the principal that I had a problem with my nerves.

"What is your doctor doing for you?" he had asked.

"I'm taking a tranquilizer but I've just started and I don't know if it will help." I responded.

He had asked me to give it a while, if I would. He hadn't seen how really upset I could get or he would never have asked this of me. And my one great fear was that I would fall apart in front of someone, especially my third graders. In fact, I had come so close to doing this that I felt relief each day that I succeeded in completing the school day before racing home to safety.

Several days later the principal had asked how I was doing. "What do they say is wrong?" he asked.

"They say I have something called 'free floating anxieties,'" I said, embarrassed.

"Is that anything like torsion ride that you get in the fancy automobiles?" he quipped. "How are the tranquilizers working?"

In response to his flippant tone, I said with feigned seriousness. "Well, it didn't seem to make a difference at first. Then I realized that they should be given to the kids, and things are *much* better!"

For a few days, things were better, but then a major panic hit me at school and I had gone to the hall, and then to the office. The tears had come as I bit my lip and said, "I'm sorry, Mr. McKenney. I just can't hang in here. I ... I ... I just need to get home ... and cry." I sat there while he went to my class. I cried softly for a while, inside the office with the door closed. After a major panic, with its sudden impact that gave knowledge of impending doom, the absolute consuming terror that made me feel I was being thrown from the face of the earth the fear would gradually recede. I would be left exhausted, with a sense of an incomplete relief that needed tears to expel the tension from the frazzled nerves. I worried about what the children thought, how I would drive myself home, what I would say to Mr. McKenney. Then the bell rang, the children left, and I waited. Mr. McKenney came back.

"I told them that you weren't feeling well. There's a lot of flu going around ..." he offered. "What do you think? Can you stay? There's only one week ... then you'll have spring break!"

I tried to explain that a spring break wasn't going to do it and I needed the pressure off completely. It was more than I could bear just trying to make it from day to day. It was like being in a sand trap with the sand pouring in all around, and no one or nothing to grab on to for survival. I feared the relief of saying to him that it was over because then I would be admitting to the failure. I heaved a sigh, knowing that I had no alternative. I knew we needed the money so I had tried and tried, but I was failing. Would Martin forgive me? Could I live with myself? I wasn't used to failure. I had a dogged determination that I dared anyone to equal. My mouth seemed to make the decision without my head. I could make it be over, finally.

The principal and I agreed that I would try to finish the week and then the music teacher would take my class for the remainder of the year. This meant no music program in the school for the rest of the year, and the added guilt made me feel even worse.

To make the transition smoother, the music teacher sat in on my third grade class for a few days. "I was surprised it was you," she told me one day. "When I heard that someone was having problems with their nerves, I figured I would have to take their class. I considered everyone in the school—except you. You always seemed so self-confident, so calm."

This didn't surprise me. I had worked hard to show an outward appearance of calm. I had always dressed very neatly, in the latest style, and pulled my hair up into a dramatic chignon. I carried myself well and put on a show of confidence. I worked to develop the outward appearance of being calm.

Now, as Martin and I entered the back office of the old hospital, I tried to put on the "calm" look and consciously relaxed my hands and face. I was going to show the nurse how very calm I was. I was not a nervous wreck and certainly not *crazy. I might be* a little upset, but I only needed to talk to my doctor. These mental health people knew all the signs to look for and I wanted them to know I was really all right. I eased slowly and deliberately into an overstuffed chair. Martin sat opposite the desk in a hard-backed, office chair while he filled in the admissions forms. I was feeling a little calmer and more self-confident, and so I tried to converse quietly and evenly with the nurse who seemed more interested in the forms. I spoke about having been here before.

"But," I said, "I was much worse then. I had insulin therapy. It really did help me a lot. I am much better. I'm having some current problems but I'm sure it's only temporarily. I probably ... just need a few talks with my doctor although ... I don't suppose he will want me to have any treatments. He'll be here tomorrow, won't he?"

The nurse ignored me, took the papers from Martin, placed them in a folder, rose unemotionally, and led us to the hallway. "You may bring Mrs. Ames' bag to the desk. I'll take her on upstairs and get her settled."

As he said goodbye, Martin seemed especially distant and hurried, almost as if he had another appointment, His last words were something about "things being all right." No doubt I had asked him at least a dozen times if they would be before leaving home and then again just before coming into the building. I assumed that he was preoccupied about getting my suitcase and then getting on home. There was the sitter, who had to go to school the next day, and he had told her that he wouldn't be long.

But we had had to make the trip after dark. It was only then that I could travel. The trip wasn't far, it was just across town but it had become so hard to go anywhere. I had to have Martin to drive and it had to be dark out, the darker and the later, the better. I felt that in the darkness the world was small. Only things nearby existed. What you couldn't see you could pretend was not there. The world was so expansive to me and so frightening. At night you only had to deal with cars and people that were in the same block and, if you drove late enough, there were few of those.

At home, the past few months, I had gotten so fearful that I closed the drapes in the dining room and living room to keep out the light, the people, and the confusion. Then, when the panics became worse, I grew too frightened to even walk past my front door with the small window in it. The past few weeks I had begun to hurry through morning chores; cleaning, feeding and bathing the baby, feeding Karen, and then waiting, in increasing anxiety, until it was time to give the children lunch and we could lie down. I would read Karen a story and then try to nap with the children. All this time I was praying desperately for the time to pass until Martin would come home from work.

I had gotten terribly upset a few times and had to call Martin to come home early, and this had made me feel even worse at my failure to deal with this insidious problem. It also made Martin more aloof and annoyed. I had always detested daytime TV but had finally succumbed to leaving the set on during the mornings to give me company and distract my anxious thoughts. It frightened me for the neighbors to come over or for the phone to ring. I was afraid I would have a panic attack and people would see me out of control.

I had even gotten to the point that it bothered me for Karen to go to play in the neighbors' yard. I would check on her from the window but worried she might fall or be injured some way. How would I get to her? I hated to even go out my own door. How could I go cross two backyards to where the preschool neighborhood children played? And what if my daughter were to be injured so severely that she needed medical attention? How could I go with her for help? I was relieved that Karen was such an obedient child and all I needed to do was to call to her and she would come immediately. I had instructed her to do so and also to stay in an area where I could see her from our own yard, or better yet, the window.

Karen seemed aware of my anxiety. She was so good and so quiet, almost as if she knew the right things to do and say for my "condition." And none of the dreaded emergencies that were so worrisome had happened—*yet*. Still, I was constantly afraid of the very worst possible occurrence. I felt that when it came I would not be able to cope. I wished that things had gotten easier and that I could carry out my motherly and wifely duties, as more normal women did, and go about my life free of fear. I was devastated that I had to give up and return to this hateful old building.

I was remembering about how hard things had become at home and how much I detested the thought of returning to this decrepit hospital as I watched Martin exit the front door of the building without looking back. I wished that he had given me at least a hug but he never liked any public display of affection. It was difficult enough for him in private.

I dutifully followed the nurse (whom I was beginning to perceive as cold, fat, and masculine) to the elevator in the center of the lobby. The nurse, whose name I didn't remember, opened the metal gates to the elevator with a key. The loud clanging startled me and refueled the anxieties that had just started to become manageable.

I had forgotten that the elevator locked though I remembered that the doors were all secured in the main building. But the old house across the street that served as an annex had no locks. I wondered why the nurse wasn't putting me in the annex. *Probably she has to wait for the doctor's directive,* I thought. Or maybe she couldn't see how well I was. I would have to be extra calm and show this nurse that I wasn't as bad off as she might think. I was so preoccupied with the different noises that I didn't notice what floor we were entering as we passed through another metal gate with another lock. As I watched the nurse finger her large ring of keys almost fondly, I realized that she was very pleased with her own importance, which was clearly measured by the number of her keys. "I guess that's how you tell the players," I told myself. "If they have a key ... they're sane." I amused myself with the thought that the white uniforms and the keys were the only differences between "us" and "them."

My attempt at dark humor proved to be frighteningly near reality. The nurse on this floor was vaguely familiar and it came back to me in a rush. I *had* seen her before. *Here!* The red hair in the same chic, short cut, the pointed nose, the green eyes with the pale, short, stubby lashes, the way she walked with her toes turned out and her knees together. It was Penny. The head nurse even called her by name. But Penny was in white now. Was she the one with a key? She had been a patient when I was here before. Or was my mind playing tricks? Was I going insane? I was tired and hadn't slept well for days. I was upset. The whole evening had played out like a bad dream. That was it, I decided. When I got very upset things became unreal and dreamlike. Conversion hysteria, the doctor had called it. Things would straighten out in the morning. Or maybe if I had another pill. Taking some medication and lying very still would make everything become settled and real again. I would ask the nurse about medication.

Penny went into the nursing station near the locked steel elevator where she and another nurse began mumbling names with accompanying comments to one another. The head nurse took my arm and directed me down a narrow irregular hall. I didn't know if the floor and walls were crooked or if I were crazy. The doors were all closed and this floor of the hospital was strangely still except for the nurses' voices that were now almost completely inaudible. We entered a very small room from the dimly lit hallway. The nurse motioned me to sit on the bed, the only piece of furniture in the room.

The nurse was heavy set with cold steely eyes that seemed to pierce into mine, but I knew how to hold her glance without wavering. I might be shook up inside but I had control of my facial muscles. From her position standing over me the nurse was intimidating in both her stares and her hovering, and in her size. She smiled but her eyes didn't "crinkle," exposing her as more "social" than truly friendly. I looked back at her with steady eyes and an equally "social" smile and explained that I was not very really "disturbed" at all, that I had anxiety attacks, felt panicky, and was having trouble being at home alone while my husband worked. I tried to sound calm, pleasant, and sensible, like someone who just needed to straighten out a few things with the doctor. I couldn't do that on the outside because of my problems with travel, I explained.

"I can get around, just not downtown and up to the sixth floor where his office is ... so I thought I could just stay here for a few days ... to see him and work out the problem," I said, speaking in my most reasonable tone.

The nurse nodded, another "social" gesture. We made small talk about weather. She asked had I eaten and told me my bag would be up soon. She seemed to agree that I was not so bad off. She conversed with me as *if* I were a sane person. She didn't seem placating or condescending at all. Maybe this visit to the hospital would give me a few days of rest and some time to discuss my setback with the doctor and then I could go home again. I was sure he could help me if I had some time with him. After all, that's what psychiatrists did. They talked to you, helped you understand your problems, and then you were able to overcome the difficulties. I felt a little better. The nurse left, jangling the ring of keys as she went.

I looked around the tiny, empty room. There was no nightstand, no closet, nothing. The light was a bare bulb in the ceiling. There were sheets and a thin blanket on the bed, and the bed—now I remembered! When I was here before *this* was the room but the hospital had been very crowded then. There was a mattress on the floor and another patient, the redhead, "Penny."

"Oh hell, I hope she didn't recognize *me*," I thought frantically. I would have to pretend I didn't recognize Penny. How would Penny react if she knew that I knew she was a former patient? I remembered the control that the staff had over the patients.

And I started to remember other things. No, Penny hadn't been the other patient in the room. She had come from down the hall, wanting to talk. She had been hysterical and incoherent, and was seeking out the patient on the floor who really didn't listen to Penny. That patient on the floor was quiet and depressed, and walked about the tiny room, stumbling over the mattress and praying while clasping a crucifix to her chest. How frightening to think that Penny, who had sought consolation from my previous roommate, was now here as the floor nurse.

I remembered going down the hall to a large bathroom with several toilets (with no doors), a couple of showers, and one large and strangely deep bathtub. The incident came back as clearly as if it had just happened. There was a very distressed young black girl in the bathroom who was making repetitive motions with her arms and hands, circling them over her head and across her body and then out to the sides as if she were some existentialist dancer. Then she had stopped, kneeled on the floor in front of a toilet stool, and looked up at me with stark anguish on her face. A strange smile had come over her face as she had said in a singsong voice to no one, "My daddy was a shoeshine boy. My daddy was a shoeshine boy." She repeated this many times and was still in the bathroom doing this when I had come back some time later. I remembered feeling angry at the confusion and the bizarre nonsense of the situation and, in anger and desperation, I had turned and said, "So what the hell? *I* used to be a schoolteacher!" as if that might be some strange kind of resolution. I wondered if the black girl were here again, also. Maybe now *she* was a nurse?

If a person is unbalanced, why inflict them with more unreality and other strange people? Wouldn't this just make them crazier and make it more difficult to bring the entire insane group back to normal? It certainly was making me feel more crazed. Why had I allowed my husband to bring me back? How had I forgotten what this place was like? More memories from my earlier stay here came flooding back. All the doors to the stairways were locked; one could only go between floors in the company of nurses or orderlies. *They* had the keys! Then there were the orderlies who ran about whenever there was a disturbance. An intercom called them, even in the middle of the night. There was only one large bathroom on this side of third floor. If this *were* third floor. Oh my God, if it *is* third floor, I'm where they put the real crazies, I though. There must be some mistake. I checked under the bed and saw the bed was bolted to the floor, a sign of the violent-ward rooms. What were they doing to me? I gasped and clutched the bed dizzily. Then Penny came into the room.

"Here's your bag. Take out what you need." Penny waited, not smiling. I watched to see if she showed any signs of recognition. Seeing none, I removed my nightgown, toothbrush and toothpaste, and some clothes for morning from the bag.

"Just take your gown and robe," she said. "I'll put the rest away. You're not to have anything in this room."

Penny stood impatiently waiting as I put on my nightgown. As I bent to take out my robe and repack my other things I noticed Penny tapping one shoe and fingering her keys. Taking the bag, Penny left me, shutting off the light and closing the door behind her.

I was glad for the light from the hallway coming through the small glass window in the door. I wished Penny had been another nurse so that I could have asked about medication. But I was afraid if I talked with Penny she would recognize me. I was too jumpy to sleep and my heart just wouldn't slow down. I wanted my toothbrush. Didn't crazy people brush their teeth? I was so frightened. How on earth could I sleep? Maybe I'd better start putting together a plan for morning, what to say to the doctor. I had to figure out a way to endure this place I had never planned on seeing again. I moved out of bed quietly and tried the door to see if I were locked in. Relieved that I wasn't. I went back to my hard narrow bed to ponder my situation.

* * *

Martin walked away from the old white building with some apprehension and also a great sense of relief. He knew he had lied to her. What else could he have done? If he had told her that Dr. Ashford said that they needed to try the insulin shock therapy a second time, she would never have gone. She might have become hysterical. Not that she'd ever become hysterical, but she did get frantic and draw things way out of proportion, like her panics. She seemed to think that the world was going to end if she didn't get out of a crowded area. She pushed and ran toward the exits as if something life-threatening were in pursuit. She would bump into people, knock things over, and leave disaster in her wake. Martin found it very embarrassing. She always seemed rational after she got out but she was so frenzied on her way.

How had he got in this situation? His family had always been very proper. They did the socially acceptable thing in all circumstances. His mother would never have dared to embarrass his father in the way that he had been embarrassed. But Laurel seemed to have little regard for the normal social niceties. She knew them. In fact, her social skills had been quit impressive before they were married. True, she occasionally said things that were questionable but only in private. She knew how to be a lady, if she wished. Her mother was different. Wow, what a shocker she was! He wondered if Laurel might become more like her mother. Now that was a scary thought.

Martin knew his mother had been concerned about Laurel's family. She had said, after meeting Laurel, that the girl seemed nice enough but that he needed to look at her background. Martin had dated her for several years before he ever asked her to marry him. He wanted to be very sure. They were engaged a whole year before marrying. He never saw any problems. And Laurel expressed her own disdain for her mother's behavior. Still, the panics were the only thing that seemed anti-social in Laurel's behavior. Her friends in college had been questionable, but she was in the art school. Those kind were always a little different, not as well adjusted as the students in his engineering classes. He and Laurel had laughed at how the "artsy" students seemed to want to shock the world. He was wondering if she were feeling too restrained in their quiet environment.

It was certainly a relief to have her back in the hospital. Their life was getting extremely difficult. He never knew when she was going to call him at work and complain that she was "shook-up" and couldn't be alone another minute. Didn't she understand what a stress this was for him to try to continue to do his job while she continually burdened him with her anxieties. Now he knew she would be with someone who could deal with her during the day and he didn't have to come home to this disturbance and frustration after work. He would have to worry about the childcare, yes, but there was still a sense of freedom in having her locked up where others could deal with her anxieties and constant need for reassurance. Maybe the break would give him some time to de-stress too. This had all been very hard on him. He wondered if she would find out that he had signed papers for her treatment when he brought her in. If she asked, he could deny it. There was no reason for the doctor or hospital staff to give her that information. He could pretend that he had signed the papers later, after the doctor had talked to him about her condition. He and Dr. Ashford had discussed the treatment and Martin knew that she was in for the whole insurance stay and for the entire series of shocks. He would deal with her reaction to this surprise later. He just wanted to appreciate the relief for now.

He wasn't too happy about having to come to visit her. She had asked him to please return tomorrow night but the crazy patients there were frightening; you never knew what their problems were or what they might be inclined to do. Laurel was even afraid of them, at least she had been the last time. Besides, he had so much to do. He needed to get the girls settled with her sister and he had no one to fix his meals or do the laundry. At least she had been keeping the housework up and the cooking and the laundry and doing a fair job at it. Why couldn't she just relax and stop worrying about the panics? He didn't think it was such a big thing that she couldn't travel or go into crowds. She didn't have to be anywhere she wasn't working anymore. He was taking care of her and the children. All she needed to do was hold up her end, but instead she was getting more and more incompetent and then complaining at that.

The doctor said that the treatments should help again, although he was annoyed that no follow-up counseling sessions were scheduled after the last hospitalization. Martin didn't think it was his fault. He thought Laurel seemed fine. Things had gone better for quite a while. He really didn't know what Laurel's problem with life was. He certainly was not prepared to deal with these kinds of problems in a marriage.

He drove on the freeway on his way toward home. It was nice to travel the way he preferred and not have to listen to someone complain about her nerves, noise, traffic, speed, etc. He looked at his watch. He had left Laurel fairly early. Checking in had not taken as long as he had expected. And it had been too late to go up on the floor with her. He was making good time. He would be home before the time he had told Sharon, their babysitter. He pulled off at the next exit. The Cozy Inn was only three blocks from that intersection. Martin really wanted and needed a quick drink, and there was time.

Chapter Two
Panic Attacks

The small floodlights from the courtyard gave an eerie picture as they reflected the vines from the stuccoed wall onto the heavily screened window. I lay watching the images varying ever so slightly with the almost still night air. The screens were a metal mesh that did not fit the old structure but, I thought, were better than bars. I remembered that the windows at Mountain View (it was hard to say the name of the place even to myself) were also well secured. The windows could be lifted, slid up to allow some air to circulate, though not easily because of their age. The heavy screens were on the outside of the building and fastened to the walls. I supposed that this was to inhibit patients from jumping to their deaths, rather than endure the menu of psychiatric treatment here. I shivered in spite of the heat, remembering how frightening the treatments were.

How had I ended up in a mental hospital and, for God's sake, why a second time? I couldn't understand how it had all come about. But my anger at my situation was muted by the inward terror of what was in store for me now. I dug my nails into the palm of my hand to keep the tears from coming. How had my sanity become a point of question? This was all so humiliating.

I certainly didn't enjoy being a mental case and wondered how it had ever come this far. Friends and relatives had always said how bright I was and talented. I painted and had had work accepted in large juried shows in the city. I had majored in art in college and my professors had been impressed with my talent, although not with my academic devotion. I had barely made a high enough grade point average to graduate because I was too busy socializing and working. I had always been very self-sufficient and had worked to put myself through my university studies.

After I had married, I had worked for a while at a title guarantee company, and then a friend had talked me into taking a job, as a teacher, at the same school with her. I had really not intended to teach but, then again, I hadn't intended to go berserk either. I had taken enough education hours that all I needed for a certificate was my student teaching. The school district arranged for these credits for me while I worked with another teacher for a number of weeks while an addition to the school was being completed. Then I was given my own class of first graders. I had hated education courses at school and was pleasantly surprised to find that they had nothing at all to do with the actual teaching. I loved the children and the job. Martin was annoyed that I spent extra time at my duties and he complained that I wasn't making money because I "sunk all my salary back into supplies" and special things for my kids.

I taught for one year, had a baby, went to New York to live for four months (while Martin took some schooling for his company), returned to teaching, grade three this time, and was teaching the second year in third grade when things began to get difficult.

The medical doctor who began treating me for my nerves when I was still teaching school, had told me that I was neurotic, but said, "Most of my friends are neurotic, I like neurotic people they're more interesting." Then he told me several of his offbeat jokes about neurotics. He gave me injections of vitamin B12 and calcium for my "nervous" condition. He was my mother's doctor and I liked his sense of humor and the fact that he belonged in the family. I also liked that he didn't think I was crazy, because I was sure that I was, or at least was headed well in that direction.

I had explained to him about my first panic attack, which had occurred when Martin and I were in New York City. We were at Grand Central Station at rush hour. A surge of debilitating fear had swept over me in a sudden instant with such intensity that I had been sure that death or worse was imminent. I had, as I described it, freaked out so totally that I felt only absolute terror and dived into a telephone booth, where I stayed until the large crowd had passed and my terror had abated. Martin, of course, could not understand my reaction. I could not understand what had happened to me either. I had been feeling fine, enjoying myself, and then suddenly the panic had just come out of nowhere, completely engulfing me to the point that I was unable to do anything other than react as a frightened animal in fear of its life.

The fear gradually abated and I was able to think again, puzzled by the experience but feeling nearly normal again.

A few days later it happened again in Macy's Department Store. But why was it on the stairwell, between floors, with no one around but Martin? The first panic I thought was probably an unusual reaction to a very large and loud crowd. The second left me completely baffled. My doctor had said it was just an "anxiety attack" that could be explained by nerves reacting to the big city, being away from home, and not fully recovered from childbirth the baby being only two months old. Not to worry.

Panics came again on an occasion, but never again in New York City. About a year later Martin and I took a trip to Florida with the baby and had stopped in Memphis. It had been a hot summer afternoon. When the panic hit all I could do, once it subsided, was to beg Martin to go back home *immediately*. He convinced me that I would recover again and so, reluctantly, I agreed that we could finish our vacation.

I had had no panics for almost another six months and then they returned, with more and more frequency. I found that it helped for me to feel I was near home and could get to "safety," a place where I could die, go insane, or meet whatever doom was surely coming, in the comfort of familiar surroundings and most of all away from spectators. I mentioned the frequency and intensity of these attacks to my family doctor, along with the accompanying symptoms that continued to develop and multiply. But the doctor hadn't been too concerned.

As the months passed, it became more and more difficult for me to make visits to this doctor, as the downtown area was growing increasingly frightening to me. And, too, his office was on the fourth floor. The ride up the elevator was panic-inducing enough, and while I felt somewhat safer in his office, the waiting itself raised my anxiety level even further. My palms would begin to sweat, I felt prickly all over, and I would tremble as if my nerves would suddenly all split apart at one time and I would be one huge mass of convulsions. When the waiting grew very long I would be overcome with vertigo and felt as if I were staggering into the examining room.

From this room I could see out the window and down four flights to the parking lot. I would always urge Martin to park in an area where I could look out and see our car. The vision of the car, my method of escape, soothed my frayed nerves somewhat. When I tried to tell the doctor how really frightened I felt, how my dependency on Martin and the safety of home were gradually consuming me, the doctor simply treated me with vitamins and calcium and told me to "just try to relax."

One Saturday morning I had had a particularly hard time going to my regular weekly appointment. It was hot. The heat from the downtown pavement aggravated the prickly, sweaty feeling that came with the anxiety and I felt dizzier than usual. Coming up the elevator was a real struggle. I felt angry with all the other passengers and wanted to yell at them for making me stop and wait at their floors. Didn't they know it could make me unable to get to my own destination if I were to lose control and have to go back to the car and then home? My nerves were in square knots before I ever got to the waiting room. I was so jumpy that I couldn't sit without squirming nervously. My eyes felt as if they were growing larger and I was unable to make them focus on any magazines. It was just as well for I wouldn't have been able to concentrate on the words as I could barely make sense of the signs in the waiting room.

While I sat there, I remembered one particularly bad panic attack that I had coming home from school the past week. I was still shaking after reaching the safety of my apartment and I felt very disoriented. I tried to calm myself by focusing on what to do for dinner but I couldn't get my thoughts to make sense. Remembering that the doctor had told me to drink some milk when I felt shaky and weak, I went to the kitchen and opened the cupboard by mistake. While looking at its contents, my eyes focused on a can of okra. I stared at it, bewildered. I had no idea what it was. In fact, I knew I had never seen or heard of "okra" in all of my twenty-five years! Here was a strange can with odd words on it, and I knew I was not just somewhat disoriented by severe anxiety. I pulled the can from the cupboard, almost falling in the attempt, and hastily began to read the ingredients. Okra, water, salt, then some strange-sounding additives. My eyes went back to "okra." Why could I read "water" and "salt" and yet not know what "okra" was?

I ran frantically to the living room and got the third grade reader from my tote bag. My hands were so shaky that I dropped the book twice before I was successful at finding a page and focusing my eyes on the words. It looked foreign to me. I stared and concentrated, laboriously sounding out each word in the paragraph, using the phonics skills I taught at school. I was relieved to find that I could read, if only at a grade three level, but I wasn't sure about what the words meant or if I were reading a story I could understand. Okay. Reading recognition, grade three ... reading comprehension? It really didn't matter. What mattered was, what in the hell was okra?

I was feeling better but still in a semi-frenzied state when Martin came home with the baby several hours later. The first thing I said was, "Do you know what okra is? Where did this can come from?" I thrust the can angrily toward his face, while turning my own face from it. I didn't want to look at it myself because it was the object of my completed slide into insanity. The can had come from my mother-in-law and, yes, he had even eaten this food a time or two. He didn't know what all the fuss was about. It was only a can of food and yet another of my anxiety attacks. I tried to explain the tension, the fear, the confusion, but to no avail. I remained angry with him for putting the can on the shelf and at his mother, who was too damned perfect and *really* calm. My anger lasted for days after the incident. If I were really and truly crazy, I reasoned, I would have blamed them for conspiring to have me put away. This situation had nearly done the trick!

While I sat nervously fidgeting in the doctor's waiting room and reliving this last week's panic episode, thinking how to relate this story to him, my doctor entered the room. He was escorting a patient who was leaving. He had no receptionist on Saturdays and it was a "first come, first served" basis. He looked around at the three or four people sitting there. When his eyes fixed on me, I was on the verge of tears, my eyes dilated with anxiety, my face strained, my tight hand frantically clutching my small purse, and visibly fidgeting. After one look, he hurried me into the examining room ahead of the others.

"What's wrong? What happened?" he inquired.

"I've tried to tell you," I stammered between the sobs. "I really get shook up ... It's *bad* ... I'm frightened ... Let me look outside for our car ... Oh, I just want to go home."

"Sit down for just a minute," he said. "You'll be all right. Just relax. It's okay. Calm down." He continued to try to reassure me as he guided me from the window and helped me to the small stool in the room. He walked to the other side of the room and picked up a phone. I jumped up and dizzily glanced again from the window to check on the car in the lot below.

"What are you doing? Who are you calling?" I insisted.

I heard him ask for a doctor, and then say something about an upset patient and that he would send her right up.

"I know what you did!" I said accusingly. "You called a head-shrinker! You think that I'm crazy now, too!"

I stiffened and tried hard not to look panicky. Maybe he would change his mind, maybe I would feel better, and maybe this would never happen again. After all it was especially hot today and I hadn't been feeling well. He walked out with me to the waiting room and spoke to Martin, telling him where to take me on the sixth floor.

That was the beginning of my relationship with Dr. Ashford, a real Freudian psychiatrist who dealt with crazy people, and even put some into a mental hospital. He was a strange short man with a large potbelly and extra thick glasses that hardly framed his bulging myopic eyes. He was afflicted with violent coughing seizures that made his eyes bulge and his face grow red, at which times he would exit the room, cough violently and uncontrollably and then return and continue the conversation precisely where he had left it. His seizures seemed to bother me more than him. I worried that I ought to obtain some medical help for *him*, and, in so thinking, lost track of our previous conversation and would sit there dumbly.

"What comes to mind?" he asked once when he realized that I had lost the train of our discussion.

I wished I could say that I was afraid that he was terminal or that he reminded me of the two owl bookends that held numerous important looking books on his large and heavily cluttered desk, behind which he always perched. He was not a personable man, but distant and analytical and, to me, more than a little intimidating.

Dr. Ashford sent me to see a psychologist; one of the few in the city that Dr. Ashford felt was qualified for giving the notorious Rorschach test. I had heard of this test in my psychology classes and understood that they could tell exactly how crazy a person was by their responses to what they imagined were in these heavy cardboard pictures made of inkblots. I thought that they were all like butterflies or other insects but I'd heard that meant my self-esteem was suffering. I had heard that you could never fool a Rorschach. Even though I didn't want them to discover my insanity, I didn't want to lie about what I saw. I did want the test to be valid since I wanted help. So I did my best to give honest responses.

But, as fate would have it, the psychologist's office was in a modern "high-rise" with windows that went clear to the floor. I was terrified when my dizziness struck and I felt that I would slide along the floor, crash through the windows, and plummet on out of the building down many stories to the pavement below. I couldn't focused on the ink-blot card while trying to ignore the gaping openness at the edge of the carpeting that could suck me toward the window, shattering it, and then dash me into the moving traffic, twenty stories down. I was so tense during the testing I supposed that if one could flunk a Rorschach, I had.

When Dr. Ashford talked to me about the results, it didn't seem all that significant. He said that I was anxious and depressed. I certainly knew that! When Martin asked me about the test, I was angry and annoyed. I truly didn't think he was concerned. He always gave the impression that he was superior because his emotions were so carefully under control. He often teased me about my super sensitivity. Once I had clipped a cartoon from a magazine for the kitchen bulletin board. It depicted a husband sitting in a chair, reading the paper, while his wife was yelling. Objects that she had thrown and broken lay all about. The caption read, "My mother told me not to marry beneath my emotional level!"

"You're safe," I told Dr. Ashford. "The tests show that I hate women and I'm angry with men."

This was new information for me, even though I was aware of my growing alienation from society at this point. I did realize, however, that my bitter response to Martin was an unfair attack on what I saw as his continual lack of warmth or empathy. But I was feeling so angry that to denote him as nonhuman seemed only a mild insult. After all, I was crazy. I even had my own shrink!

A few weeks after this, I found the anxiety so increased that I could no longer go to Dr. Ashford's office or to my medical doctor. I could barely handle driving through the downtown area with Martin. I talked to Dr. Ashford several times by phone and, among other things, he cautioned me to avoid getting pregnant as it could cause additional problems.

So I floundered along, doing my best with my panics. I had been through the trauma of having to quit my teaching not even making it to spring break. I was being an absolute failure and letting down my students at school. I was trying my best at home to be a good housewife and a mother to Karen. But Martin and I had bought a modest home and I was good at growing flowers and had made my own draperies for several of the rooms. Dr. Ashford had told me to stay busy. He had said to "bake a cake" when I felt panicky—some weird kind of Freudian philosophy about "creating something causing sublimation of repressed sexual desires." I didn't understand it and felt that the doctor didn't either, as it was not very effective. The only help was that it served to occupy my mind at times. I wasn't as apt to panic if I stayed busy.

At times Martin and I were even able to go out. I had learned that nighttime was best for outings as I felt unobserved and the night darkness hid the distance from home that we had gone. Things were difficult but manageable for me until I did become pregnant.

Fearing that this was the death sentence for my recovery, I became progressively more anxious. I worried about the fact that I could not get to the doctor's office and was not receiving regular checkups for my prenatal care. How could the baby be healthy? I had Martin call Dr. Ashford and let him know of our "goof-up." I had never overcome my fear of Dr. Ashford and was afraid of his anger, and afraid of what his prognosis might be considering my new "condition." Martin told me the doctor said I would be all right and just to try not to worry. Martin lessened the impact of the doctor's original concern by saying that Dr.

Ashford only meant that I should probably wait until I was better to have another child, that I was so nervous it might make me worry more. But, as soon as the baby came, I would surely be better. It might even be helpful, in that it would give me something to think about other than myself. Although this seemed logical to me, it didn't seem right that the doctor would almost reverse his opinion about pregnancy. I wondered if those were Dr. Ashford's words or Martin's, but I was afraid to call the doctor myself. He always seemed impatient and acted as if I didn't have any sense. And too, I was depending more and more on Martin to handle difficult things for me.

I stayed busy with housework, did some sewing, and visited with the neighbors in my immediate block of homes. I was able to see my medical doctor only twice during my pregnancy. I had had a very painful and difficult labor during Karen's birth, but I was more afraid of hospital confinement than of the childbirth. With my panics, the thought of being stuck or trapped in a public place, such as the hospital, was terrifying.

Some of my neighbors were aware of my problems. They seemed genuinely concerned and offered any help that might be needed. I believe they saw me as high strung and nervous but seemed to appreciate my sarcasm and wit, perhaps thinking I seemed interesting and different. People saw Martin as nice and always amiable. So Martin and I were frequent guests at neighborhood barbecues and parties. I was fairly comfortable in my own home and at social gatherings in the home of some neighbors, since I could hurry home if a panic struck.

Having friends and relatives come to the house was more difficult for me. If I were the hostess, there was no getting away if my nerves became overwhelmed. My own relatives seemed to sense my uneasiness and phoned often but only visited by invitation, which I seldom offered. But my in-laws were frequent visitors, especially on weekends. I often cooked Saturday or Sunday dinner for Martin's drop-in relatives. One of Martin's brothers was particularly bothersome even to Martin. It seemed as if he, his wife, and three children were there all the time. I would duck into the bathroom and take deep breaths or cry quietly for a few minutes, wash my face with a cool cloth, and then emerge again, trying to look unruffled. Apparently I was successful as Martin's mother remarked once, "Laurel seems to prepare meals so quickly and it seems effortless for her." When Martin related this to me, I was aghast. Didn't the lady know I was on the verge of complete insanity, that any minute I could become a raving maniac?

Martin and I went places less and less frequently. Occasionally, on weekends, we would go across town to his mother's home and stay all night so that I could ride a shorter distance to see my own mother or go shopping the next day in a small quiet store. This also gave us both more of a change from our four walls that were now beginning to close in on Martin also. And then, too, the grandmothers could see Karen.

It was on one of these visit weekends that I went into labor. We had stayed Friday night at his mother's, and Saturday morning I awoke with regular pains already minutes apart. I called the doctor and he said for us to go on over to the hospital where he would meet us. I dressed quickly and woke Martin. He seemed annoyed, as usual, and I carried my bag downstairs to the living room to wait for him. He came down a short time later and asked me what I wanted for breakfast. I was already plenty nervous and this really irked me.

"You don't eat when you're going to deliver a baby!"

"Well," he snapped, "*I'm* hungry!"

"Can't you eat after you take me?" I pleaded. I was getting more and more anxious and Martin had gone to the kitchen to start to fix something for himself.

"I don't think we've got much time. The doctor said to go right away."

Martin slammed a pan down on the stove and shut off the burner. He clearly felt annoyed and thwarted but left with me, giving me the silent treatment. Thirty minutes after we arrived at the hospital I gave birth to a second little girl.

Initially I was very panicky in the hospital but I was momentarily distracted from anxiety attacks while experiencing childbirth. My anxiety was so strong that the pain of the delivery was nominal. Then, of course, I wanted to go home immediately. The staff tried to treat me like the other patients, who were to stay three to five days. But the hustling around by the nurses and movement in and out of my room made me extremely agitated and jumpy and served to remind me that

I was in a public place. All I really wanted was to go home since I was in a constant state of extreme anxiety. I was sure that I was all right, physically, after the delivery. And I needed some relief for my nerves away from the noisy business of the public hospital.

When a nurse brought my baby in to me, I checked her fingers and toes. I recognized that she was an unusually pretty baby and genuinely wanted to hold and admire her. But I felt so nervous and jumpy that I couldn't cope with her crying, and I was afraid that my own thrashing about on the bed would dump the baby to the floor. I rang for the nurse and had them take the baby back to the nursery. My self-judgment, that I was an unloving mother and didn't give the baby proper cuddling and attention, made me angry with myself, the hospital staff, Martin, and eventually the entire world. I became excessively depressed and tense. I ate almost nothing, as I felt too anxious to chew. I just waited, longing desperately to go home.

I was afraid even to get up to use the restroom. And I was extremely fearful of trying to walk around in the room much less the hallway. I was in such a public place and, even with medication; I was shaky, jumpy, and terrified. I was unaware of time. I did know that Martin had been there, as had my obstetrics doctor. But I was very surprised when I looked up to find Dr. Ashford standing at the foot of my bed.

"She said she'd be more comfortable at Mountain View," he said to my medical doctor, who had also just entered the room. Mountain View was the local funny farm, but I was even more angry because he spoke of me in the third person as if I weren't even present.

"She said she'd be more comfortable at home!" I said angrily, wondering why Ashford was quoting me when we had not even spoken. The medical doctor told me that I was too weak and needed to be up and around before being released.

"Well, if you're waiting for me to get up and walk around *here*," I said, "it'll be a cold day in hell. I'm not walking around in this place. It's public ... and too busy ... I'm scared and I'm not leaving this bed ... except to go home."

I got my wish. I was released the following day. Martin took me at night, as I requested, so that I could travel all the way across town with less trauma. And he even stayed home with me for a couple of days as he realized that I was a total emotional wreck. When the baby cried I jumped a foot, and her continual crying upset me so that *I* dissolved into tears also. It seemed as if the cries were amplified by so many decibels that the windows would crack, along with my head.

Martin hired a nurse so that he could go back to work although we really couldn't afford her for more than two weeks. It was obvious I was in no condition to be left in charge of Karen and a small infant. All I did was fret and cry while the nurse did all the baby care. In fact, she hardly let me touch the baby! She didn't like the way I held her, "like a sack of potatoes." And she seemed fearful that, as jumpy as I was, I might drop her. The nurse was reassuring about my condition, however, telling me that she cared for many new mothers and babies, and my continual crying was only a "post-partum depression," which was a frequent result of childbirth.

I knew it was more than that, however. I'd been told I had postpartum depression when Karen was born. But that depression had been minor. It was depression without the continual sobbing and had been quickly cured by my getting out and around, and my returning to my teaching job. Now I couldn't stop the tears and I felt completely overcome with a deep dread, a feeling of dark gloom, and complete sadness. There was also the feeling that every nerve in my body had blown a fuse. I was continually tense and was not sleeping or eating. The depression and anxiety didn't pass.

Before the nurse's two weeks were up, I called Dr. Ashford in desperation.

"You're right!" I sobbed, "I think I need to go to Mountain View."

I had told Martin that I might as well do this and that it looked as if I had no choice. He checked into our insurance and then agreed with me.

Our children were taken to my sister's and I went to the hospital for their "thirty-day insurance wonder treatment." This was my first trip and I had been devastated by the idea that I was in a mental hospital. Dr. Ashford assured me that I would be fine, and that the treatment would take care of my nervous condition.

I was on the Third Floor for several days, where severe cases were put. Dr. Ashford had told me that there were no other available rooms and apologized, saying that he would move me as soon as possible. After I was thoroughly traumatized, I was transferred to the old house, across the street and one-half black away, which was a part of the hospital. The Annex housed the less severely disturbed patients and a few of these patients, including myself, were walked to the main building each morning for the daily insulin therapy treatment. We walked in nightgowns and robes, and I wondered if the neighbors were amused by this strange parade of mental patients coming down the street each morning at seven and back again at noon. I had an irresistible urge to do something very bizarre, for their benefit, just in case they were watching.

Insulin therapy involved injections of insulin, which lowered blood sugar and put the patient into a coma. Then glucose was infused in the body by rubber hoses through the nose into the stomach. This caused the patient to regain consciousness. This shock to the body was supposed to cure anxieties, depression, and overall craziness. Dr. Ashford had seen many such cures. I sincerely hoped this was true. It was certainly no spa or restful recuperative procedure. I was fearful of the treatments and wondered why no general physical exam was given me prior to the initial insulin injections. What if I had diabetes or something? After all, diabetes ran in my family. But at least I only had insulin treatments. Some of the patients had a combination of insulin *and* electroshock.

The first few days in the main hospital were terrifying. The "crazy" and out-of-control patients were very frightening to me. Dr. Ashford moved me to the Annex to help allay my fears, and because I was not "as sick" as the others. I could see some problems with the patients at the Annex, but they seemed more neurotic rather than flat-out crazy. I felt better identifying myself as one of them. One thing that really worried me was the number of the patients I came in contact with who were there for a second or even a third time. One lady, a doctor's wife, had reportedly returned once or twice a year for a number of years. The nurses said they could expect her at least once a year, and then they made cryptic remarks about her husband being culpable.

I vowed that I would make myself be well and *never* return. The last several days of my stay were almost enjoyable. There were no more treatments, I chatted with my doctor daily, sat under the huge old shade trees on the lawn of the rather charming and antiquated three story house, that served as the annex building, and got better acquainted with several very nice patients my own age. Some orderlies, employed by the hospital, lived in the upper rooms of the old Annex, and they were there for meals and gossip. They talked rather freely about returnees and even told me that some of the nurses had become patients. I didn't believe this. I thought that they were either trying to shock me with their war stories or wanted me to know that I was not alone in mental illness. They smiled but insisted the stories were true. One orderly even remarked that there was a nurse on duty at the main building who was working there to pay off a hospital bill for earlier incarceration right here at Mountain View!

Nevertheless, I was feeling more relaxed than I had for a long time and hadn't had a panic attack for a couple of weeks. As a matter of fact, I felt almost euphorically calm at times as I sat under the old trees and listened to the birds. I was excited about getting home to my family and enjoying my cure.

Back home, in suburbia, I was still much more relaxed and life was gentler on me for a while. I endured various responses from my neighbors, relatives and friends. The woman directly across the street from me had gone to have electroshock therapy in a regular hospital shortly after I returned home. The lady had told me, "It's just for my nerves. My doctor said I'm just nervous ... it's menopause. I'm not 'crazy' like you were." I guessed the place of treatment was the determining factor, or how you felt about yourself. My neighbor was very depressed and I thought *anyone* who sat all day and watched game shows on TV had to be demented. But I was willing to remain the insane person in order to continue our rather impersonal relationship since I was hurting for friends and entertainment.

At times it seemed to me as if my own IQ had slipped twenty or thirty points, at least. I actually found it almost pleasant to clean house and do laundry. As I sat blissfully pulling weeds one morning, I pondered the inner quietness and told myself, "Now I *am* crazy. Who would be content to wash diapers, pull weeds, mop floors, watch an occasional game show with a nutty neighbor, etc., unless they *were* crazy or had been given an undisclosed lobotomy?" My temperament had always been one of unrest, driven activity, intellectual pursuits, and creative inclination. This dull existence and lack of frustration with it really made me wonder. I did seem dulled and forgetful, and was slower to respond and less quick-witted. I was reading less and was less creative. My mother had even commented that "they" had made me dumber and asked anxiously about the one real positive reward that I felt I had gleaned. I was really enjoying being a mother to the girls. I sewed pretty little matching dresses for them, and truly found satisfaction in caring for them.

I also worked in my garden through the end of summer and early fall. The asters that I had planted in early spring were gorgeous shades of pinks and purples. I loved working in the yard and actually enjoyed the neighbors. Travel was less difficult, but by late fall my anxiety had started to build once again. After placing my oldest daughter, Karen, in kindergarten, I began feeling increasingly frustrated with my day-to-day mundane existence. With just the baby at home with me I had less to do. I found that I had all the housework completed by nine A.M. and sat about restless or visiting with the neighbors over coffee the rest of the morning.

The afternoon was even a bigger bore as the baby napped and Karen was in school for the entire day. I tried to get back to painting but felt bored and uninspired. I had no transportation to get around, even to the local shopping centers. Daytime TV was terrible. Martin and I seldom went out anywhere (he said we had no money as it all went for my past hospital bills). We did go occasionally to his mother's or to the drive-in theater, taking both girls in the car with us.

By winter I was feeling hemmed in, frantic, and anxious. All the symptoms returned bit by bit until just making it from day to day was a struggle. I felt that if spring would come and I could get back outside again I could relax. Winter precluded even occasional neighborhood parties, which were a welcome relief for my restlessness.

A young man living several houses to the south was reported to be suffering my same ailment. Neighbors urged me to go and talk with him. His name was Frank and he, too, was an artist. When I visited with him, I thought he seemed genuinely crazy. He was afraid to go out of his door and had difficulty carrying on a sensible conversation. He never looked anyone in the eye and seemed strangely preoccupied with something he never discussed. I wondered if I appeared that strange and crazy to others. We talked about art, shared ideas when he was more communicative, and both entered a juried art show at the city's large art museum. Both of us had our work accepted but neither of us could go to the opening of the art show. Me, because of the crowds, and he, because he rarely even went outside of the house. I wondered if this strange ailment, which Frank called "agoraphobia," was contagious as I began to have intensified symptoms that more and more resembled his. I was becoming more apprehensive at going out and away from my home. By spring I was having difficulty walking more than two houses from my home to visit neighbors. I was again very afraid to ride across town with Martin, except at night. Neighbors had quit talking about Frank but I knew that he had left the house that he had been sharing with his wife and her parents.

As summer came, I worked some in the yard but it was hard for me. I had planted asters again and they were growing quite tall. I felt the blooming of my flowers might strangely portend a visit to the loony bin a second time before the asters opened since I had been preoccupied with their care the previous summer when I was at Mountain View. I had put such effort into planting several flowerbeds, even making maps of my design for the colors and heights of the plants. Martin had teased me about my diagrams, "Is that how you tell where you are?" The query seemed to be a not so subtle reference to my overall instability. He seemed less and less supportive of my efforts to retain some sanity.

I had asked Martin several times to call Dr. Ashford and let him know my condition was worsening. He always reported that the doctor said that I would be all right. One day when I was particularly upset and depressed I went to the bathroom, closed the door, opened the medicine cabinet, pulled out a razor, removed the blade, stared at it for a minute or so and then said softly to myself, "You don't want to do that ... you want help ... you want some relief. Let's try to get it in a sensible, mature way." I replaced the blade and razor and cried briefly with the door still locked. I had heard something about Frank having made a suicide attempt. I hoped he had gotten help. Then I dried my eyes and resolutely went out to find Martin.

Facing him squarely I said, "*We* have a problem, we need to talk. There is something very wrong here."

Martin said he was busy and to give him a few minutes. Later, when he came inside the house looking hurried and impatient, he frowned as he approached me. His tone was annoyed when he spoke. "What did you want to say?"

I threw up my hands in despair. What had I obtained? *I* always talked, confided everything, thoughts, fears, hopes, and ideas. Martin always listened, not always interestedly, but he seemed to listen and then never shared anything of himself. I didn't even know how he felt about my illness, except that in one of his very infrequent expressions of out-and-out anger, he had said, "You're like a ball and chain around my neck!" That had really hurt and I imagined many such angry feelings were in him often, and he just had never let me know.

I had tried even harder after that not to be a burden, and not to impose on his time and energies. He had begun leaving on Saturdays and Sundays and not saying where he was going. I had gotten to the point that I was terrified of being alone with the children. I was afraid I would go completely crazy and scare them, or at least not be able to meet their needs. But I wanted desperately not to be responsible for Martin thinking that I was chaining him, so I said nothing when he left. Occasionally, when I got extremely upset and desperate I would call Martin's mother. He was usually there or his mother would know where he was. I felt rejected and very left out.

I was able to cope only until mid-July. After a very difficult weekend and several previous weeks of having had to call Martin at work to beg "Please come home!" I was emotionally exhausted. The constant fear, the shutting out the daylight, the inability to go anywhere, and the worrying that I couldn't handle it anymore, forced my long-dreaded decision. I called Dr. Ashford and said, "I think that I need to go to Mountain View again. I really need to talk to you and I can't get into town to your office." Dr. Ashford told me that it was a wise decision and to have Martin call him to set it up.

I cried all day prior to my going that evening. I was so distressed at having to leave the children. How would they do at someone else's home? Would they be well cared for? My sister could watch them for a while and maybe Martin's sister could take them. I didn't want them shuffled back and forth. How would they react to my absence, or maybe they would be better off? They must have suffered some effects of my constant anxiety even though I had tried desperately to hide it from them. And how would I get along without *them*? They seemed to be all that was important to me now. I started to pack the eight-by-ten recent portraits of them that were still unframed but changed my mind. I knew that if I looked at them I would be inconsolable and could not bear their absence from me. Martin got the teenager across the street to baby-sit and arranged to take a day off to transfer the children to my sister's house until I could come home again. I expected to be away only for a few days. And Martin hadn't told anyone differently, as that news must have to come later!

I returned to the loony bin at ten in the evening while it was dark and the streets were fairly deserted.

Laying on the stiff narrow mattress in the small room at Mountain View, reliving this past year and my second sweep into insanity, I prayed and told God that I needed a minor miracle to help me and the doctor pull me together and make me normal.

I knew that I had to come back to this place again but there must be a way to solve this problem, make me well, and let me live a normal life. I was sure the doctor would know how to do this. In the meantime I must be calm and optimistic. I closed my eyes, envisioned myself, Martin, Karen, and "Sissy" (who had never received a name in all this confusion) being the ideal, happy, loving, well–functioning American family. "I'm doing this for *my family!*" I told myself, and in total mental and physical exhaustion I fell asleep.

Chapter Three
Insulin Therapy

Daylight did not awaken me. I had lain awake ruminating and listening to the occasional screams that came from below my window for so long, and was so exhausted, that my late sleep had been a deep one. A nurse entered the room noisily at about six A.M. My eyes blinked open. Fear entered with the dim morning light. I remembered where I was, and depression and fright churned together until I was numbed, but I obediently rolled on to my stomach as requested.

"I have a shot for you. We have to start your insulin early, as you need two shots each morning for it to work."

I was not fully awake and felt muddled by the nurse's business-like announcement. Why were they giving me insulin? Why had I rolled over to let the nurse shoot me in the fanny? I hadn't talked to my doctor. He probably didn't know about this. And Martin, he would be upset, too.

"I don't think I'm scheduled for treatments," I said meekly. "I haven't seen my doctor yet. He hasn't made any decisions."

"Oh, yes, you're on the list," the nurse responded briskly, "and we have special orders that you get two shots. One at six and then again with the others at seven."

"Why two shots?" I was waking slowly and feeling more and more unsettled.

"Your shots didn't work last time, so we're trying a new procedure. Apparently you didn't have enough insulin before. But we do need to give it in two dosages."

The nurse had become slightly more friendly but was still not smiling. I thought her rather informative conversation was so that she could seem important and not for any tender feelings for her patient.

I was now very distressed. Did two dosages mean larger amounts or did it mean a new method of injecting the dosage. I wished Martin were here or that I could call him so he could check on this new treatment. I knew that in my prior hospitalization I had not gone into a coma, and although the doctor had increased my dosage numerous times, I never "went out." But the doctor nevertheless felt I had received great benefit from the subcoma relaxation I had experienced, and he thought that was sufficient.

At least this was what Martin reported to me. Maybe because I hadn't been comatose, I hadn't been "cured." Anyway, it looked as if the choice were not mine to make right now. I knew you couldn't argue with the staff here. There were large men in white coats just to insure that you didn't. I was fearful but since I already had insulin in me I decided I might as well let them do their thing today. I would argue with the doctor when he came and enlist Martin's help if that failed.

The nurse left the room saying, "I'll be back to take you to treatment at seven." As I lay waiting for her to return all kinds of worries floated in my head. I worried about the dosage, the procedure, the doctor's inaccessibility prior to decisions, and how long they might keep me.

I had been hoping to talk the doctor into a short stay only. So I needed to see him, or rather, let him see me before the insulin messed up my mind anymore. I had read about insulin therapy when I was at home following my first treatments. I was relieved that I had gleaned this knowledge *after* my treatment, rather than before. Insulin therapy had a certain incidence of death! It was low but it was there. What if the insulin killed me before I could stop the treatments? I felt so helpless.

The nurse returned. "Time to put on your robe and get your second shot," she said. This day nurse was fairly pleasant but extra efficient and very hurried. The patients who were receiving insulin therapy were all herded down a locked, back stairwell to the second floor where the insulin room was located. We went down the narrow dark stairs, the confused, even stupored women, all in their night clothes with robes covering them, stumbling almost blindly over the steps, bumping into one another and being hurried by several nurses and orderlies barking orders. The stairwell had one small, uncovered bulb at both the top and the bottom of the stairs. There was also a bulb and a narrow door at the landing between floors. The bulbs were dim and gave off very little light and made the off-white walls seem grimy and the bare wooden steps more worn. To me the muddled mass of expressionless, grim faces in the hurried procession resembled a fire drill from some bizarre dream sequence out of a horror movie.

All of a sudden one of the men who had entered the strange parade with several other men at the landing bolted from the downward mass of humanity and headed back upstairs, knocking aside the others as he went.

"Stop him!" the nurse shouted. He was quickly followed by two very muscular orderlies, who also knocked people about, grabbed the runaway by both arms, and shoved him back into the pack. He gave some feeble resistance but, seeing the opposition, he succumbed.

I was momentarily amused and remarked to the nurse near my side, "That took a lot of guts. I'm real proud of him. I'd try it myself but you guys would just overpower me too ... and more easily too."

"That's right!" snapped the nurse. "Don't even think about it!"

She moved closer to me and took my arm although I didn't know if that was to prevent me from running or because I had already been injected and was somewhat dizzy and obviously staggering.

We entered Second Floor, the entire herd, through a locked door with a glass window in it. That's a little unsafe, I thought. Someone with *real* intent could break the glass, but then, what would an escape to a stairwell serve anyone? It was locked at the other end. Unless—and the idea was exciting—one could do it during an exodus, such as this, confuse the staff, and get into an unlocked door as the men were entering. I wondered if they had ever had any escapes here.

On the other side of the door on the Second Floor was a small room with numerous chairs, all old and made of ugly and uncomfortable vinyl, as well as a couple of inexpensive small tables. Beyond that room were two doors, one of which led to the Insulin Room, which was a long, narrow, tiled room with gray-white walls and nondescript-colored asphalt on the tiled floor. Cots were lined up from one end to the other on the left side of the room. The cots were the simple metal fold-up variety, with thin mattresses. Each cot had heavy cotton flannel sheets and a pillow with a heavy cotton pillowcase. The cots were separated by pale green curtains that were on tracks that ran the length of the room; the curtains also separated the cots perpendicularly on both sides of each cot.

I remembered hating this room. It reminded me of a terminal ward in an army hospital near the front, where the casualties had curtains to provide some privacy and dignity in their dying. The curtains were at the foot of the cots. At the head of the cots stood the wall, with a window here and there. Past the curtains at the foot of the cots was a long counter that ran almost the length of the room. Behind the counter were medications (probably gallons of insulin), charts, records, and staff equipment for which I could only imagine the uses. At each end of the long counter was a door that went into other rooms that I knew nothing about.

The procedure was this: You were to remove your robe and pajamas or gown, and put on "insulin pajamas" that were handed to you as you entered, and then you were directed to a cot. These new pajamas were of very heavy cotton, like the sheeting, and were grayish white (as if the hospital hadn't noticed all the detergent ads touting "whiteness and brightness"). When you were clothed in these garments, a nurse or orderly came and shot you in the behind with a needle full of insulin, and usually put your clothes on a hook on the wall in your cubicle. I was assigned to a cot with no window, received my second insulin shot, and lay staring at the green curtains.

"I hope I can stay awake," I thought anxiously. "I don't want to have a coma, and with luck, this may be the only crack they have at me." Time passed and I grew groggy and dizzy and started perspiring heavily. I almost dozed off a time or two but laboriously focused on the staff conversations; I tried to keep my mind active by making pictures and patterns of the shadows and lines in the curtains. I became damper and groggier. A nurse or orderly pulled back the curtain at the foot of the cot, from time to time to peek at me. I smiled at them and felt a little superior knowing they hadn't put me out. After a long period of time a nurse pulled back the curtain, handed me my clothes, and said curtly, "Dress and come on out." I rejoiced inwardly knowing that I was still alive and conscious.

The next event in this insulin process was to stop in the room with the tables and chairs that we had passed on entering the Insulin Room. This was the only halfway pleasant part of treatments, as I remembered it. The earlier bared tables were now covered with coffee makers, mugs, ashtrays, and several covered trays. No tablecloths or napkins. None of the niceties; everything was just functional. Here the patients were given a sweet roll with coffee, or with a nauseating, overly sweetened "shake" made of glucose and who knew what else. I enjoyed the sweet roll, but not the shake. I was one of those chosen few who were given a shake and was watched to see that it all went down. I hadn't remembered the drink tasting so sickeningly sweet. The patients sat around in groups looking vacant and being uncommunicative. Some were smoking cigarettes, others just staring. A nurse ushered a group out of the door and up the stairwell. I watched, feeling a bit nauseous, but nevertheless trying to enjoy the sweet roll.

A doctor came in from the Insulin Room and sat by me. I knew he must be the doctor as he was dressed in his street clothes, and I recognized his voice as one of those present while I was trying to stay awake on the cot. He started to talk to me as the door to another hallway on Second Floor opened. A nurse emerged but was pushed aside by a very distressed female patient who made a dash toward the doctor. The patient was pushed back into the hall, and the door was locked again behind her. As the doctor made another attempt to start a conversation, the same door was unlocked by an orderly. The patient reentered, got closer to the doctor this time, and frantically pleaded with him to do something.

"They just keep flying all around me ... in front of my eyes ... I can't see ... they won't go away!"

The doctor looked annoyed. He was still trying to get some basic information from me: my age, how long ago I was here, what had transpired since that time. We were interrupted several more times by the same patient. Each time the door was unlocked, the patient pushed by nurses or orderlies and asked the doctor to "help get these flies away from my face, I can't stand it anymore!" The doctor rose, escorted the patient to the door, and then, in great irritation, scolded the nurse, saying, "Now don't let her in here again!" He turned to me and apologized for the interruptions then started to explain.

I cut him off pleasantly. "Oh that's all right. *She* doesn't bother me. It's just those flies."

The doctor looked at me a little bewildered and then smiled

hesitantly. I guessed that maybe I wasn't funny or maybe he suspected me of possessing the same mental aberration. A nurse came and hurried the rest of the patients and me back to the stairwell and up to Third Floor.

Back in my room, I stretched out on the bed, still a little dizzy and very nauseous. The floor nurse came in and told me to hurry if I wanted to bathe, as lunch was coming promptly. I followed the nurse to the large bathroom where the nurse turned on faucets for the shower. There were no handles and the nurse held keys, or a wrench, something that I could not see.

"For heaven's sake!" I wondered, "Are they afraid the patients will drown themselves in the shower?"

The shower was quick and the water temperature was cooler than I liked, but I was still in a haze and accepted whatever was happening to me. I felt in such a stupor that it took a while for me to realize that the water temperature was what concerned the staff. Were the patients so dulled that they could scald themselves? Back in my room once again, I was given my suitcase and told to get my clothes. I dressed and went back to the bathroom to comb out my wet hair.

While I was there another patient entered the bathroom, muttering something about being in here and wanting to get out and wait until she got a hold of her husband since it was his fault. I looked at her. She was a small, rather muscular lady, with very unkempt, graying hair, probably in her early fifties. She appeared very tense and her angry expression exaggerated the wrinkles on her face.

"What did your husband do?" I asked.

"He tried to kill me, that's what he did! He belongs *here*, not me. Don't you think a person is crazy if they try to murder someone ... for no reason? He meant to ... I know he did. He didn't fool *me*."

I asked how he went about it.

"He filled the basement with water. That's what he did. He knew that I would go down there."

"How would that kill you?" I asked curiously.

"Well, if there are bare electric wires in the water, where you can't see them, if you walk into the water—it was deep so that you wouldn't suspect anything—if you went to find the problem and walked into the water, it would electrocute you, now wouldn't it?"

I was horrified. The poor woman, her own husband had tried to kill her with this evil plot and *she* ends up in the locked ward. Maybe no one believed her story and he ...

"He's going to try it again when I get out. I know he is. He knows I'm on to him ... and this time I'll know."

A nurse interrupted our conversation, and we both were hurried out to go eat lunch.

My tray was on the bed since there was no other furniture in my room. I picked at the food. The glucose shake was still lying just under my throat, and I wasn't sure that it wanted to stay there. The shaft of the dumbwaiter, which carried the food from floor to floor, was in the wall adjoining my room, and the banging and clanging made me jumpy. I was becoming a little more alert, and my senses were starting to respond with the usual strong super-sensitivity.

There were more trays, which were followed by more noises in the wall. The noise level was mounting and I couldn't stop from jumping nervously. A nurse came in and took my tray, remarking about the waste, and made her contribution to the clatter of dishes and banging of trays. I thought that if there were one more stop of the dumbwaiter I would be unable to suppress a scream.

Then someone did scream. A loud piercing scream that went on for several seconds. An urgent call came over the intercom. "Orderlies to Third North!" I jumped up from my bed and closed my door for protection, just as two orderlies came running down the hall headed toward the opposite side of the bathroom from my room.

"It's Martha," I heard a nurse say.

After things quieted down, I reopened my door to rid myself of the claustrophobia from being in such a small enclosure. The orderlies and the doctor I had seen in the coffee room came walking quickly past me. The doctor was carrying a black case and had a small rubber hose in one hand. I wanted to speak to him, to ask him about Martha, but he was in a hurry and didn't seem to notice me so I went back to my bed. I sat on the side and then lay down, curling myself up and burying my head in the hard pillow.

I sobbed quietly. It relieved some of the fear and the tension that had built up from the loud clanging and banging. But my depression was growing more intense. The loud noises in the wall persisted; they were unbearable. I tried covering my ears, but the muffled sounds were even more frightening.

A while later the early morning nurse came in and told me that the patients were going to the garden and asked if I wanted to go. I shook my head. I said I didn't feel well, but in reality, I was far too afraid. I was confused with directions and frightened just going to the bathroom. The thought of being outside, in the daylight, terrified me. The noise from lunch trays had subsided and I wished only for silence and rest. I remarked that I was nauseous and dizzy, and the nurse looked intensely at my eyes. She appeared to notice something.

"I'll have some juice sent to you," she said.

Another nurse brought the juice a little later, and I lay on my bed the entire afternoon, waiting for my doctor. I spent the time alternately crying, getting up briefly to go to the drinking fountain in the bathroom, and very tentatively exploring the area in my hallway.

With the patients out in the garden, the floor seemed somewhat stilled. I appreciated the silence and tried to relax. An orderly came and gave me a pill that I supposed was for my nerves. I tried extra hard to be calm, now that I knew what happened to anyone who screamed. Beyond my room was the dumbwaiter, then the bath, and then several rooms, small ones like mine with windows in the doors. I didn't look in because I was too frightened. But I assumed that some of them might have patients. I was right. That was where Martha came from, and later that afternoon there were two more calls from the intercom, and two more processions of orderlies, followed by the doctor with his black box going down the hallway.

The patients came in from the garden. I could hear noises from the halls and nurses were walking by my door. Dinnertime came and went with the same unnerving noises of trays and dishes right outside my door and the continual banging in the wall. I was feeling a little hungry now but was still too jumpy to get much of the food to my mouth or concentrate on chewing. I guessed that I had spent most of my time crying. Everything looked so black and hopeless. My nerves were completely frayed from the sounds of feeding time.

It was getting dark outside. I could see the vines' shadows starting to form on my window screen. Chills went up my back as I remembered how alone and frightening it would be in my small, spooky room. And I was so fearful of what might be down at the darker end of the hallway where the orderlies and doctor went. I knew better but imagined that the green demons from my childhood nightmares could be lurking there. I must have been crying and dozing off and on for hours. I heard someone on the intercom say that visiting hours would be up in ten minutes. What had happened to Martin? And why hadn't my doctor come?

Martin came through the door a few minutes later, just as the speaker announced that visiting hours were over. I sobbed in relief as I reached out my arms for him and for comfort. Martin was stiff and apologetic.

"I'm sorry, I couldn't get here any sooner ...got off work kinda late ... had to go in this afternoon ... for a while. I stopped to see the girls ... and now it's already time to leave."

I started crying again. "Martin, they gave me insulin today. What is happening? Didn't you talk to them? You've got to stop them. They could kill me! They are giving me *two* doses! I wasn't even going to have those awful treatments again. Didn't you tell the doctor I didn't need them? Wasn't it agreed? Can you call Dr. Ashford tonight? I don't want to go down there for another one tomorrow. Please do something. This place is awful. The dumbwaiter is right in that wall, and it is so noisy in here that I can't cope with it. When they bring up the food it's like living in a construction site. I get so jumpy that I can't even eat. You know how loud noises upset me. I'm *so* scared. Oh *please*, you've got to help me!"

Martin put his arm around me stiffly and tried to tell me it was all right.

"But why are they giving me treatments? You didn't sign for them. It wasn't arranged.... Martin, did you sign?"

Martin was looking guilty. He started moving toward the door. "I've got to go. I had to, Laurel. They wouldn't admit you unless I did.

They have to have permission to give treatments or you can't be here. And the doctor knows what he's doing."

I was almost angry as I said accusingly, "You just got here. Why didn't you come earlier? You didn't even talk to the doctor, did you? You said that you would tell him that I wasn't so bad this time and that he wouldn't give me the insulin therapy. Martin, what happened?"

Martin was at the door and trying to pull away from me as I clutched desperately at his arm.

"I've got to go now. Visiting hours are over. They just let me in for a minute because I explained that I got hung up. I guess that the doctor decided you needed to have the treatments. Maybe he had already made up his mind. I had to get you in and they insisted I sign the papers or you couldn't be here. I guess they do that for all patients ... get permission for treatment."

He was pulling away and heading into the hallway despite my pleading and following after him.

"Goodbye. I'll call you ... or come ... tomorrow ... got to go ... got to go now ... It's all right."

Martin went down the hallway while I followed, trying to plead with him to change things. We rounded the corner near the nurses' station. I was apprehensive at being so far from my room, so I waved hesitantly and started backing down the hall toward the security of my room. I realized as I stumbled in my backwards movements that this hallway really *was* crooked the walls *and* the floor. But the knowledge that I was not so out of it the previous night was of no consolation to me now. I lay down on the bed, pulled my knees to my chest, and cried some more. I tried to say a prayer but couldn't focus on thoughts or words.

I stayed in that position for some time until the night nurse—not Penny, luckily—came to my room and suggested firmly that I go to bed. I needed to be up early in the morning for my treatment. She took my temperature and counted my pulse. This was the first indication I had seen of any concern about my medical condition. It wasn't much, but at least they would be able to tell that I wasn't dead ... *yet*.

I sat there oblivious to the nurse. I was devastated. How could Martin have done this to me—actually sign papers for them to do this inhumane treatment? When had he done this? I had sat there, unsuspecting, as he admitted me to this place and told me that I would be "all right." He had said that they would only keep me a few days. Had he been lying to me?

The doctors still didn't even know my physical condition; no one had given me even so much as a blood test. The treatments could actually kill me. It would be Martin's fault, but he had been so calm about it, saying the doctor knew what he was doing. Martin should have them do this to him. Then he wouldn't be so sure it was all right. He had betrayed me. He hadn't spoken to the doctor in my behalf. If I couldn't count on Martin, then who could I?

I was so terrified, so sad, so deserted. The room looked even more frightening to me. The scary vine's shadows were on the windows. The unfriendly light from the ceiling had made the nurse's features look harsh and she had seemed even *more* threatening. The intense fear was causing other symptoms that I had to endure. My hands and feet were feeling disconnected from my body, my head was aching, and I had a choking feeling in my throat. I was trapped here, and I was with crazy people. I felt so distressed and so helpless.

I undressed in a trance, having to give double directions to my hands to make them perform. I gave the nurse my suitcase. The nurse left without saying anything more, and I crawled into my hard bed, pulled my knees to my chest, and quietly sobbed myself to sleep.

Chapter Four
Martin

Martin was embarrassed as he got in the elevator. He suspected that some of the visitors had seen his wife pleading with him. He didn't like her trying to make him feel guilty. He probably should have told her earlier about the decision to give her treatments, but he hadn't been sure how she would react. He was sick of dealing with her histrionics. When he and Dr. Ashford had talked, the doctor told him that they needed to start all over. Last summer had helped her some. She had been better for a while, but the problem was that there had been no follow-up therapy sessions.

But it wasn't his fault, Martin defended himself. How could he afford to pay for sessions at almost a hundred dollars a shot? The doctor certainly had an inflated idea of his worth! Martin's company's insurance policy had been stretched to the limit with Laurel's hospitalization. Good God! He had the whole family to think about feeding and housing.... Laurel needed to get a grip.... to grow up.

The elevator jarred to a stop on the Second Floor. The old mechanisms were probably about ready to give out. Martin's eyes widened in alarm as a rather portly, baldish man headed toward them to board the elevator. He was with a group of four visitors leaving the Second Floor and was partially obstructed from Martin's view by an elderly, plump lady. Martin lowered his eyes, trying to look inconspicuous. The balding man looked like one of the men from his downtown office, but he wasn't sure. He didn't want to be seen here by anyone from his work; it could jeopardize his job ... probably. As they climbed onto the elevator the man had pushed forward into the space right in front of Martin. Thank God, it wasn't who he thought it was. But should Martin feel so concerned and uncomfortable? After all, it was Laurel who was nutsy, not him. Still, at this point it was an embarrassment just being her husband.

He was still feeling angry toward her as he got into his car and headed for the highway. He was not going to let her make him feel guilty about the treatments. He just was not! That was final. He had had to make the decision for insulin; Laurel was simply not capable of doing that right now. At least that was what the doctor had implied. They needed to get something done, and Ashford was one of the best in the business. He said she needed more shock. Damn it, let him explain it to Laurel. Martin didn't want the blame. He was just doing what he was told by someone who knew about these kinds of things.

Maybe by his next visit she would have had enough shocks to make her forget to blame him. He was sure that he was a damned good husband ... and father. He took good care of his family. They had what they needed and then some! He had just signed away his life on a large mortgage for their new home. A home that was better than what most of his acquaintances his same age could provide for their families. He sure hoped Laurel wouldn't screw this all up with her mental problems.

She hadn't seemed to have problems when they were first married. She had always been a little high strung and emotional. His family was more sedate, more refined. They didn't get theatrical over every little thing as Laurel sometimes did. His mother had been skeptical of Laurel before they married. But she had been very nice to her, and she continued to be nice even when Laurel was rude and unappreciative. Damn, but she had caused him a lot of stress lately. He pulled off the highway. He surely needed a drink this evening. He headed again for the Cozy Inn.

There weren't a lot of people in the small bar. Definitely a slow night. He sat at a booth and ordered his drink and lost himself in trying to sort out what had gone wrong in his life. It wasn't his fault. He had studied hard in college and gone on to further training for his company. When Laurel had joined him in New York, she had seemed a little unhappy there. Sure she was cooped up in the apartment all day, but she had things she could do, and the baby needed a lot of care. Later, her teaching had seemed to help her, but he didn't like it. He wanted her home taking care of the house and the kids.

He still didn't understand what caused her to start having the anxiety attacks and the panics. He supposed that she had inherited a mental weakness from her mother. She had always said she feared she might go berserk just like her mom. He guessed she had. What to do now was the problem. He had married her and needed to stick by her. He knew that was his duty. But it was so embarrassing to have a wife in a mental hospital.

His drink came and he noticed the waitress was rather cute. She had a very nice figure, good breasts, pretty hair, and a flirty way of talking. He paid for his drink and wondered if she had good mental health.

Martin thought about his brother. Michael had been having some problems, too. His wife had talked him into taking accounting and business classes when he was in college and they had been engaged. But Michael wasn't a businessman. He had no skills in that area. He hated selling. He hated figures. He should have been a writer. Everyone in the family knew that Michael was talented and very sensitive. He should have stayed in the liberal arts program and been a college professor or writer or both. Instead Michael had joined a large firm based in Chicago. He was one of hundreds of employees doing accounting in a huge office. No individual offices, just row upon row of desks and more desks. Michael couldn't take that kind of environment. It was too meaningless and too "dog-eat-dog." Michael was just not competitive. He began to smoke two packs of cigarettes a day, then three. He drank cup after cup of coffee. He had trouble sleeping nights. He worried how he could take care of his family when he hated his job so. Martin knew how that felt. Michael had finally had to quit his job he was having such severe problems with stress. But it was his job that was the problem. It was not a mental problem. There were no mental problems in Martin's family.

Once, a long time back, Martin's oldest sister had started feeling scared, insecure, somewhat like Laurel. She was afraid to go to work, afraid to leave the house. Martin's mother had kept her home to rest for a few weeks. His mother had read to her from their religious books and they had prayed a lot. Then Martin's sister had got her courage back and she returned to work. She hadn't had any problems since ...

So what was it with Laurel? His mother had tried to help her. She had tried to read some of the religious writings to her once, when Laurel was having a panic attack, but she did not even try to listen. Laurel had not only been unappreciative, she had been out-and-out rude. His mother had left her alone after that.

It had been awful going to see Joe, the department head at work, and telling him that his wife needed to be hospitalized. Martin had hoped that there would not be any questions that could point to her specific problem but Joe was nice enough. He gave Martin the papers to fill out and didn't get too personal. Everything had gone okay until Martin had turned in the papers and the name of the hospital was on them. Martin hoped that Joe would not read them, that they would be given directly to the insurance underwriters. But, as Joe looked them over, he read "Mountain View" aloud and looked up at Martin. How mortifying, to have someone look at you and know that your wife was in the local hospital for crazy people. Joe had mumbled something about "sorry about this" to Martin, but Martin didn't want to hear. He had left the office with a deep shade of scarlet covering his face. He now dreaded going to the main office, and he felt as if all his coworkers were discussing him behind his back. Damn Laurel, why couldn't she hold it together? Life isn't easy for any of us, he thought, but Laurel always made a big deal out of everything.

Martin sipped his drink, noticing that a rather swarthy looking man had entered the bar and was looking furtively around the small group. He was wearing a brown leather jacket, which seemed strange for this late summer evening, and an old worn pair of jeans. Martin was startled by a sudden shout....

"Okay, everyone. Put your hands up!"

Martin, the barkeeper, the waitress, and the others obediently put their hands above their heads. The man had taken the gun from his pocket and was holding it rather awkwardly. He circulated among the few patrons and had them hand him their wallets. He asked several of them, including Martin, to remove their watches. He then took what little money there was in the cash drawer from the barkeeper and rushed out of the place before anyone from the kitchen or back rooms could alert the police.

When the police did arrive, they could only take a description, a statement from all of the victims, and a detailed list of the stolen items. Martin had had only thirty-five dollars with him, his credit cards, and driver's license. He was relieved that there had been no violence and that so little money was lost.

The robbery had distracted him from his anger and frustration at Laurel. When he returned home he made a quick call to check on the children and let his sister-in-law know that Laurel was "doing great."

In the next evening's newspaper was a short article about the robbery at the Cozy Inn. Martin's name was listed with the patrons, the amount of his loss, and mention of his watch. His brother called and asked him about the incident. His family usually excused each other's shortcomings They would

understand even though most of them did not drink. He had a right to stop
for a drink. He had a right to try to find relief from the hell that he was
dealing with in his private life. He was fairly sure that his mother knew,
but she would probably never mention it to him.

But he worried that Laurel's family would see the article and wonder
what he was doing in that part of town ... and in a bar. None of them were
drinkers. Well, if they had to worry about Laurel they'd probably need a few
stiff drinks themselves. In fact, he decided to have one himself.

Chapter Five
The Great Outdoors

The thin green drapes shifted slightly with the movements of the staff going back and forth between the insulin-drugged patients. I could hear Martha in the background talking incessantly. I fought hard to stay conscious and not let the insulin take effect. I was perspiring more heavily this morning as I tossed and moved about on the cot to stay awake. My consciousness was spotty as I entered strange dream states and would reactively shake myself awake in fear. Much of what I heard going on about me had the feel of distinct unreality. Martha continued talking incessantly as she had when I had gone to my own cot at the start of the session. Then, when it was nearly time to get up again, I could hear Martha in the background. It seemed as if the whole treatment consisted of sweating, fighting consciousness, and listening to Martha.

I was no longer feeling any hope or trying to have a positive attitude about my hospitalization. The nurse had taken my pulse and temperature last evening but I knew that no blood tests had been given, at least to me. I had not had a physical exam for a few years and I had a nagging fear that if I had something wrong, they would never even know it. It bothered me that Martin didn't seem concerned about the treatments. I had described them to him and had even looked up information about insulin shock in the encyclopedia after my treatments during the last hospitalization. I had seen the incidence of fatalities—I didn't remember it, but the fact that there was one was scary enough. I was sure that Martin would never want to take insulin shock but it was okay to sign me on. I was annoyed, frightened and feeling very alone. With the sound of Martha still in my ears, I arose from my cot, took off the damp pajamas, put on my own clothes again, pushed my damp hair away from my face and neck, and started for the coffee room.

Martha was at the counter still talking nonstop. She was going on and on about her toothbrush. I had no idea why Martha would have brought it with her to her treatment. She had put it right here. See? Just before she had lain down on her cot. Now it was gone. Where could it be? No one else would want to use her toothbrush, now would they? It was not sanitary. But then, it was right here and someone had to have moved it because she had put it right here. Had anyone seen her toothbrush? She was asking yet another person, a patient who was probably too confused to know what a "toothbrush" was and who was just looking at Martha dumbly. I passed the counter about then and Martha swung toward me, ready to direct the same questions to me, for the untold time.

"Martha, for cripes sakes, forget it! Just be glad that you still have your teeth!" I growled as she passed me.

Several of the staff snickered and I wanted to tell them it wasn't funny, that it was lucky that everyone was still alive, and to please keep Martha out of my physical range. I could almost forgive Martha's husband for trying to electrocute her.

Maybe because treatments weren't so rushed today, or maybe as a reward for shutting up Martha, the floor nurse offered a tub bath to me. I needed to have something to make me feel soothed and so I gladly accepted. It was in the great bathtub. I figured that this appliance must have dated back to the decades when large water baths, alternating hot and cold water, were used for the insane to calm their anxieties and hopefully save their minds. The nurse had to fill the tub, as it, like the showers, had no handles on the spigots. But I was allowed to tell her how hot to make it, and the nurse did put a lot of water in. I lay back in the warm tub and closed my eyes. My fingers were puffed with swelling on the ends, my nerves were tingling throughout my arms and legs, and my head was confused and angry but I was relieved to be able to try to relax. Bathing was one of the few pleasures that had remained for me, and I often used it at home to try to relieve tension. For a few moments, I felt happy. I tried to pretend that I was in a bubble bath in an exquisitely decorated bathroom, at an expensive estate, and that soon my maid would bring me a soft luxuriously large towel.

Then I opened my eyes as the nurse called my name. She handed me one of the hospital's coarse off-white linen towels. I had not even enjoyed any privacy; the showers had been busy and the toilets didn't even have doors in front of them. The nurse also handed me my razor to use, but said that I must use it while she watched, as razors were a forbidden item on Third North.

After bathing, eating lunch, and crying once again from the nervous jangling that the dumbwaiter, dishes, and tray noises were inflicting on my senses, I lay on my bed with my eyes red and swollen. In my body every nerve was vibrating, and it seemed that the clamor would *never* stop. All the noises were intensified and lost together in one great roar, punctuated periodically by a tremendously sharp bang that felt like a physical blow to my spinal column. I stifled the impulse to scream out when I glanced up and saw Dr. Ashford standing over me.

"How is it going?" he asked.

I was momentarily relieved at seeing my doctor and the impact of the noise seemed to lessen. On rethinking his question, I became angry. The nerve, I thought, to ask me how it's going, just like it's any day, any person, and any place. Did he expect some trite "fine, how are things with you" response? I burst into tears.

"I can't stand this place. Why are you giving me insulin again? Can I please get away from this floor? I'm with the very most disturbed patients. And the noise, the noise is so dreadful ... I can hardly think ... and I'm so jumpy."

Dr. Ashford looked very solemn.

"Well, you are a very disturbed young lady," he said. "I will move you when you are better ... and you need these treatments. You are extremely depressed and crying all the time. You need to be here, on this floor, where we can keep an eye on you."

I tried to explain to him that the noise from the dishes and the serving kept my nerves on edge, and that I was crying because I was so unsettled, jumpy, and frightened, and that a mental hospital should be quiet and secluded to provide rest. And would he please get me away from the noise, away from the back wards with the night screaming coming from the yard below. Then I would be better, faster. Just then, as if to prove my point, the last load of dishes was loaded and sent clanking through the wall. Could he hear that it sounded as if it were right in my room? I had jumped and clenched my arms to my body in a reflex to the loud noise. Dr. Ashford nodded and said he would try to make arrangements, and I didn't get a chance to ask him about dosages or treatments. He left as suddenly as he had come.

When the floor nurse came a few minutes later and inquired about my going to the garden, I tried to make excuses again but the nurse was more demanding this time.

"The fresh air will do you good. You need to get out. I'm going to insist today. I'm sure that your doctor wants you out there."

I put on my shoes and went to gather with the herd to be loaded in and out of the locked elevator. This was the first time that I had gone in this front elevator since my arrival. It was fascinating, yet frightening, to see how groups of ashen-faced, expressionless people were all clustered into groups and loaded into the car like cattle. On the main floor the nurses and orderlies ushered them out the back door of the hospital into the yard.

It was not much of a garden. There were a few petunias, several rose bushes, and lots of small evergreen bushes, benches, and numerous trees. The trees were all surrounding the yard probably, I thought, for privacy. Beyond the trees was a very tall fence. One could not even see over the fence. It must have been seven or eight feet tall. On top of the fence were some lines of barbed wire. Mountain View had all the charm of a prison, consisting of the tall, stuccoed walls with heavy-duty screens at the windows, barbed wire fences, and guards.

The nurses and orderlies were interspersed among the patients and were ever vigilant. The patients sat around on benches, walked about, or played at a large shuffleboard court. I sat on a step just outside the doorway and watched the "crazies." I tried to stay near the building; the heavy structure made me feel more stable. If I were to stray out into the open bright light I would feel unprotected and more dizzy. Here I felt a little safer. The nurse came over and insisted that I come on past the cement courtyard, out onto the grass.

"I need to keep an eye on you," she said.

I was puzzled. Dr. Ashford had said they needed to keep an eye on me, too. I wondered what they were expecting me to do.

"Why do you all need to keep an eye on me?" I asked. "I'm not planning to do anything."

The nurse smiled in a condescending manner, "You're having a lot of insulin so your doctor wants you watched for any reactions."

Great. As if I weren't concerned enough about what they were doing to me. That explained the long look that the nurse had given me the previous day, when I had said that I was too dizzy to go outside. Of course, and that was the reason for the extra juice treat. I wondered what a reaction would be like. It must be something related to dizziness. But then I was nearly always dizzy. It went with the anxieties. I sighed, took a deep breath, stood shakily, and made my way toward the lawn area. I found a bench that was the closest to the building and sat down very tentatively.

Several orderlies were playing shuffleboard with a few of the more alert patients. Many of the men and women just milled around, not talking, and looking at nothing. The entrance to the courtyard from the alleyway had a large gate that was part of the fence. It could swing open wide enough for deliveries and even for ambulances. I smiled sardonically as I told myself, "This is quite a place to be. If only my friends and family could see me now." I felt tears well up as I indulged a little in some self-pity. The orderlies seemed to be enjoying *them*selves, I observed. Too bad if the patients were not real excited about their lot.

The nurse interrupted my musing by asking me to come walking with her. I was feeling so nervous and shaky that all I wanted to do was to sit, move as little as possible, and wait quietly there until we were all taken back in. My fingertips were feeling swollen and sensitive as they did when my anxiety was at its peak. My head felt strange and stuffy and I was experiencing so much dizziness. It was very warm outside and I had no socks inside my loafers. My feet were swollen and sweaty and my legs were wobbly but I rose to walk with the nurse. I wanted to make an impression of being better, so that the doctor would move me away from the crazy hallway where the orderlies and the house doctor ran up and down to the locked rooms. I didn't remember all the patients being so completely out of it when I was here last summer.

Apparently the nurse felt her job was to get the patients moving, maybe get a little exercise with the fresh air. She gathered several other patients to walk along with us and the group was growing. I was disappointed. I had hoped that the nurse was going to talk with me. I

had tried numerous times since my arrival to engage the staff in conversation, but they were either too busy or discounted the patients as
unworthy of their time and attention. Sensible conversation here was
probably hard to come by but the staff didn't seem too bright either.

I was silent as we walked, listening. The patients who were talking really weren't making much sense as they ruminated over whatever
their main concern happened to be, not unlike Martha looking for her
toothbrush.

Chapter Six
Dorothy

Unexpectedly, a woman spoke to me as the nurse led her group of patients around the garden. I had recognized the tall lady with red-blonde hair who was on the same floor with me but the shock of a normal-sounding voice caused me now, since I was feeling unsteady anyway, to stumble on the broken old sidewalk and lunge to keep my balance.

I learned that her name was Dorothy. She had been here for several weeks, getting electroshock. That explained why I had not seen her in the Insulin Room. She was older. She had no children nor indeed had ever wanted any. She was not getting along with her husband, as he was crazier than she was. I thought that it was getting to be a common occurrence, husbands who were crazier than the wives they had committed.

Not getting along with her husband was nothing new to Dorothy. She had been married five times and divorced four times. She had been married each of the five times to the same husband, Harry. They would have terrible angry scenes, even physical violence, and then Dorothy would divorce him. Anytime from two weeks to two years later Dorothy would reassess the situation, and they would remarry. I was amused. What did Dorothy's family and friends think? They, of course, thought that she was *crazy* but then she must be, else why would she be here? I supposed that if Harry and Dorothy wanted to marry again and again, that was fine; it was their business, if rather zany, and kind of interesting.

Dorothy knew all about the hospital and some of the patients. She couldn't stand Martha either. Not all of the patients here had to have treatment; some just came here to consult with their doctors. This was unsettling to me because I had believed Martin when he told me that he had had to sign for treatments or the hospital would not admit me. Some patients got insulin therapy, some got electric shock and insulin, and some had only electric shock.

Electroshock was usually done in the basement treatment room, in the morning. It only took a short time. You were given an injection to put you out, and then you were wired to an electric box with some contraption that they fastened on your temples. You went into convulsions for a few seconds and it was over as soon as you woke up. It made you forget things. No doubt that was what was wrong with a lot of the patients; their brains had been fried. But the psychiatric theory was that blocking out unpleasant memories was part of what made you "well," since then you could focus on other things and be more amenable to therapy.

I learned that some patients were even given an electric shock when they were in a coma with the insulin. That information was less than comforting to me. I hadn't been consulted about the insulin; what if they decided to give me both? Dorothy didn't know much about insulin therapy, except that they took all morning to do it, and it didn't seem to affect your memory as much. So I explained the procedure to her and it felt good to tell someone who was listening what they were doing to me and how scary it was.

We circled the garden and I didn't even notice how far from the building entrance I had gone. As we started around again, Dorothy shared with me some bits of information about various patients and staff. Martha was here because she had gone into a psychotic break during menopause. The very tall, gangly blonde lady, walking alone and skulking around the bushes, had just come in last night. She was from Wyoming and had been in a boating accident. Her husband and her twelve-year-old son had drowned, but the lady had managed to save herself and her small baby. She was now suffering from total amnesia. She didn't even know her own name. The two old ladies who sat over by the shuffleboard were permanent residents of this place. They both came from very wealthy families and were both senile. Their families wanted them to be well cared for and not have to worry about anything. They both had rather nice private rooms around the corner, near the nurses' station on Third Floor. I didn't think putting your old relatives in a loony bin to save them from care and worry seemed like a very charitable thing to do. The older, fat, blonde woman, who walking in the group with the nurse, was in because her husband had committed her for bothering him so much at work. She was going through menopause, too. I had heard of women who had lost their minds during the change of life. But it did seem unfair that the husbands got to decide *when* their wives were crazy.

Dorothy also knew Penny and didn't like her at all. I didn't tell Dorothy about Penny having been a patient, as I hadn't yet assessed my trust level with my new friend. Dorothy liked the day nurse on Third Floor all right, but thought the nurse in charge who sat in the office was very cruel and unfeeling. And Penny and the other floor night nurse were both more than unpleasant. Dorothy could even tell me about some of their out-and-out cruelties. She cautioned me to stay as far away from them as possible. The orderlies were nice enough, though a little silly and immature. Dorothy would probably have been at the Annex with the less disturbed patients, but she was here under court order and had to be locked in. She was upset about that and didn't elaborate further.

Dorothy also shared some information about the hospital itself. The rooms that were locked in the back part of Third North did have patients in them. You could sometimes hear them scream at night. And when the orderlies and the doctor came running, it was to administer an electric shock to them right in their rooms to quiet them down.

So that was what was in the black bag that the doctor carried—a "shock box." The rubber tubing he was waving around was used to tie around the patient's arm to help him inject a knockout dosage of sodium pentathol.

The screams that I heard from my window above the courtyard probably came from the Second Floor, where the alcoholic patients were kept who came here to be sobered up. The hospital had originally been built for the treatment of alcoholism. The drunks screamed during their delirium tremors, hallucinating, and yelling for more alcohol.

The Second Floor alcoholics were mostly all men. Second Floor South was a men's ward. Second North had a few women on it. The skinny brown-haired lady, walking with the nurse just ahead of us, was in here for alcoholism. She had abused the substance so badly that her brain was partially destroyed. If you talked to her, she would make perfect sense, and then her eyes would sort of roll up and she would forget what she was saying, sometimes right in the middle of her own sentence.

Dorothy and I had fallen back behind the walking procession and had come around the shuffleboard court a second time. One of the orderlies called to Dorothy to come and join the game. I sat down on a nearby bench and Dorothy went out on the court, where she stood talking with the orderly. Neither of them witnessed what I could see from my vantage point. The Lady from Wyoming had come out of the bushes and had picked up a shuffleboard pole. She was holding it like a lance and coming at a running charge toward the back of the orderly.

"Look out!" I yelled, but too late. The woman had jabbed the stick right into his backside. A second orderly had also witnessed the deed, but was also too late to prevent it. The first orderly doubled over in pain and then in laughter. Then he turned to me. I sat startled with my mouth gaping, and he said, "I guess that's what you would call a 'shuffleboard goose.'"

A nearby nurse hurried over and relieved the lady of her weapon, giving both orderlies a scathing look. Dorothy and the orderlies went back to playing shuffleboard as they tried to stop smiling, which was much easier for the orderly who had been struck as he was still feeling some pain.

Angrily the nurse directed the Lady from Wyoming to sit on the bench, just like a kid in "time out." The woman sat down briefly but then, being excessively restless, she bounced up and paced about the lawn, stopping periodically to do arm stretches and knee bends. The nurse watched with apprehension. I watched with amazement. I was so absorbed by this bizarre behavior that I didn't hear the orderlies blowing a whistle. Apparently this was the signal to come to the door and wait to be loaded into the elevator.

Only some of the patients could go in the elevator at a time. Those loaded for the Second Floor went first as there weren't nearly so many of them. As I looked at the other patients, I wondered why men were not as predisposed to insanity as women apparently were. Maybe men just all got drunk instead? Dorothy and I went up in the third load and there were still patients waiting. The whole operation seemed archaic and inhumane to me. I was glad that I had found someone with whom to converse. It distracted me from my fears. I was amazed to think that I had managed to move away from the hospital building without having a dreaded panic attack. My anxieties had still controlled most of my thoughts, but the unusual goings-on had been a diversion to me.

For dinner I went to Dorothy's room, where I had some relief from the noise of the dumbwaiter. Dorothy was also on Third North but she was closer to the front of the hospital and the nurses' station. The Lady from Wyoming was in the room next to Dorothy and had a quiet little mouse-like patient for her roommate. I glanced in their room in passing but both ladies were sitting expressionless on their beds. Dorothy said that most everyone in this building was in that mindless condition, but not so at the Annex. Dorothy had been at Mountain View before and she said that this was nothing to be worried about. The patients would start thinking again once they stopped receiving shocks. Dorothy hadn't had shock treatments before now, but her doctor was trying to make her so well that she wouldn't want to marry Harry again if she divorced him a fifth time.

"I guess he thinks I'm so crazy I don't know my own mind. I guess that's right. But I have fun anyway ... and the doctor won't change that. I've forgotten some things but I still know that I'm very angry with Harry. But I'll get over it. I always do."

When I went to the bathroom that evening, Martha was in there ranting. Dorothy had come in just as Martha started telling her story to me again. Martha had already told several of the patients in the bathroom that her husband had tried to electrocute her by filling the basement with water.

"It was like a swimming pool," she went on. One lady asked Martha why her husband would do such a thing.

"Well," said Martha, "you know what you have down here?" Martha made a sweeping motion with her hand circling the pubic area in front of her own body.

"Cobwebs?" remarked Dorothy.

Martha seemed too confused to be incensed, "No, pubic hair. And as you get older ... it gets thinner ... and then they don't care anything about you ... and you end up like this ... in *here*."

Dorothy and I exchanged smiles, but Martha seemed oblivious. The nurse entered and I tried to share the joke with her.

"Did you know," I began, "that our mental health is all dependent on our 'PH'?"

The nurse looked angrily first at me and then at Martha. "Come on, get on back to your rooms, ladies!"

"Really," I continued, "Martha said we end up here because of our 'PH' or Pubic Hair. If your 'PH' count isn't high enough, you'll be locked up in a crazy ward. Right, Martha?"

But there was no reaction from the nurse other than to hurry us off to our rooms.

Dorothy and I got ready for bed and talked until Martin showed up the usual ten minutes or so before visiting hours were over. I didn't say much to him as there wasn't time and I was still feeling betrayed. Also, I now had a friend I could talk with, one who listened to me and even seemed to care. I asked Martin about the girls, said I had seen Dr. Ashford, asked Martin for more clothes since it appeared I'd be here a while, and told him again I didn't want to be here. I let him know, in conversation, that some of the patients were not receiving treatment.

"Well, I only know what they told me about your situation," he said defensively.

When Martin left, I went back to the large day room near the elevator where I had last seen Dorothy. The TV was on but Dorothy had not yet come back. I sat and watched TV for a few minutes but the program wasn't very interesting, and I wished that the patients had elected to watch one that I liked. As I looked around the room, most eyes seemed focused on the set. People appeared to be watching, but the laughter at the jokes came only from the sitcom's studio audience. All the faces remained passive.

Oh well, I thought, maybe they didn't catch on to the jokes. Then, too, the jokes really weren't that funny. If they don't like the program maybe I could change the channel. I looked around to see who seemed interested. No one did. I asked a few ladies if they minded if I changed channels. They either didn't answer or they shrugged. I got up, changed the channel, and looked around for any objections. No one seemed to notice.

Great! I decided. I'll view whatever programs *I* want. I watched a show until Dorothy came back.

"Watch!" I said to Dorothy. I got up and changed the set. No one responded. "See!" I said. "The TV is ours! We can watch whatever we like."

About that time Martha came over and changed the set back to a channel where the president was giving an address.

"Don't you care what your president has to say?" asked Martha.

Dorothy looked at me and shrugged her shoulders. "You shouldn't discount Martha," she said.

The address was nearly over, and as it concluded, Martha made numerous comments about her own patriotism, her president, her loyalties, her country, etc.

Later that evening, as TV went off the air on an early channel, Martha insisted that everyone stand, place their hands over their hearts, and listen as the band played "The Star Spangled Banner," while a flag waved on the TV set.

"Ah, a touching moment in the funny farm!" I remarked to Dorothy.

Dorothy shook her head, "I've heard that when you're truly crazy, you go 'off' on politics, religion, or sex. Martha's off on all three!" she commented sadly.

Only one of the patients stood up, responding to Martha's insistence that they give proper respect for flag and country. The others weren't aware enough to comprehend the shame that Martha tried to put upon them.

The night nurse, Penny again, walked around the TV room, taking all the temperatures and feeling all of the pulses. Dorothy and I looked knowingly at each other and made no comments. I looked around me. The room was huge, two or three times the size of my own living room. The large arched windows had no curtains or draperies on them, either to discourage patients from climbing from the windows, using the drapes as ropes, or possibly to prevent serious suicide attempts by hanging oneself from them. The large windows were on the front of the building, and the elevator was in the center of the building across from the windows. At one side of the room was an old upright piano, probably as old as the hospital itself. The TV was not a large set and sat at an angle in the corner, on the side of the wall where the nurses' station adjoined the TV or day room. There was a long glass window between the nurses' station and the day room for observation of the patients. There were a couple of card tables set up and a few comfortable chairs here and there against the wall. Two well-worn old couches sat near the window. The rest of the furniture consisted of stiff, hard chairs placed around the periphery of the room, so all of the blank-faced patients sat, mostly staring, in a large circle. Some of them were smoking, but only Dorothy and I were actually conversing.

A nurse announced that it was time to go to bed and began overseeing the putting out of cigarettes and checking of ashtrays. The room vacated slowly with Penny having to do some physical encouraging. I observed that Penny seemed loathe touching the patients and had an odd manner of retracting her hand as though they were infected. I wanted to announce to the group that Penny was actually one of them, but only Dorothy would have been able to appreciate this, and she had already left for her room.

As I climbed into the narrow bed, I pondered the weird inability that these people seemed to have to deal with life, myself included. Dorothy was fun, but truly nutsy. Penny was an unhappy and critical bitch. Martha was "way out." And the poor confused Lady from Wyoming ... what would happen to her? What would happen to me?

Chapter Seven
The Many Colors of Thelma

The old carpets and sagging walls were more depressing in the daytime, as were the many vacant and distressed countenances of the inmates. There was one nice surprise, however, when I returned from wrestling with insulin treatments the next day. I found that Dr. Ashford had indeed ordered my room changed. I was still on Third North, but just barely. The new room was just around the corner to the North Wing. The hallways were still narrow and did not seem to sit straight on the foundation. I had been bothered by this but couldn't tell if this was because of my dizziness, or if the structure was so old that it had heaves and cracks that had been repaired, leaving high and low places and angling walls. The carpet was old and frayed and the pattern was muted with age and worn-in dirt. My new room made me the nearest patient to the nursing station, as I was just across the hall and around a slight corner. The Lady from Wyoming was in a room adjacent to the nurses' station, Dorothy's room was next, and then a room with a new patient. I felt safer being close to the nurses. If I got faint, which I often did, a nurse would always be nearby.

I had noticed the new patient when I was passing through the hall after treatment. The lady was about my age and was sitting up in bed leaning against several pillows. (This made me wonder how to get extra pillows.) I walked passed the new patient's room several times, trying to find a way to meet her and killing time while waiting for Dorothy. When Dorothy didn't come, I took my lunch tray to my own room and ate alone. My new room was slightly larger than the one near the dumbwaiter. There was no window in the door so I could have privacy. There was a small portable closet, which would end the annoyance of living out of my suitcase and having such rumpled clothes. My suitcase was there on the floor, and on the small end table were the few toiletries that I had brought, but which the nurses had been keeping. There was also a small inexpensive lamp on the bed table. No more jumping into bed with only the hall light to see by. There was no outside window, but then I was still suffering from the anxiety that seemed to come in through the outside world or with the daylight. I sat on the one chair in my tiny room and ate from the small table next to my bed, feeling very privileged.

After lunch I bathed, returned to my new room, and dressed with my door closed. I put some cream on my face and a little lipstick, using the mirror in my cosmetic case. I had noticed that the new patient seemed very well coiffed and was wearing makeup. Now I felt more presentable for a self-introduction. The lady's door was partially opened. I walked slowly by and smiled in. The lady looked up and nodded back. I stopped and pushed the door open a little further.

"Hi, I'm Laurel. Did you just come today?" I said a little shyly.

"Come on in," said the lady. "I'm Thelma ...Yes, I just came a few hours ago. I'd like to *leave* again just as quickly."

I went on in and we exchanged small bits of information about ourselves. Thelma had been brought here by her parents. She had gone through a nasty breakup with a boyfriend, and she was devastated. She didn't know what treatments she might be given. She didn't even know what the treatments were all about. Her father wanted her here and had arranged it with the doctor. She was seeing Dr. Ashford.

"Oh, no!" she said excitedly to me. "He's your doctor, too? I can't stand his face. When he gets all upset he turns so red in the face ... and his eyes bug out!"

I laughed. "I try not to upset him," I said. "I'm afraid he'll have a coughing fit."

Thelma looked very serious.

"Do you know what that is all about?" she asked. "I'm sure it has to do with my father's paying his bills. The coughing ... I mean ... and the red ... My father is very strict ... doesn't pay when it's not warranted. He's strict about everything. He didn't want me to date my boyfriend, Gary, to start with. When Gary won the golf championship, my father was sure that he would use that to keep seeing me ... on the sly. Gary is careful. He doesn't like my father ... but I'm supposed to keep that a secret ... as well as the fact that my father can read almost everyone's mind."

I was a little confused about the intrigue, but I was fascinated with Thelma's looks. Thelma had beautiful red hair, a nice red, almost auburn, and no freckles. She had large blue-green eyes with very long lashes. Her skin was perfect and beautifully tanned which was very unusual for a redhead. Her nose was narrow at the top but swooped down into almost a flabbiness near the nostrils, and creases from her nose spread out to either side of a very generously wide, yet narrow-lipped, mouth. Her hands were smooth with moderately long and well-manicured nails. Thelma wasn't beautiful, but she was extremely attractive and very poised.

I could tell that Thelma had been crying, as her eyes were all swollen and reddened. This made her nose seem even larger. I wished that I could look so elegant while suffering a complete nervous collapse in the local mental hospital. Thelma had on a lovely, finely knit matching cotton top, jacket, and slacks. Her clothes hadn't a wrinkle and she was lying in bed. I self-consciously smoothed the top of my faded blue cotton dress that was growing increasingly tighter. The insulin treatments, and all my sugar intake, were putting back on the pounds that I had lost after my visit here last year. I felt like a washer woman and imagined Thelma to be a fine lady in distress, with a love who would come back to her, declare his undying love in spite of Thelma's tyrannical father, and take Thelma, all cured, away to live with him.

In our ensuing conversation, we found that we had gone to high school and college at the same time and in the same city, although at different schools. So we had some acquaintances in common. Thelma's father managed a local country club where Thelma met Gary, who was a golf pro and gave lessons there. Her father disapproved of the relationship and had forbade Thelma to continue to go to the club. But the young couple had managed to continue meeting at the club whenever Thelma could sneak in. Thelma lived in an apartment that was connected to her parents' home, and she was carefully watched. She thought that her father had had her phone tapped and that he followed Gary, trying to catch him with a wealthy lady who came to the club for golf lessons. Thelma had found out about the woman and was trying to find a strange connection between the lady and an opal necklace, which Thelma had seen as a young girl. Thelma didn't know why her father wanted her here. She supposed it was to get her away from Gary. I thought it was a great length to go to break up a romantic relationship.

Thelma told me that she had been distraught and that she had been crying for several days. Her father had grown sick of it and asked to have her hospitalized. This made me think that her father was very insensitive to poor Thelma's needs. Why on earth would he want her to recover from a severe heartbreak in a mental hospital? He must have wanted her locked in to keep her away from Gary, I decided

I stayed until the nurse brought the medication and then I left, closing Thelma's door so that she could rest. I went across the hall and down to my own room, but still no Dorothy. I was feeling a little unsteady. Thelma was upsetting, but I didn't know why. I was feeling fat and ugly and unwanted. I looked down at my rumpled, tight dress and grimaced. My fingernails were stubby and the cuticles torn. And my hair! I had recently given myself a home perm, and I had to cut it myself, since going to sit in a beauty salon was out of the question even if Martin would let me have the money. I surely wasn't the fashion plate that Thelma was, and Thelma didn't really seem crazy either, just upset about her love affair. I stretched out on the bed, listening to Martha jabbering down the hallway. After a time the nurse came in and asked me if I weren't going outside.

"Where will Martha be?" I asked snidely.

"She's going out, but the yard is large. *Come* on!" said the nurse impatiently.

"No, if she's out, I'm in," I said with finality.

After the nurse left I stayed on the bed. I was pleased with myself for being so assertive with a nurse. I hoped to nap before Dorothy came back, as I was feeling sad and rather shaky. I tried to sleep, but anxious thoughts about my illness began to run through my mind. I could feel my heart beating. It seemed way too fast. I felt a tightness in my chest and my palms were sweaty. I had my shoes and stockings off, and I pulled my knees to my chest in the position that I assumed when I was most upset. I felt my feet. They were damp and swollen like my hands.

I got up, staggering a little, and went to the drinking fountain down the hall near the seclusion rooms. I heard some strange noises in one room at the very end of the hall. It sounded like someone thrashing around on the floor. I was frightened and quickly headed back to my own room. My dizziness overtook me, and I fell against the wall. Catching my balance, I lunged for my room and fell face down on the bed. My heart was still pounding and it wouldn't quiet down. I took deep breaths and tried to concentrate on something—the faded wallpaper, the creases in the lamp shade.

Maybe I should call the nurse. I could. I was close enough now. Maybe I should have gone outside? No, if I had an anxiety attack out there, everyone would stare at me. But what did that matter? Most of them didn't know anything anyway. I got up shakily and started to go to the nurses' station. Maybe they would give me another pill or something.

I got halfway out of the doorway, when my nerves gave way completely and I started to cry, little short whimpering sobs that I tried to stifle. Then there escaped one large gasp that was very audible. The nurse, who was coming in the hallway, took one look at me and pushed me back into my room and led me to the bed, where I let out another frightened but stifled sound, louder this time, and nearly a scream.

"Lay down!" the nurse ordered. "I'll be right back!"

I felt relieved. It *was* good to be so near to help. I was sobbing quietly, worrying about all of my strange bodily feelings, when the nurse returned.

"I'm having an anxiety attack," I said shakily and very apologetically.

"I know, said the nurse. "Turn over!"

I rolled over, and the nurse raised my clothing and stuck a needle in my backside. Within seconds I was out.

When I awoke again it was near dinnertime. The halls were quiet, as most patients were napping or in the day room. I listened for noises, any noises. I couldn't bear loud noises, but complete silence was also difficult for me, because then I focused on my own breathing or my heartbeat. Sometimes I was bothered by the ringing sounds and strange noises in my own ears. My door was slightly ajar. I could hear Martha all the way from the day room. I thought that Martha was supposed to be in the garden, but I was too sleepy to care. A nurse came in and took my blood pressure. I wanted to get up. I felt very relaxed, but I was extremely weak and could only think about it.

I listened to the hospital sounds. Several messages came over the intercom. Some patients passed by my room without looking in. I wondered if Dorothy had ever come back. Maybe they had finally killed her while shocking her this time. I heard the nurses talking. There was something about a "shot" ... probably mine. The nurse, who was talking, said in a very stressed voice, "I think that I would call about that."

Aha! I thought. She wasn't supposed to give the shot to me, and now she's in trouble. I strained to hear more. The nurse was talking on the phone.

"Yes ... I know ... but her pressure is already seventy over fifty two. Yes, I've already given the shot. I know. But I supposed that you wanted me to report it.... Okay. Yes.... we are keeping an eye on her."

Oh my God! my mind raced. They are killing me! My blood pressure is wrong.... I bet I'm dying. I staggered off of the bed and grabbed onto the closet to help me to the door. I felt my way around the hallway and to the door of the nurses' station. Both nurses looked up, startled.

"What are you doing here? Get back to your room!" said the nurse who had administered the shot.

"But I heard you talking. I'm in trouble. My blood pressure is bad! What can you do? Will I be all right?" I asked.

"We weren't talking about you. That was someone else. You're fine. Go back to your room and stop trying to listen to everything."

The nurse was angry. I knew it had to be me. How many shots did they give in an afternoon? And wasn't it my blood pressure that had just been taken? I started to argue, but the nurse took me by the arm and led me back to my bed. I was still very groggy and weak, too weak to build up a good anxiety, so I just lay there resolved that I would either live ... or I would die. I would just have to wait and see.

It seemed I lay there for hours. The nurse had closed my door so that I couldn't eavesdrop anymore. They had peeked in on me once. After a long time, I got up and went to the drinking fountain. I was a little steadier on my feet. The nurse brought in my dinner and asked how I felt. She told me that I could go to the day room if I wished. I guessed that this meant the crisis was over. I would live for yet another insulin treatment in the morning.

Dorothy was in the day room. She had stuck her head in my room when I was out cold.

"What did you do?" she inquired.

"Just got frightened ... and upset," I said with embarrassment.

"I thought that you had to get violent or scream at them to get a hypo," said Dorothy in a puzzled tone.

"Well, I *almost* screamed," I said. "Anyway, now I know not to let them know if I'm shook up. They could kill you around here ... and not even bat an eye."

I related the blood pressure incident, and Dorothy agreed about their incompetence and need to cover up. They had not even tried to recheck my pressure; they must have thought that I would relate the information to my doctor.

There were no good shows on TV, and Martha was sitting in the middle of the floor being her usual gabby self. Several other patients sat on the floor with Martha, but not really knowing, or caring, what Martha's one-way conversation was about. Dorothy and I didn't know or care either. It seemed that all of Third Floor had come to the day room this evening, and there weren't enough chairs or couches for all. Dorothy and I sat on the floor with the two other ladies who were sharing a light from their cigarettes with Dorothy. Only the nurses had matches. They would light patients' cigarettes for them, and the patients would often take a light off another cigarette from a communicative patient. Dorothy was a chain smoker. I had tried it a few times, since I had come but couldn't learn to inhale. So I watched, wishing I had something to do with my hands.

"Let's go to the OT shop tomorrow," said Dorothy. "They have lots of interesting things to do there ... all kind of crafts ... since you want something to do with your hands. Lets get productive ... kill the damn boredom."

I hoped that something could liven up this depressive place, other than hypos and my preoccupation with my anxieties. Occupational Therapy, or OT as we called it, might be just what I needed to distract my thoughts.

A nurse came on duty, one that I hadn't seen before, and she started taking temperatures. She started at one end of the day room and was working her way toward Dorothy and me. Both of us were bored and just sitting quietly. Mae, one of the old senile permanent residents, was bending down from behind a couch and talking to several of the patients.

"See," she said, smiling and so pleased. "That girl over there, isn't she lovely? And so polite. She is my daughter."

She was pointing proudly to a very quiet and pretty young girl who was smoking a cigarette and watching the smoke curl toward the ceiling. I looked at Dorothy.

"Are they related?" I asked.

"No," said Dorothy. "Mae just likes her looks."

The nurse taking temperatures approached me. I reached out my arm, and the nurse silently counted the pulse rate while I held the thermometer in my mouth. As the nurse removed the thermometer, she asked, "Did you have a bowel movement today?"

I brightened, my whole face lit up into a smile.

"Why, yes," I beamed. "Did you?"

"I was just trying to find out if ... I'm supposed to ask you this because we need to know if you're constipated," the nurse stammered.

"Oh," I said, looking completely crestfallen and putting my lower lip into a childish pout. "I though that you were trying to start a conversation."

Dorothy looked at me and smiled, ever so slightly. I tried to keep my face sad and ignore Dorothy's possible disclosure of my joke.

"Oh, I get it," said the nurse. "Okay. If I need a laxative, guess who's going to get it?"

All three of us smiled; and Dorothy and I instantly liked this new nurse.

When Martin came for his usual hurried ten-minute visit, I again pleaded with him to find out about my treatments, to talk the doctor out of them, or to try to get me out of this place if the doctor wouldn't change his mind. Martin said that the doctor had been definite. The treatments had to continue. I shouldn't fight them or I would be here longer. It seemed that twenty to twenty-five comas were necessary to insure a successful treatment. I should cooperate. Time was passing. I had had three treatments already and no coma yet. Would I please try? Think of the girls and him. He said that he wanted me to get well. I walked with him to the elevator, crying quietly.

"Please come and visit," I asked, "Don't just run in and out. I want to talk to you."

All temperatures had been taken, the senile ladies put to bed, and visitors were gone. Martha was sitting at the piano stool, silent for a change. She looked all around the room, carefully examining every patient with narrowed eyes. I was looking at the TV set, but not really watching it. Dorothy and two other ladies were talking about the Lady from Wyoming, who was near the elevator, and pacing back and forth. Suddenly Martha came over to me and bent over to speak.

"You know," she began, "if it weren't for the fact that you and I are here, I would think that the reason we are all in this place is because we smoke!"

"Probably," I said. "So then, I think we should ask to be let out."

Martha nodded and smiled knowingly. I got up, hoping to avoid further conversation with Martha, and went to Thelma's room. Thelma was still sitting on her bed, propped upon her pillows, but a man and a woman, obviously her parents, were there with her. Thelma very graciously introduced her mother and father to me. The parents were quite polite.

"How are you doing?" her mother asked.

"Okay," I responded.

"Are you feeling all right? Have you had any treatments?" her father asked.

"I have been taking Insulin Treatments. I don't feel very well," I responded

I excused myself but her parents said they were leaving and should have left earlier, "Would you please stay and talk with Thelma?" her mother nervously asked of me.

I watched the goodbyes. Thelma's mother was obviously very upset and worried. Her father seemed very severe and almost angry. I could see why Thelma talked about him with some awe in her voice. He reminded me of my own grandfather, who had always made me feel intimidated and on edge. Thelma had a large bouquet of red roses sitting on her bed table. These were the first flowers that I had seen in this dismal place. I commented on how lovely they were and asked if they were from Gary. Thelma didn't answer; she smiled slyly and raised one articulate eyebrow.

"Wouldn't you know that they would be red?" asked Thelma

"Well, of course," I said, assuming that they were from Gary, and that "red" roses meant "I love you."

"Did you see how my father looked back after he set my bag down?" Thelma questioned, her brow knit in contemplation.

"Yes," I said, "He did do that."

"Well, he knows something and he plans on keeping it from me. Besides he had on that brown suit that he knows that I detest ... and you know what that's about!" Thelma pulled a cigarette from her vanity case. "I wish that I had a light," she said, and then demanded, "Do you have a match?"

I explained that only the nurses could have matches in this God-forsaken hole and that you had to track down a nurse or take a light from someone else's cigarette. I took the cigarette and went out in the hallway to procure a light for my friend. When I returned, we talked about the inconveniences and lack of comfort and elegance in the appointments. This ultra-social focus seemed appropriate in dealing with Thelma, the dramatic princess in distress. I took a cigarette, offered by Thelma, lighted it off hers, and tried again to inhale. It looked so sophisticated on Thelma.

"Did you know that if we all stopped smoking we could get out of here?" I asked my friend.

Thelma's eyes lit up and her well-formed eyebrows arched expressively. "Is that so?" she asked.

"That's what Martha told me," I said. Then I proceeded to explain all about Martha. Thelma smiled and laughed now and again, appreciatively.

"Well," said Thelma, "I really don't want to be here, especially if everyone is such a bother like Martha. I like your visiting, but I hope *we* are left alone. I bet my father knew what it was like in here. He probably wants me to be uncomfortable ... to teach me a lesson."

"Your mom seemed nice," I volunteered.

"Oh, yes, but she can't handle him either. I'm actually better at it than she is. I'll figure out something. It may take me a while."

Thelma squinted her eyes. They held a faraway look that made me almost shiver. I excused myself and left Thelma sitting up in bed, inhaling her cigarette thoughtfully, and studying the various objects in her room.

Later someone at the very far end of the hallway screamed. A call went out on the intercom. "Orderlies to Third North!" and the usual procession came by my room. I was sitting in bed, trying to read a magazine that I had found in the day room, but my head was too confused and my eyes wouldn't focus right. I was feeling a lot of anxiety again, but I knew it was best to keep it to myself. A nurse came in, looked closely at me, and returned with some orange juice that was nasty with sugar.

"You're having an insulin reaction," she said.

This was strange; how come an anxiety attack could bring you either a hypo or an icky sweet glass of juice? Perhaps the nurse was afraid that I would report her to the doctor. I had learned from Thelma that Dr. Ashford was the head of the hospital. That, I reasoned, almost precluded knowledgeable decisions on the premise.

Just as I was feeling hostile toward the whole staff, the new nurse, with whom I had kidded earlier, came into my room and sat on the bed. She was a small slender woman a few years older than I, with fine brown hair and smiling eyes. Her uniform seemed more neatly pressed than most and yet less heavily starched. She wasn't really pretty, but had nice even features, and wore little or no makeup. She told me that her name was Margaret and that she had just returned from a vacation with her husband and two daughters. She usually worked nights, but more often on Second Floor. She confirmed that the drunks were brought in to Second Floor for detoxification. She didn't mind working there, as they were all locked in their rooms until they were calmed down with "anti-buse" and then they were usually a lot of fun. They were more communicative on Second Floor and even played games, after they were quieted, of course. I said that I was glad to have Margaret on Third North, and wished she would try to work this floor again.

I recounted the story of the hypo, and Margaret looked serious but said nothing. Margaret laughed about Martha, seemed concerned about Thelma, and seemed truly sad for the Lady from Wyoming. Inwardly I praised myself for doing a good day's deed by helping Margaret catch up on all the new patients and occurrences. It seemed that this new nurse was truly kind and wanted to help others the way people expected nurses to be. Then Margaret left, as it was time for report and she was to meet with the nurses coming on duty to fill them in on medications and events of the day.

It was a long time before I was able to fall asleep. I thought about Thelma, and then I worried about what Martin had said regarding the twenty to twenty-five comas needed to make a person well. I decided that I would have to go into coma and I would try to get all those comas behind me quickly. Still, I wished I didn't have to "go unconscious."

Chapter Eight
What Cheryl Did

Another new room assignment was given to me when I returned from the insulin floor the following day. The nurse met me as I entered Third North from the narrow stairwell and directed me around past the day room to a room on Third South. It was a double room with much more space; it even had a small table and a couple of chairs. My roommate, Mickey, was in and out of the room, always looking very concerned and businesslike. I had some difficulty getting acquainted with her. My roommate didn't seem to focus on anything or anyone around her. She did keep asking me the date.

"I think it's the seventh," I said. "But I've lost track since I came in. There isn't much use for the date in a mental hospital."

Mickey made no comment, but only frowned more intensely and retreated back into her own thoughts. The two ladies in the room across from Mickey and me were also insulin patients. There was also a very distraught patient down the hall. She roomed alone and stayed to herself. I spoke to her on the way to the new bathroom.

There were several smaller bathrooms on this side of the third floor. Each one had a tub that patients could fill for themselves. I thought, I must remember to ask Martin to bring me some bubble bath. Long, warm, sudsy baths were one thing that made me feel calmer and more relaxed. I could probably use the bath in the afternoon, when the others were either napping or out in the garden. I wondered, hopefully if the doctor had ordered me moved again because he realized that I was not so bad off. But I supposed it had something to do with the nurses' desire to have me out of earshot. Anyway, it was a nice lift to my spirits, after again failing miserably in my attempt to go into a coma that morning.

After lunch, Dorothy and I went with a nurse to the OT shop on the first floor, north of the lobby and offices. I found some pillowcases to embroider and Dorothy had a key chain to braid. We took the objects back to Third Floor for completion, after promising to return the next day and learn some leather tooling. I got the impression that the occupational therapist was lacking interested clientele and that she had found some live ones with Dorothy and me, as we had been the only ones in the shop, except for a very quiet and nervous man who was about the same age as my father. He was doing leather tooling, and the therapist said she could teach us all together.

Dorothy hadn't said anything to me until dinnertime, but she was moving to the Annex the next day. She had been shocked enough that she was more compliant and was even going out for the evening. I made Dorothy promise to come back, if only just to go to OT with me.

I visited for a while with the "insulin ladies" across the hall. One lady was about thirty-something, the other well into her forties. The younger lady had very little to say and only repeated her concerns about how unfair her boss had been to her and how very hard she had tried to do her work to his unattainable satisfaction.

The older lady was very tall and large boned. She towered over me and was aggressive and frightening in her mannerisms. She didn't like the hospital, her family, or her doctor. She didn't understand why she had to be hospitalized. She simply was not sick. She suspected that her husband was trying to keep her there because he was having an affair with the secretary at his office. Jeannie, as she introduced herself, had been making threatening calls to the secretary, often times leaving angry messages. This, she averred, was not crazy behavior; she was just protecting her marriage. She admitted that she had recently discontinued her own job and begun cooking for her family and keeping up the housework in order to preserve her marriage. And look at what her efforts had garnered her. Her family was all in favor of having her hospitalized while the secretary was now given the opportunity to pursue her husband, unfettered. If only she had access to a phone! Still, she was glad she was taking insulin therapy. The lady in the next room had electroshock therapy, and she just went downstairs for about an hour each day. Jeannie got to go to Second Floor and nap all morning.

I said that I went to the "naps" also, but really didn't know which treatment I preferred. I would certainly rather have none. I couldn't believe how uninformed Jeannie was about what was happening to her. I thought Jeannie was spooky because of her anger and because she was so large. I felt a little inhibited and rather eager to go back to my own room. Jeannie said that Mickey, my roommate, and Cheryl, a quiet patient on down the hall, had no treatments at all. We wondered about treatment selection for a while, and then I excused myself in order to go find a less stressful situation. I walked on around to Third North to check on Thelma.

My new friend was very agitated and was moving restlessly about her room, smoking one cigarette after another. I observed that the gorgeous bouquet of roses was sitting, blooms down, in Thelma's wastebasket. When I inquired about the roses, I was told it was because they were red, of course! She was impatient with me for not knowing that. Thelma was fuming about her father and how he was in league with Dr. Ashford. She confided in me that her father had "bugged" her car, but that she had thwarted his efforts by bashing in the glove compartment with one of her father's hammers. Wasn't that ironic? His *own* hammer?

"Has he always spied on you?" I asked, more for information about Thelma's thinking pattern than for conversation, as I was beginning to understand why Thelma was here.

"Of course," said Thelma. "He's never let me do anything on my own. Now he's upset because he can't control my relationship with Gary. And then he comes here and wears that brown suit just to spite me."

And I had thought that Jeannie was scary! I was beginning to be worried about Thelma, too. But I found Thelma very likable and Jeannie was just upsetting. I asked if Thelma's parents were coming this evening. I remembered that Thelma's mother had wanted me to talk with Thelma. I wondered if Thelma's mother understood her daughter's bizarre thinking, and I felt guilty for being so envious of Thelma.

"I'd like to see my mom because I need different clothes, but I don't want my father here. He knows about that opal necklace, and he never did tell me, even when it was all obvious. He really upsets me."

"Did you tell Dr. Ashford that ... about the necklace?" I asked, concerned that Thelma was becoming more agitated.

"No, I wouldn't dare! He'd just get all red in the face and I couldn't stand it," said Thelma, starting to smile.

I sat down and relaxed somewhat while we discussed dinner and the small uncomfortable room. I remarked that Thelma's clothing was very attractive and inquired why she had to have "different" ones.

"This outfit is *red!*" said Thelma showing annoyance. "And *you* know what that means."

"Yeah, I sure do," I agreed.

We looked at each other knowingly. Dr. Ashford came in and so I left, asking, as I went, if the doctor would be coming to see me also.

"I'll check with you tomorrow, after insulin therapy," he said briskly.

I was disappointed. I wanted to tell him about Thelma, her car, the color red, opal necklaces, brown suits, and other strange comments, things that I knew Thelma was keeping from him. But then, it really wasn't my business and he might be annoyed at my intrusion. I was determined to find some way to help Thelma. I didn't think that the nurses would care about my inside information, as the only one who even seemed to converse with the patients was Margaret. Maybe I should tell Margaret.

I was preoccupied with saving Thelma as I went around the corner in the hallway. Martha was carrying on in the day room. The senile ladies were staring at the TV, and several visitors were getting off and on the elevator, as I passed on through on the way to my room.

"What is today's date? Do you know?" Mickey asked me for the second or third time for the day.

After I responded she seemed unconvinced and stopped me again.

"Are you certain?" she questioned.

I wondered why the date was so important to Mickey, but after conversing with Jeannie and Thelma, I was afraid of what kind of response might be forthcoming if I questioned Mickey. I picked up my embroidery and went on down the hall to see Cheryl, the quiet patient who kept to herself.

At Cheryl's open door I knocked lightly. Cheryl invited me in but didn't smile. She had her rosary in her hand, so I asked if I were disturbing her prayers or anything. Cheryl said I wasn't and that she would like company. I sat down on the old hard wooden chair and started to embroidery while I got acquainted with Cheryl

"How long have you been here?" asked Cheryl.

"Less than a week," I answered, puzzled.

"Do you read the papers? Watch TV?" Cheryl questioned.

I said that I did, and then Cheryl began crying as she went on.

"You probably won't want to talk to me when I tell you who I am. I'm Cheryl Houssand ... the monster who killed her own child."

A chill went up my spine. I remembered the story in the papers, but how could this be? Cheryl was quiet and appeared frightened, and she seemed so sweet. The picture of the woman in the paper made her look like an angry animal. It was worse than any driver's license photo and made her look deranged or like a poster of an escaped convict. The story in the paper said that she yelled at the reporters and threw things at them. She had supposedly smothered her handicapped infant and then gone to the police and told them about it.

But this Cheryl was subdued, crying off and on all the time. I knew. I had heard her at night. She stayed to herself, saying her rosary almost constantly. She was even sort of pretty, under all the redness and the swollen face. I lied, saying that I didn't care why Cheryl was here, that "we all have our problems to work out." When Cheryl asked if she could tell me the real story and get my opinion, I was very uneasy. I really wanted to go back to my own room. Why had I sought out yet another patient? I was frightened by all the problems here and by all the angry distraught patients. My own difficulties seemed minor now. Cheryl really wanted to talk to someone and I felt duty-bound to listen. I had embroidered only a couple of stitches and now I sat frozen. I wished that I didn't need to accommodate Cheryl, but I felt very sorry for her, even though I was feeling afraid of her and worrying about my own anxiety. There was nothing I could do now but listen.

Cheryl had married young and had four children before she was twenty-five. She was exhausted with childcare and had not been very healthy during her fifth pregnancy. When the child was born, she was severely handicapped. She had a double cleft palate (I didn't know what "double" meant but was too frightened to ask) and since the palate was open from the center of the nose to the chin, it was a distasteful job to feed her. It was a job only a mother could do since it took great patience to get any food into the baby's stomach without choking her.

Cheryl and her husband were told that their baby was severely mentally retarded and would never be more than a "vegetable." The doctor suggested that they apply for placement for the baby at the state home for the severely retarded. They made the application for placement when the little girl was less than a week old. The child lived until the age of eighteen months, when Cheryl suffocated her, and still she was on the waiting list. Cheryl never left the baby's side for the entire eighteen months. She didn't trust anyone else to feed her or watch her. Cheryl's mother tried to help some but she mostly assisted with care for the other four children, while Cheryl devoted her entire time to the baby. Many times the handicapped baby would awaken, choking, during the night, so she was kept in the parents' room. Cheryl had trouble talking between sobs, as she explained.

"You would think that she was ugly, but I loved her. And just a few months ago she smiled, actually smiled. It would probably have looked ugly to you. Her funny little face with the large gaping mouth that wasn't really a mouth ... and the way she twisted the muscles to finally make a smile. You would think that it was grotesque, but it was really, truly, beautiful to me. I was so happy that she learned to do it. And she was smiling at *me*. She loved me. I loved her ... and that smile ... it made me so happy that day.

"But then everything was so sad. The baby never was well; she had lots of respiratory infections. And she got worse. She was sick ... so sick. She had pneumonia and the doctor said that there wasn't anything he could do for her. I think that he wanted her to die ... but he said that she would get better care at home than at the hospital. And I wanted to be with her. I was *always* at her side. I'm the *only* one who could get her to eat. She got so sick. Her breathing was so difficult. She would gasp, and I would lift her head or change her position to help her get her breath. I hadn't had any sleep for several days.

"I had to take care of her. *I was the only one who could do it.* That day my husband went to work and the other children were outside in the yard. The baby couldn't breath. She kept gasping. She was so sick and so uncomfortable. Her color was so bad, and she was crying, at least *trying* to cry *all* the time. She made strange gurgling gasps for air, and whimpering noises because she was so weak ... she couldn't even cry out loud. I couldn't stand to see her suffer anymore, so I took her blanket and threw it over her face, and ran out of the house and down the street.

"We live about two blocks from a police station. I told the policeman at the desk that I killed my baby, and then I started crying. That's all I remembered until I was back at home, and a doctor gave me a shot. Then the press started coming to my house. They were there from early morning till late at night. We had to keep the blinds drawn because they tried to look into the windows. My lawyer told me not to talk to them. I yelled at them to go away once and then threw the morning paper at them. I was very upset, and they were upsetting my other children. My other children had suffered enough. They really hadn't had a mother for the past eighteen months. My lawyer said that I should have no expression at all on my face when I came in and out of the house ... past the press. Did you know that they can print any picture of you that they want and put any caption under it?"

I remembered the picture that I had seen in the paper. It didn't look like this poor, pathetic creature. I didn't remember the caption, but I did remember that the story was horrifying.

I was not a "touching" kind of person, but I felt that I needed to put an arm around Cheryl. I felt so intensely moved by the story, and so very sad for Cheryl. Cheryl cried some more and told me that she had been sent to the locked floor of Mountain View to keep her away from the press. She asked me if I thought that God would judge her harshly for killing her own child. The doctor *had* said that the autopsy showed that the baby was dead from the pneumonia, not suffocation from the blanket. It was hard for me to respond. I was nervous and shaky seeing Cheryl's emotions and hearing the account ... and I felt so sorry for Cheryl. I got up and went over to her. I put my hand on Cheryl's shoulder and patted her gently, reassuring her that God knew the truth and that the press should be punished for the way they had harassed Cheryl and her family. I told Cheryl I believed that the baby had died from its illness, and I didn't think Cheryl was to blame. I privately wondered if the doctor had told her the correct medical results from the autopsy or if his words were intended to help assuage Cheryl's deep feeling of guilt. I wished that I could do something to right the injustice inflicted by the press. I reassured Cheryl several times and excused myself on the pretext of using the bathroom. I actually needed to go somewhere to cry. I didn't want to upset Cheryl further by unleashing my own emotions with Cheryl's

I cried quietly in the bathroom, with the door closed, for a little while and then regained my composure. I was feeling a hard gripping sensation in my stomach, and some nausea and dizziness. I realized that I had dampened my embroidery and tried to use this to help myself smile a little. In truth I was so unnerved by Cheryl's story that I wanted to go lie quietly on my bed for a while. My spine was shivering and I was on the verge of another anxiety attack. I was ashamed of myself. I couldn't even handle *other* peoples' problems.

When I got back to my room, Mickey was sitting on her bed staring at the wall. I was afraid that she was going to ask what day it was for the umpteenth time, and I didn't feel up to dealing with it. But Mickey just continued to stare at the wall, with that deep frown on her face. I lay down and tried to relax. It was visiting time but I didn't care. I surely didn't want to see anyone, not even Martin. I wanted out of there. This place was getting to me. Then I felt very guilty. How could I feel sorry for myself? Cheryl was someone with real problems. I had a nice little family, a good husband, and everyone was healthy except me. Why couldn't I cope with my own life? I sat up. I knew I'd better find something pleasant to occupy my mind or I would drive myself into an anxiety attack for sure. Then would come the "hypo." I took my damp embroidery and headed for the day room.

A strange new patient was going up the hall looking into all the rooms. I had seen her stop at a stairwell and try the locked door. Apparently she was looking for a way out. When I reached the day room, another patient I had not seen before was standing by the elevator. The patient watched as the elevator was unlocked from the inside and several visitors emerged before the nurse locked it again and went to the nursing station. The patient looked at me.

"Did you know that the elevator was locked?"

I answered that I did. The patient asked if I knew that the doors in the hallways were locked. That was *two* loonies trying to get out, I thought, trying to find some humor yet feeling annoyed and frustrated with my own situation and all the insanity around me.

"Do you have keys to this place?" the patient continued.

I turned and said sarcastically, "No, they haven't seen fit to give me my keys yet. Don't you have yours?"

The lady was puzzled. "I don't understand it. They haven't given them to me either. Every other place that I have ever been they've given me the keys. And I usually get them long before now. I've been working here much longer than a lot of places. I wonder why they haven't given them to me."

"Why don't you ask them?" I suggested.

"I did. They said it was for 'security reasons.' Well, if you ask me ... the security is all on *their* side."

"I believe you're right," I said.

"What security?" continued the lady, glad to have someone to help her deal with her dilemma. "Why, if we had a fire, we couldn't get out, those of us *without* keys. Why, we would all be burned!"

"Go tell them about it!" I suggested, moving away.

I didn't want to hear about a fire in the loony bin. Things were far too upsetting already. Martha was still going on about her problems, or those of the world, in the day room. The senile ladies were still staring at the TV, and different visitors were coming and going through the elevator, though I was glad to see Margaret, the night nurse I liked, coming on duty. The embroidery and the poorly selected TV channel were not enough to distract my chaotic thoughts and move the time quickly. I didn't even mind when Martin came for his usual very hurried visit. I told him about Cheryl Houssand being in here, how awful the press had been, and how really sweet and sad Cheryl seemed. I cried a little again, although I tried hard not to, and Martin acted interested and amazed about a "celebrity" being right here where he might see her.

Dorothy came back very late from her evening out and stayed up and talked with Nurse Margaret and me until everyone else was in bed. Margaret didn't encourage either of us to retire for the evening, as she wanted company, too. When I finally went to bed, Mickey was still staring at the wall. She was in pajamas with the lights out and still just staring. I didn't turn on the lights to undress because I wanted to avoid any conversation about "what day it was" with Mickey. Morning would come too soon and the nurse would be there with insulin. I need to find a way to "go out," suffer through twenty to twenty-five comas, get along without Dorothy, try to help Thelma and Cheryl, and get home again *safely*.

Chapter Nine
Just for the Summer

Some of the anxiety I had felt at night was relieved by being on Third South. In many ways the patients on this side of the building were less disruptive and it seemed that more of them slept through the night, though some nights, if I were asleep, the piercing screams or wailing and moaning sounds would awaken me abruptly. The sounds curled into the courtyard and up the stuccoed walls, filtering with somewhat less intensity through the heavy screens, the open window, and moving angrily across my pillow. Now, on Third South I heard only the softer, though restless, sounds of feet carrying sleepless worriers to the fountain for drinks or to the bathrooms down the dimly lighted hallway. There were stifled sobs that permeated the night and let me know of anguish other than my own.

Despite these sounds, I preferred to leave the door to our room open. I felt less imprisoned that way. Mickey seemed of no opinion; her main, and probably only, preoccupation being upon the current date. Knowing that I wasn't within the earshot of the sudden screams from deep in Third North, I felt some ease and relaxation. My window somehow deflected the noise of the drunkards from Second Floor back to the floodlit cement courtyard.

At night I lay quietly savoring the semi-quiet, listening to see if the horrors had actually left the second floor or if they were only more barred now from entry. I could faintly hear the cries and dulled screams, but only if I strained. Closer were the noises that came from the hall, all muddled together, preventing me from knowing whether "That's Cheryl's sobbing" or "Jeannie can't sleep and is venting her anger to that pathetically withdrawn roommate." I thought those sobs might be Cheryl's, but there were others with them, and then, from time to time, there was the longed for silence.

I hugged the bedding closer around my neck. I liked to pull myself well into the bedclothes. There was protection and comfort there. Suddenly footsteps that had been hurrying in the hallway entered my open door. I pulled back the covers from around my chin and raised my head enough to allow me to identify the intruder. In the faint light that squeezed in from the dim hallway, I could make out a figure standing over Mickey's bed. Whoever it was had an urgency to talk with Mickey and was whispering, though not too softly, so as not to disturb me. I squinted so that, from my eyes and ears, I could determine the identity of the invader. Oh no! It was Martha! I had thought that Martha, and her night noises were something from which I had gratefully escaped.

I sat up meaning to make a protest. As Martha realized I was awake, she made less effort to stifle her noise. She was still whispering, as she didn't wish to alarm the entire floor, but her voice was certainly audible for several rooms. Martha had a way of making her presence known. She was telling Mickey that she was sure of something and how wonderful it was. I was curious for good news.

"What is it, Martha? What has happened?" I inquired, even with some friendliness.

Martha turned and walked over to me.

"I thought I was!" she said excitedly. "Now I know it! It's so strange, but I felt it ... just a little while ago. Look! You really can't tell too well yet, but I felt it! I actually felt movement!"

She crossed back over to Mickey's bed. Mickey was sitting up and listening, but had made no comment.

"Here, put your hand right here, feel that? Can you feel it move? I can! I'm going to give birth! I'm pregnant. Isn't it exciting? I hadn't expected to be a mother again. I'll have to tell my husband. Won't he be excited? I kinda think he'll like it. But he'll sure be surprised!"

I was more confused than excited. I was *sure* that Martha's husband would be surprised. Dorothy had said that Martha had been here for quite a while, months in fact, and that she had been separated from her husband for some time before her admission. Then, too, wasn't Martha too old? A nurse came into the room and scolded Martha for waking the inhabitants here, and insisted that she return to her own hallway *and* her own room. When Martha tried to explain her own excitement to the nurse, the nurse was clearly annoyed.

"Martha, forget it! Wait until morning ... we can discuss it then. You're waking the whole hallway. Get back to your room ... *now.*"

Martha was pushed from the room, and Mickey looked over at me.

No smile. No comments. No reaction from Mickey. Mickey rolled over and turned her face to the wall, her most common position, and I went on thinking about the events of the day and evening while waiting for sleep.

Dr. Ashford didn't come after treatment the next day, as he had promised. I was hurt and annoyed. I had wanted to talk to him about Thelma. And Thelma was even stranger the next day. She had asked me what "yellow" meant.

"Hell," I said, impatiently, "I haven't figured out 'red,' yet!"

Thelma had looked upset and a little disappointed to hear this. But nevertheless continued to tell me her suspicions that her father was doing many things behind her back and that he had some devious plot to separate her and Gary forever.

Cheryl had told her story of her infant's "murder" to a number of patients and was getting some support, as well as some fearful avoidance from other listeners. Martha seemed quieter about her pregnancy but still seem convinced that she was. I had been ignoring Jeannie, who had begun talking a lot to Mickey. I wondered why the other patients sought out Mickey. She really didn't listen. She just worried about the calendar. Maybe they all just wanted to talk, and Mickey just sat and looked at them.

Chapter Ten
Occupational Therapy

When I met Dorothy at OT, she reported how comfortable it was over at the Annex. Occupational Therapy, or OT, was pleasant respite from the loony bin. The patients here really didn't take advantage of the program. The room was empty except for a man who wanted to do leather tooling and a little old lady who said little but sat quietly painting a small paint-by-numbers picture. The old lady worked intently, asked no questions, and didn't seem to want to be bothered.

Dorothy and I selected a project to work on, after being shown pictures of different kinds of designs and the objects that could be decorated. I wanted to do a belt for Martin, but the tooled belt looked very Western, and I knew that Martin would never wear it. But I would do one for myself later, I decided. Right now I wanted to do a small purse I could give to Karen. I had already completed the pillowcases that I had bought here earlier, so I got a second set to embroider just to entertain my brain while I was upstairs on the "disturbed" floor.

I also got a very small paint-by-numbers picture. I was intrigued with the colors that were premixed and the way that the areas of color made the picture come to life. It was gimmicky but clever, and besides, I had learned that sitting and doing small movements with my hands could help control my anxiety. At least it worked *sometimes*.

Dorothy wanted to tool a belt for herself. She didn't like embroidery and had no patience for painting. I was afraid that Martin might be upset at the cost of materials, but the occupational therapist said that costs were nominal. Sanity did have to have some price, I supposed.

We practiced making marks on scraps of leather, in order to be more proficient when we began on the real items. Dorothy and I shared humorous stories about Dorothy's "husbands," her treatment at Mountain View, and the things that the patients and staff had said or done.

Several hours passed quickly, and I almost enjoyed this time, away from the zany courtyard or on the floor with the other patients. Afterwards, Dorothy went back to the Annex and I reluctantly returned to Third Floor. A nurse had to escort me, both coming and going to OT because of the locked elevators and the confined floor whereas Dorothy could come and go at will. That must have felt "freeing," I had remarked enviously to Dorothy. We agreed to meet again the next day.

The house doctor came into my room that afternoon, seemingly intent on getting acquainted. I supposed that if the head of the hospital wanted someone to do his "rounds" for him, the house doctor couldn't very well refuse. But I was still annoyed that Dr. Ashford wasn't all that enthralled with my case.

"Hi," he said, "I'm Doctor Jennings, the house doctor."

"Oh!" I said, with feigned surprise and sarcasm. "Didn't recognize you without your rubber hose and black box."

The doctor smiled appreciatively. "Are you more comfortable with your new room ... on this side of the building?" he ventured.

"Actually I miss the screaming ... and I'm sorry that Martha couldn't come with me. She's pregnant, you know."

"That's what I hear." Dr. Jennings smiled widely, and then he looked at me very seriously. "I understand you are worried about the insulin therapy."

It was my turn to smile. "Well, wouldn't you be if it were you?"

"Well," he said reassuringly, "I might be a little concerned, but you seem to have an unusual fear of the treatment."

"I don't think that it's so unusual!" I was defensive. "The treatments are very frightening."

"Look at the other patients," the doctor continued in an even, quiet voice. "They're not frightened. Why should you be?"

I opened my mouth, dumbstruck. "The other patients!" I said angrily. "The other patients don't know what's happening to them. Ask them. They actually think that they go downstairs and take a nap. Why, Jeannie, that dopey creature across the hall and her dumb room-mates are *glad* that they have insulin therapy because they 'get to sleep all morning.' Of course they're not frightened. They don't have sense enough to be frightened."

"So what do *you* think happens?" the doctor asked me, still talking low and quite calmly.

"I *know* what happens," I said impatiently. "You inject us with insulin, which lowers our blood sugar enough that we go into a coma. You leave us in a coma for a prescribed period of time. I don't know how you judge the amount of time, but at a certain point you put glucose water into our stomach to get the body and brain active again and we 'come to.' However, *if* by some chance you were to blow it, forget the patients, or bring them out at the wrong time, we'd be goners. Of *course* I'm frightened! I *would* be crazy *not* to be frightened. Go explain the procedure to the other patients and see if you don't get some fear! But some of them wouldn't even understand, they're so out of it"

"Okay, you've got a point," admitted the doctor. "But we know what we are doing, and you are safer than you think. Try not to worry so much."

He patted me on the shoulder, reassuringly, told me he would come and talk with me again, and left.

Mickey had been out of the room while Dr. Jennings was there, but was coming in just as he started into the hall.

"I only have a few more days!" Mickey said anxiously to the doctor.

"I know," he answered her. "It's going to be all right ... very soon."

Mickey looked a little relieved but still had that perpetual frown. She looked at me and said, "Today is the eighth, isn't it?"

"I think so," I said.

"It will all be over ... one way or another ... on the tenth," continued Mickey. "Do you know the incubation period for rabies?"

I said that I didn't. I really didn't care but kept *that* information from Mickey.

"Well, I've called the public health department, veterinarians, and medical doctors, and all of them have been telling me two weeks. So I guess I'll have to believe it is two weeks."

This was the most I had ever heard Mickey say. I was intrigued. Maybe there was more to Mickey than I thought.

"Do you know someone infected with rabies?" I asked.

"*My* husband," replied Mickey. "He was scratched by a cat that had rabies. He will get rabies in two days, and it will all be over. Rabies is a horrible death. I have to wait two more days ... and there is nothing I can do. And the whole thing is my fault."

I thought that the doctors were probably treating Mickey's husband, and I was sure that there was a way to save his life. Mickey must have just been admitted because of her inability to cope with his possible infection from rabies, I decided.

Chapter Eleven
Coma

I made even more effort to sleep the next morning on my hard, damp, insulin cot. I lay quietly, remembering the twenty to twenty-five comas that I needed to have. Unconsciousness had always been very frightening to me. I had almost fainted once in junior high. I was in the Christmas choir on a very closed-in stage. There was absolutely no circulation and I had a bad head cold.

The choir members all carried candles and all the electric lights were out. I remembered that the music had drifted away, slowly, and then the individual flames all blurred together and moved as one pretty wave. A teacher had come and helped me off the steps, after the choir members in my row had handed me, one to another, to the exit. The teacher had told me that she had noticed one candlelight swaying back and forth in each direction.

The sensory experience had been almost pleasant, but I was devastated. The other choir members had been annoyed that I had all but ruined the pageant. I was relieved that I hadn't fainted completely, but I was also aware that, if I had actually fainted, the reaction of my peers might have been more sympathetic.

Being unconscious, judging from my own experience, must mean that you have no senses. And so, a coma must be even closer to actual death. Or, maybe it's just like a sleep, I thought, a very deep sleep. A person is not conscious in sleep, and they come out of that alive. Didn't I see all those insulin patients come back with me each morning, some of them even saying that they had been "asleep"? Some of them must be going into coma and living through it. I lay in one position and tried to think pleasant thoughts, which was very hard with all the *un*pleasantness about me. I tried to relax my muscles, one at a time, and then tried to "drift off." I was sweating heavily, feeling very damp and groggy, and felt as though I were growing smaller and smaller. I knew I should feel frightened, but I was too comfortable even with the dampness and the dizziness.

I closed my eyes and opened them again several times. Sleep was almost there, but still teasingly elusive. My eyes focused hazily on the pale green curtain. I watched it move, ever so little, from the air about it. An ugly color, I reflected, but very soft and filmy.

Sleep had almost descended to push my eyelids closed when the curtain parted. I observed a nurse staring at me, and then coming into my cubicle to look even more closely. The nurse smiled. That was nice, I thought. They don't often seem pleasant or friendly around here. The nurse went out, and I hadn't even returned her smile, I thought. How rude of me. I heard the nurse calling to others. The voices were a little distant.

"Come and see Laurel. We did it." Several nurses and orderlies were entering my private cubicle.

The first nurse was ahead. "Look," she said. "Laurel has finally gone into coma."

She was still smiling. So that was what had pleased her. Well, won't she be surprised when I smile back at her, in front of all of them. I told my mouth to smile, intent on the embarrassment I would cause. But my mouth didn't obey! Oh well, I told myself, it will be even funnier if I wink at her. What was wrong? No wink. My eyes were open. I saw them all smiling at me. I told my face to form a smile, my eyes to wink. Again I commanded. But my face and eyes wouldn't obey. Cry out! I told myself. Tell them that you are not "out," that you can see them and hear them. Oh, dear God! Why doesn't my body work?

The nurse came closer to me "Just look at that!" she gloated

Is she stupid? I wondered. Can't she see me looking right at her? I was trying to think of something clever for my mouth to say but again I couldn't. The nurse was standing right above me, looking back into my open eyes. I was sure that those eyes were open. You couldn't see through your lids, could you? The nurse slapped my cheek. It stung a little and made me angry. Why would she do that—to see if I'm really awake? Then I should certainly tell the witch something that will really put her in her place. The hand struck my cheek a second time. I wanted to blink, curse my assailant, and stop this mad charade. I couldn't do anything; I was sure my body was *dead*. Would my mind go next?

I watched the people smile approval and exit. The offending nurse started out behind them. I was terrified, but my heart wouldn't even race, and my muscles wouldn't tighten. I *knew* I was frightened. I was dying. I was dying and they were smiling and slapping me. And my useless body was just lying there taking it. The green drapes were still gently moving and getting a little blurry. Oh, God, I thought, I know what it is like to be dead.

Unconsciousness must have completely overcome me, as I didn't remember what occurred next until I was sitting up on my cot with a nurse standing beside me. I felt muddled and wondered why I didn't remember sitting up. Luckily, the nurse beside me was not the one who had struck me in the face. But then, anger was too difficult to pull from my brain and put on my still half-dead face. Speech was distant, like my feelings. No wonder these people had all seemed so much like zombies to me. Now I was one of them. I let the nurse help me, as I pulled off my pajamas wet with sweat and put my own dry clothes back on my still disconnected body. It's a good thing that walking and dressing become automatic to us, I pondered; otherwise, I would still be sitting on the hard, wet cot, staring at those damned green drapes. I followed the nurse out to the coffee room.

I had succeeded. I had been able to go into coma. But there was no victory here, as I really didn't want to be comatose. Who would? The staff. *They* had succeeded by putting me under. Theirs was the victory. I was growing increasingly bitter about the total situation. I felt over-powered, not in control of my own destiny, and demeaned by my position as a mental patient. I felt very sympathetic for some of the patients and very annoyed by others. This was a judgmental attitude I found embarrassing. But the staff, that was another story. I felt justified in hating most of them. They were, after all, the persecutors of the vulnerable and the victimized. Most were rude and uncaring to the patients. Some were even cruel in their comments and attitudes, though there were a few exceptions, Margaret, the OT instructor, and possibly the house doctor. I was withholding judgment on him for the present.

Having succumbed to coma made me feel very depressed. I didn't want to go to OT that afternoon but knew that Dorothy would be disappointed. I went down, worked an hour or less, and then excused myself. Dorothy and I did not have the usual exchange of funny jokes and anecdotes. I had already told her about "Martha's pregnancy" and the ladies trying to find unlocked doors, as well as those "dumb-oes" across the hall that went for "naps." Thelma's preoccupation with colors and her strange irrational relationships were somewhat humorous, but I felt a loyalty to Thelma and did not feel I could discuss her. Cheryl was so pathetic that I would never tell her story. It was not even an option. I had not told Dorothy about Cheryl, as I didn't think the world should discover Cheryl's hiding place. I was even sorry that I had mentioned it to Martin, but I was upset and needed someone in whom to confide.

Martin had just seemed so overwhelmed by it all, and I was worried that my illness was hard enough on him. Then, too, there was a fascination on his part that seemed unrelated to empathy for Cheryl herself. He often seemed uncomfortable around all the patients. Was he afraid they might be harmful? He had let *me* stay here with them but maybe insanity was something that he just could not handle. But who could? Even the staff here seemed to be making strange decisions, reacting with hostility toward "illnesses" and not seeming to have any real feelings for tragic situations.

I hadn't thought of one funny or ironic situation during the entire OT visit. Dorothy and I learned a few new methods for marking the leather with some other tools, and we decided we would start our projects the next time. Dorothy seemed somewhat subdued also. She finally told me that she had to make some decisions and was troubled. No other explanation was given. It was probably a good thing that we both had an "off" day at the same time.

When I got upstairs, I went to my room and just lay on my bed. It was still early afternoon and the patients were out in the garden. One of the nurses who had just come on duty asked me if I wouldn't like to come on outside. Perhaps the sunlight could lift the gloom that I was feeling. I was also rather weak and shaky. Anxiety, I suspected. When I mentioned it to the nurse, she immediately looked into my eyes, then said that we would stop on the way outside for some sweetened juice.

Outside, the patients had dispersed to various parts of the ill-kept garden. I didn't want to talk to anyone I knew since I didn't see Thelma there, and Cheryl was never allowed outside. The depressed lady who went around checking door locks was there, but now she was trying the doors to get in. I sat on a bench near the entry and watched her for a while. She was a well-dressed woman in her early forties; she wore her hair neatly pulled into a bun behind her head and wore carefully applied make-up. Her hair was obviously dyed. The rather overwhelming black color didn't quite match her sallow complexion. She seemed oblivious to other patients and very preoccupied with locks and doors. A nurse I didn't know came and sat on the bench with me.

"She is so depressed!" the nurse commented to me.

I almost responded with "Aren't we all?" but I was so surprised that a staff member would initiate a conversation with me that I turned and gave a half-hearted smile instead.

"Yeah," I said. "She never does anything upstairs except go around trying all the doors."

"Are you on Third Floor?" asked the nurse.

"Oh, yes," I sighed, "I'm one of the *real* loonies." I expected that this information would terminate any further conversation, but I had underestimated this rather friendly nurse.

"She recently lost her son," commented the nurse.

I felt a hollow sensation in my upper stomach. I was damning the staff for their insensitivity and I, myself, was worse.

"Will she get better?" I asked.

"They've only started her treatments, but her prognosis is good."

The nurse answered me like an equal and in such an accepting manner that I was truly touched. We conversed about a number of things to do with the hospital. How long I had been there, my problem and treatment, how long the nurse had worked here, how stressful the job was, and how there were so many different types of patients. I let the nurse know that the staff was perceived by the patients, at best, as uncaring. The nurse agreed, but pointed out the heavy caseloads and understaffing. She usually worked nights herself on Second and was just putting in an extra shift.

The nurse glanced away, and then said she was keeping an eye on the Lady from Wyoming, who had amnesia after a boat accident. The staff was concerned about her behavior. I hadn't noticed the woman earlier, but now I could see her over near the side of the building that was visible from this bench. Realizing that the nurse wasn't really seeking my companionship, just sharing a bench located where she could do her job, I felt let down.

Meanwhile, the Lady from Wyoming was alternately walking and running about the bushes. She was silent in her strange maneuvers and had not seemed to arouse anyone's interest except for this nurse, who must have been designated as her personal "keeper." Wyoming would stand still every once in a while, and then, as if by some unseen command, she would begin a series of calisthenics. Hands would fly up over her head, then down to the grass, as she bent at the waist, keeping her knees straight. She would then do a series of eight to ten "jumping jacks," after which she would look around her furtively and dash toward the bushes. Then she would come slinking back from the bushes and begin the sequence again. What an unusual and nonsensical demonstration, I thought.

An orderly approached our bench and offered to relieve the nurse if she would oversee the shuffleboard game for a while. The nurse left and the orderly said nothing to me. I got up slowly and walked toward the building, hoping it would soon be time to "load the cattle" into the elevator and return to Third Floor. I wondered if Martin would come earlier tonight.

Martin did come after dinner and slightly earlier than usual, but still with little time to talk. He seemed uncomfortable with Mickey being with us in the room, asked about Cheryl, and then watched anxiously out the door to the hallway, asking if any of the passers-by were Cheryl. I was missing my daughters and so was relieved when Martin told me they seemed to be doing fine. They were enjoying being with their cousins, but of course they missed their mom.

I sat in the day room until late that night doing my embroidery. I was in no frame of mind to hear how close it was to Rabies Time, and I didn't want to see Cheryl. Cheryl was still staying to herself in her own room. She carried her crucifix with her always. When anyone approached her door, they were often aware that they had interrupted her saying her beads. I had looked in on Thelma earlier and had seen her parents there. Later, when I could have visited, I hadn't wanted to deal with her.

Margaret had come on the three-to-eleven shift but had been busy and had not found time to talk with me. After all the temperatures were taken and the patients were either in their rooms or appearing to watch TV, Margaret came and sat beside me. We updated each other on various events. Martha was still pregnant, Thelma was still taking electroshock treatments, the Lady from Wyoming did calisthenics, and Dorothy liked the Annex. Not much was new. Tomorrow, though, was when Mickey's husband would go into a rabies seizure and surely die. We both smiled. Margaret asked me how I was doing. I let her know that I was down today, annoyed with treatments and somewhat discouraged.

Margaret said, hesitantly, "Excuse my asking, as I really don't know, but what is *your* problem? You've never said anything to disclose it, and I saw nothing on your chart, except the treatment notations. You know your doctor never reads the charts. He believes that he can tell all about his patients from just looking at them. I don't think he believes that the nurses know very much, either. We keep the charting for him—we have to—but I've never seen him read anything.

"Anyway, as I was saying, it is very obvious what is wrong with most of the patients here. And if you're around them very often, you usually know what is going on with almost everyone, just like the people we've been talking about. But I really want to know what's wrong with you? I've never seen you act or say anything weird ... or anything that would explain your problem. Would you tell me ... what's wrong? Why are you here?"

I was feeling so crazy that day but even this didn't really lift my spirits being told that all the covering of my anxieties and thoughts was effective.

"Nothing really!" I responded airily in a relaxed theatrical voice. "I only come for the summers."

Margaret laughed with me and then I looked at her seriously.

"I was here last summer," I said almost apologetically. "Maybe I don't seem too crazy in here, but put me out on the street ... in public ... and I'd probably go bananas. In my own way, maybe I'm crazier than all of them. At least they can come and go in public, and not have to feel scared to death and incompetent when they're not all penned-up."

Margaret seemed genuinely understanding of me and reassured me that she didn't think this was such a serious problem.

"You're still rational. At least you know what's going on about you," she said. "This is just a form of anxiety that I'm sure should be easily cured."

I was a little lifted by that comment.

"So, you only come for the summers?" Margaret laughed. "Well, I'm sure that we won't see you next year."

"You bet you won't!" I said, with finality. "They'll have to catch me first to ever get me in this God-forsaken place again."

Chapter Twelve
More Insulin Therapy

With a reverberating bang, Betty, the morning's floor nurse, slammed her heavy hip against the partially opened door, banging it against the adjacent wall. She was making her entry for the purpose of administering the patient's early insulin shot at six. No doubt she calculated that the noise would awaken her patient and cancel the need for verbal exchange. Already the morning had not gone well. Two patients in the North Wing had become overly agitated, and Betty had had to call down to have them sedated. At least she hadn't had to call the emergency paging and awaken the other patients, and cause more confusion in the halls. She was peeved that she had to give two shots to this patient ... more steps ... back and forth ... and the morning treatments were so tiring. It seemed there was never time enough to bring them all out of coma, wait while they had coffee, and get them back on the ward in time for lunch trays. And this special case! Why did it have to fall to her? She could hardly wait until she had enough seniority to request an afternoon or night shift ... that was so much easier. She motioned her patient to roll over.

* * *

I was already awake and had reluctantly turned over and pulled my pajama bottoms down, to allow the shot to be injected. Sleep had again been elusive, and I had been one of the wandering spirits walking the halls, restlessly pretending to need to use the bathroom or get a drink at the hall fountain. This was an improvement of sorts, as I was always so frightened of being away from the security of my own room and bed, especially after dark. My trips to OT and visits with the other patients had been a conscious effort to appear and possibly become normal. The nurses and orderlies were my motivators for the dreaded garden visits. The more aware patients avoided the night nurses, as they were even more unapproachable and punitive than the day nurses. It was best to ask no questions, stay out of the way, and cause no problems. Word of mouth was that the night staff was quicker with the hypo needles. The staff found it easier to call for assistance at night, as there were no visitors or doctors to hear the intercom, and there was not as much traffic in the stairwells, elevators, or hallways. Besides, many of the night personnel had other jobs, and wanted this time to relax, read, write, watch late TV, and generally just not be bothered.

After Margaret went off floor duty at eleven, I usually sought the safety and comfort of my own bed and of sleep, but my recently increased worry and depression made a restful night unobtainable. Early evening talks with Margaret were now of little comfort. Mickey slept fitfully, and the slightest noise jarred my balance between sleep and the real world. One less coma to deal with; that was small comfort. If only I could live through the other twenty-one or so!

At least life was not boring here. It was more like an ultra bizarre presentation of Theatre of the Absurd. Any patient would be fearful and disturbed in this environment and treatments, and my "free floating" anxieties only made it worse.

* * *

Mickey awoke confused and annoyed. All the commotion in her room! And it was so hard to try to remember what the date was. She scowled at Betty and Laurel, tried to organize her thoughts, and plan her actions. How could she help her husband in here? She needed to get out. But that was impossible. It was locked up tighter than a drum! She was going to have to enlist some aid from someone, but not someone wielding a needle! She turned her head to the wall and wished Laurel out of the room so she could settle her thoughts on her own problems.

* * *

I pulled on my robe over my pajamas and waited, already feeling woozy from the effects of the insulin long before Betty came to take me with the others to the treatment room. We walked in the usual strange parade, down the stairwell, all the zombies, all our shuffling, causing the antiquated stairs to creak. The only voices were those of the staff, repeating their terse orders.

Wouldn't it be something, I thought, if we all greeted one another pleasantly with comments such as "Good morning to you!"? "How are your comas coming along?" "Good to see you here again today!" "Won't this be a great experience?" "*I'm* surely proud to be here." I mustered a half smile at the thought.

Betty noticed the smile. This was the first positive thing that had happened all morning. I could see by the look in her eyes that she thought the depressed, frightened, little thing (me) was coming around!

"You're doing better, aren't you?" she commented, almost kindly. I just shrugged.

* * *

The insulin patients filed solemnly into the treatment room. Some went automatically to their accustomed cots; others waited for directions. One man slipped and fell against the patient near him. Two orderlies were quick to usher the men to their places and avoid any conflict. The larger, rather muscular patient was unsure of what was occurring, and the orderly remembered reading on his chart that the patient had struck at a patient the prior evening, and then threatened an orderly. The patient had received a hypo and was still a little unsteady this morning. Too bad they had to give him a treatment so soon after, but time schedules were important in order to conclude treatments during the limits prescribed by the insurance coverage. The orderly indulged in self-commendation, for such immediate action and presence of thought…. "Got to keep ahead of the nuts," he smiled to himself.

* * *

The nurse in charge of the treatment room ordered the Third Floor nurse to lead me into a different area. I glared at the charge nurse for the low regard she held for either my intelligence or cooperativeness. Why couldn't she go directly to me with the commands? The other patients and I were guided to one of the small rooms at the side of and behind the counter area. This room had six or seven cots in an irregular pattern about the room. No curtains to separate the patients here, just cots. One small window with a heavy screen let in dust-filtered light rays and gave a rather weak illumination to the stark, dull-sheeted bedding and pillows. There was a small dressing room attached where the women could change to the insulin pajamas. The men had come to the room already dressed for treatment. Everyone found a cot. Everyone but me seemed to know what to do. I watched, and then dressed methodically and wandered across to the far side of the room, where I took the extra cot. I had no idea why I was here, but assumed that it had something to do with my previous treatment, and the fact that they had finally been able to induce coma.

There was little privacy in the main room, with the green curtains shielding each cot. The staff was in and out of each cubicle, but at least the patients could not see each other's faces. No privacy existed in this small room, but the beds were alternated so that their faces were not in such close contact with one another. Still, in order not to peer at each other, some turned their faces either to the wall or away from those nearby. The tall, gangly blonde lady from Wyoming was also assigned this treatment room. I shivered. Did everyone go into coma at the same time? If not, did they witness one another's unconsciousness? I didn't want to see their "dead" faces, such as my own had been the day before, and I wished for the green curtains.

* * *

The Lady from Wyoming had forgotten what she came here to do and was looking intently from one face to another. Then, beginning to remember the procedures, she smiled knowingly and arranged herself rather deliberately on the cot, turning her head to create as much privacy as she could. She wished she could sleep and complete the morning as soon as possible. Overwhelming anticipation, directed at everything, had been consuming her for days. She knew there was something that she must finish, or tend to, but she was confused about what it was. There was a purpose in her being here, if only she could recall it. A dark anxiety about something unknown lurked in the back of her mind, but she was too confused to pull it forth.

She lay down and tried to concentrate on what she was expected to do.

She needed some structure to the great mass of disorganized movements and events in her mind. Something terrible had preceded all this but it was gone. She couldn't remember exactly, but she knew the people around her were all wrong. Nothing fit.

Now she could feel her heartbeats quickening. She was beginning to feel a little dizzy, and she was remembering that this was the way it went. You close your eyes and sleep comes. The morning passes quickly, and then they will take everyone to the garden, where it is spacious, and you can get the restlessness from your body. Run, stretch, and fight back at the confusion. Please come, Sleep.

* * *

A nurse came, pulled back the drawstring drawers of the insulin pajamas, and injected the shots, one at a time, into all the fannies thus exposed. No one spoke. The patients all obediently raised their behinds, in sequence, as the nurse approached them, in acceptance of her needle. I received a second shot as well. Then everyone dutifully pulled their sheets up over themselves and lay quietly, most still trying to turn their heads in a direction away from one another.

I was near a wall, so that it would have been easy not to watch but I was so curious and awestruck. Was this like the war camps during the Holocaust? If you told these people to take a shower and then turned on the gas, would they blindly do what was expected of them? I supposed that they knew what happened if you refused the same way that I knew. And I was obedient. A hypo that had taken me into oblivion was sufficient incentive for being tractable.

I was disgusted with myself. No, I was only obedient in order to help myself get well. But then, perhaps everyone else had the same motivation. Except that I knew at least one person in this room, Jeannie from my floor, did not even think that she was sick. I looked at each patient carefully, trying not to stare. No one seemed frightened or sad or happy, just preoccupied. Most had closed their eyes. I turned my head toward the wall. I didn't want them to go into coma ahead of me. I didn't want to see their unconsciousness.

I wasn't sleepy, just weak and dizzy. I tried some relaxation techniques to put myself to sleep, but the newness of the situation, and the fear of the "dead" feeling, had further raised my anxiety level, and I could not drift off. It seemed that the harder I tried, the more awake I remained. My eyes were burning with the dryness and stinging sensation that accompanies lengthy periods of poor rest. The time crawled by, as I lay listening to an occasional restless patient turning or breathing differently.

The stillness engulfed the small stuffy room, which was beginning to smell of insulin sweat. The staff frequently joked about the stench in the treatment rooms. I knew how fortunate I was that I had a poor olfactory sense. But soon the pungent odor was sufficient, in this oppressing space, to alert my entire body toward nausea. I pulled the heavy cotton flannel sheeting higher, burying my nose in the smell of a strong disinfectant soap that lingered in the stiff, rough fabric. Beneath the gray-white linens I listened to the room with eyes closed. The room was quiet. Just low breathing noises. Had they all succumbed to the insulin except for me?

I heard a noise. A patient was moving. It was a prolonged movement, not just someone turning over. I turned to see if someone had decided to rearrange things, or even possibly get up and deny the treatment. The Lady from Wyoming was in the bed next to mine and it was she who was moving about. Lying on her back, her eyes open wide, she was rising slowly, very slowly, from her head on down to her waist, into a sitting position. Then she would slowly lower herself down until she was completely prone on the cot. Then she methodically rose again. This time she thrust out her tongue as her body came up. She extended her tongue gradually, in sequence with her rising body movements. As she lay down, the tongue would curl upward and backward into her widely opened mouth. Then she began the rising again.

This rhythmic procedure continued. My heartbeat quickened. Is this what a coma was? I glanced furtively about the room. The others seemed subdued, some with eyes open, others in apparent sleep. Didn't they notice what was happening, or didn't they care?

I turned my face to the wall again, trying to still the pounding in my head and ears. My heart was beating so loudly I was sure it could wake the dead—or even the merely comatose. I tried to breathe slowly and closed my eyes, wishing desperately for sleep or coma or *something*.

* * *

Dazed, she continued to sit up slowly, as her tongue crept gradually from her mouth, in time to her rising. And then the curling retraction moved, in concert with her body's reclining. Oblivious of her surroundings, she fought her chaotic dreams, visions of water filtering in and out through them, a boat, faces contorted, and thrashings of arms and legs. Would she remember any of this upon awakening? The inner self in anguish was trying to communicate to gain assistance. With the next opening of her mouth, for the tongue thrust, a low gurgling sound emerged from the depths of her throat. It began almost inaudibly, and then raised in tone and intensity of volume until, at its conclusion, it became a scream.

* * *

A few of the other patients moved in physical alarm but remained unconscious. Several staff members had entered the stench-ridden room to continue with their duties. They had not yet noticed that I was still awake.

I lay there, sweat beginning to exude from my entire body, listening to Wyoming's rhythmic movements and now her screams. I squinted my eyes in revulsion, wishing again for the green curtains, yet curious about was occurring. I turned my head without lifting it and tried to look through the loose strands of mussed hair that stuck to my now sweaty face. The house doctor and orderlies had straps of cloth that they were brandishing about. They stopped here and there to tie the ankles and wrists of some of the patients to the metal undersides of their cots. I wondered how patients were chosen for tying and if I would be one of those selected. The doctor approached Wyoming, and the orderly secured her feet with the white cotton straps, as Wyoming continued her meaningless sit-ups.

The thin slits of eyes that I had been peeking through opened wide as I observed the doctor putting the dreaded black box on the floor near the woman. The orderlies came and stationed themselves on either side of the victim as the doctor connected wires from the box to the woman's temples. As two orderlies each held an arm, the box was tuned on. There were crackling noises, and Wyoming twitched violently all over her body. Her screams had stopped. The jerks were dramatic, pushing her head and feet from the cot, and raising her body up and down, while the orderlies held her down, preventing her from coming off the cot. Then the forceful movements stopped, and her body settled into a stiff mass, her glazed eyes still staring vacantly, while her arms and legs continued vibrating slightly. All the while, the strange wires were hanging at each side of her pale head. The orderlies released her. Her body stilled, as if its life were drained away. My mouth gaped open in disbelief.

Suddenly the doctor became aware of my presence. "Quick!" he called angrily. "Laurel's awake! Bring a screen *now!*" He looked at me in sudden contempt, as if he had been caught at a misdeed and it was my fault. "Turn around!" he ordered, still angry, just as the screen was being hastily erected between the cots with much noise and scrambling on the part of the frantic orderlies. The convulsion was over, and the Lady from Wyoming was now lying still, at last relaxed and eyes closed.

Too late, I thought. I've seen it anyway. I was regretting that I had not had the presence of mind, and self-discipline, to turn my head away. You don't think too well when you're full of insulin and in a semi-stupor, I told myself cringing, hearing myself make excuses, as if it *were* my fault that they had allowed me to witness this torture session. I could hear more moving about, and the crackling and the jumping noises on the cots, and I knew that *he* was inflicting that black box on others.

After what seemed like hours they left and the muggy, stinking room was comparatively still again. I was drenched with sweat, and the stiff flannel pajamas had lost their hardness and now clung, damp and cold, to my body. How I wanted them removed from my tingling skin! I also wanted to get up, look around, and see what havoc the marauders had caused and check to see if any patients were dead. But I was too shaky and weak to move. I lay there terrified, listening, head to the wall, trying to distract myself by forming intricate, minuscule pictures in my mind from the shadows that floated across my eyes. Almost gagging on the foul, suffocating odor, I waited and waited and waited.

At long last a nurse came into the room, mumbled something gruffly and handed me one of their "shakes." It was especially large and nauseating. The screen remained up around me. I was told to stay on my cot while the other patients were being awakened. I wasn't sure how that awakening was accomplished but I was content with my ignorance. At last my screen was removed, I was given my clothes, and I began dressing with the other women. I pulled on my worn pajamas and my faded blue robe. The women had gone from the room. "Anderson," as the larger man was addressed, was the only one who had anything to say on leaving. He was stumbling and complaining of a headache and wondering why his pajamas were wet.

I exited with the Lady from Wyoming, who seemed remarkably active, though a bit jerky in her movements, considering what she had just experienced. She almost pushed me out of the doorway, moving hurriedly and with little coordination, past the long counter and on toward the coffee room, bumping into others as she went.

I walked slowly and stopped behind the desk area on my way. I was still in shock from what had occurred, and did not feel very lively or alert. I tried to focus on things around me as I tried to keep my balance and instill some calmness into my surroundings. I glanced about at the walls.

Suddenly I caught sight of a chart with names and numbers. I stopped to read it, focusing on the detail and concrete things about me, in an attempt to erase the emotional shock of the past several hours. I assumed, correctly, that this was a list of the insulin patients and their prescribed dosages. I was scanning the chart for my own name. I found it. Laurel Ames, 450. I looked to see what other figures there were, and how they compared to my own. Good heavens! There were numbers of 20, 60, 40, 90, 80, 125—all small in comparison. I had scanned the entire chart before Nurse Betty noticed what I was doing.

"Get Laurel!" she commanded excitedly. "She's reading the charts!"

One of the orderlies came to pull me away. I just stood there in disbelief. "Anderson" was the one with the next highest dosage. His was at 200. Anderson was a huge man at least six feet tall and built like a football linebacker. He was only getting 200 "whatevers" while I, who was short and still rather slight but getting fatter from their shakes, was receiving 450. No wonder they didn't want me to see the chart! Why wasn't I dead? How could they know what they were doing? It was all so unreasonable to me and frightening.

As I was led reluctantly from behind the counter, I tried to ask first the orderly then the nurse in charge what was going on. But they were all intent on vacating the treatment areas. I was stunned. No one wanted to discuss this with me, but I realized that they had no say in the administration of the doctors' orders. I needed to talk to Dr. Ashford and stop him while I was still able. I glided dreamlike into the coffee room, was given more "shake," and stood with a sweet roll in my hand, unable to concentrate enough to eat it.

The Lady from Wyoming, whom the nurses called "Madelyn," was having quite a different problem. While I was slow and unable to get myself moving correctly, Madelyn was bounding about the room. She went from one table to another, changed ashtrays a number of times, dumped several ashtrays into wastebaskets, and refilled her coffee cup at least three times. She had begun talking also and was commenting about various unimportant things in a loud and abrasive manner. I had been trying to think but with Madelyn's commotion, it wasn't easy. Madelyn was almost as bad as Martha had been. Martha, by the way, had recently become rather withdrawn, and she rarely spoke after her treatments. I hadn't even noticed her.

* * *

Madelyn was starting to feel more agitated. She didn't like "being awake" and feeling so apprehensive. She wanted to get on with things, have the coffee, bathe, eat, and get outside. She wanted to see the sky and the trees. She was cooped up no, locked up in here, and she didn't know why. They told her she was ill and needed to get better. She wished she could remember! She felt fine and had lots of energy, too much energy, in fact. She wanted to run, yell, and throw her arms about. If only she could relax and sit for a while. She tried to talk to Anderson and then crossed the room to tell the nurse about her cigarette. It seemed that no one was interested in her or her comments. She was puzzled at this but not overly concerned.

* * *

Anderson was sitting across from me, with the other smaller man from their "coma cots," and drinking coffee. I watched him with interest. I wanted to go over and ask him if he knew that he was getting 200 "somethings." I wanted to question him about what he thought insulin did for him and see if he minded the treatments. He seemed quiet, too quiet. What would he say if I told him that I got 450 "somethings"? Would he be in awe of my physical endurance? Did this make me a bigger person with stronger resistance? Or was I going to get a stranger and stranger reaction in the physical feelings that went with a coma? What if my blood turned completely into insulin? I didn't see how anyone could drink enough glucose shakes or enough sugared-up juice to combat 450. Anderson didn't look ill, just a little shy, confused, and inoperant. The staff was probably "poisoning" *him* more slowly.

I was feeling extremely disoriented and quite crazy. Oh, *how* to fight this system? If I weren't so groggy and confused, I knew that I would bolt and run. If only I could be like Madelyn, I could knock the nurses away. Yes, even the larger orderlies ... escape with someone's keys and head for the main door.

When Madelyn knocked over a cup of coffee, she was directed, along with several other patients, out of the room to the stairwell. Anderson and the other man left. I stood there, still holding the sweet roll, and a nurse came and took my arm to hurry me to join another group of about five women, outside another door in the coffee room. We entered a large room on Second Floor, where I had never been before. I assumed it was a day room. It had a large pool table, a TV and some chairs. This must be the men's ward, I thought. At the center of the room was the locked elevator. The nurse remarked that she was taking everyone on the elevator, as it was late and they needed to hurry. I was still feeling stunned by my newly discovered dosage information, and didn't talk to anyone and went quietly to my room. Still puzzled, I planned to sort it all out, and *then* take action.

Chapter Thirteen
Mickey and the Rabid Cat

Lunch was being served on Third Floor, and the other patients and I went to pick up our trays in the day room. Mickey indicated that she wanted to talk to me. It was "Rabies Day" and Mickey had told me that her husband did *not* die.

"The cat must not have been infected," she said with great relief. We went to our room, and Mickey asked if I wanted to hear the Whole Story. I nodded although I couldn't feign much interest. My "450" was still in me and I wanted to concentrate on getting enough food, glucose, and sugared juice to fight the "450" for my life.

Still, Mickey had a very interesting story. Her husband had been scratched by a stray cat, and Mickey had tried for days to find the cat, describing it in vain to all of the neighbors. She walked the alleys, and streets nearby, and even drove about for hours in her car, seeking the cat. No one could help her. They didn't know to whom it belonged. They hadn't even seen it.

Mickey was terribly distraught. She assumed the cat had rabies; she didn't know why else it would have attacked and scratched her husband. She worried so much that she couldn't sleep nights. She took their two small children on lengthy walks and drives, looking unsuccess-fully each day, and sometimes in the evenings. Still no cat. She worried frantically. She researched rabies and found that it was a terrible disease and, when contracted by humans, the resultant and unavoidable death was horribly painful. Possible survival from an almost equally horrible treatment did not seem to be a good alternative.

Mickey could not let her beloved husband endure either. She had tried her best to find the cat and had not succeeded. When she realized that there was no way to prevent him from the disease or drastic treat-ment, she knew that, as his devoted wife, she must protect him from the dramatic and painful choices that awaited him. Mickey's husband, who had more than noticed her morbid preoccupation with the cat, went with her to several doctors and psychiatrists. They all tried to reassure her that everything was going to be all right, but Mickey could not be consoled or pacified.

Mickey realized that she must work out something on her own. She devised a plan. She went to a pawnshop and purchased a small pistol for a nominal price. She asked her husband to go out "on a date." He was very excited, thinking that romance was the motivation, and Mickey *had* been less than amorous lately, what with all her fretting. Also, he saw this as a move away from her obsession. Two of the psychiatrists had interpreted her exaggerated concern as a strong need for psychiatric care and had told him that she could be dangerous. The apparent change in her interests came as a welcome relief. Mickey's plan for their "date" included a nice dinner out, a movie, and then a long drive into the country. Her husband, Mickey told me, seemed very happy, especially about the drive into the country, assuming that Mickey was feeling better, and in the mood for a more intimate relationship; since the babysitter was at home with their kids, they could make the most of the evening.

He was particularly pleased when she asked that they stop and park, whereupon they both got into the back seat. As her husband choreographed his next moves in his mind, Mickey expressed her love and concern for him. Then suddenly she jumped over the seat into the front, lunging toward the glove compartment, from which she quickly retrieved the pistol and shakily pointed it at his head. She announced that she was going to shoot him, explaining that she loved him so much she couldn't bear to watch as he died the horrible death that was awaiting him. He cried a little, and then talked her into giving him the gun, assuring her that they could find a better solution (fast thinking on his part, I thought).

"What do you think of the story?" asked Mickey.

I was incredulous. What could I say? That Mickey was a real nut case? That I was afraid of her? Or that I was so glad that it turned out the way it had?

"Well?" pressed Mickey

"That's a very interesting story," I started hesitantly. "I can see why … you were so very worried about the calendar date. I'm glad that he didn't get the rabies. And … I'm relieved that you didn't shoot him."

114

"Oh!" said Mickey, with a smile that I had never seen on her face before, "*my* doctor said that I'm not capable of killing. If I were, I would have pulled the trigger when I had the chance." Mickey seemed very relieved about the outcome and appeared to know that she needed help. It was clearly reassuring that she was neither insane nor a murderess.

I was relieved that I wouldn't have to be questioned about what day it was anymore and that Mickey hadn't been a killer *yet.* I was also very uncomfortable that Mickey was *my* roommate.

"Well, isn't it great? I don't have to worry anymore that he's going to die, and I get to go to 'insulin' starting Monday. What do you think about my sharing my experience and problems with the other patients? Do you think that they will see me as crazy? Or would they be afraid of me? I'm so relieved! *Should* I tell them?" Mickey blurted out all these questions at once.

When she finally waited for my response, I advised that she keep the story to herself for a while, at least. Some of the patients might not understand, I said, and it could upset them. I found it amusing that Mickey saw it as a privilege to be assigned to insulin. She'll have to learn for herself, I thought. How could she *suppose* that anyone could see her as *crazy*? Didn't she have a clue as to where she was? I just looked at her wondering why I had had any doubt of Mickey's "depth."

Mickey left the room, humming a little to herself. Her new self-confidence irritated me. Just wait till the treatments get her. Damn! After all, what good news did I have to boast about? I didn't even *want* to know Mickey better and was sick of everyone's problems forcing themselves into my private thoughts and personal worries. I lay down on the bed, feeling shaken, both by Mickey's story and the terrifying 450. I was also feeling nauseous from so much glucose. A deep sense of depression swept over me. I could almost expect one of my severe anxiety attacks, if I had the strength to have my pulse race and the fear build. I lay quietly until Jeannie and her roommate came into the room. Jeannie was complaining about a dance where she had been this morning.

"What was it all about?" Jeannie asked me and I turned toward her, frowning in annoyance.

"I don't know what you mean," I replied irritated.

"That dance, the one that we were all at. We were all dancing the entire morning! You know. *You* were there. You were *in* it! What was it all about?"

I raised my eyebrows and heaved a sigh. I didn't know if she had a dream or if this was a hallucination of Jeannie's.

"I'm just not real sure what the whole damned thing *was* about," I said, slowly and tersely. "But it certainly was strange, wasn't it?" I remembered Madelyn and her gyrations. I imagined the whole Insulin Room full of drab-white, insulin pajama-clad patients, all finding their own movements and rhythms. Bodies undulating, writhing, eyes vacant and wild, the smelly heavy air being pushed about by arms and legs in strange and unnatural positions, and the movements all being orchestrated by clean white-garbed orderlies and nurses wearing evil half-smiles and glaring through narrowed eyes. While the swirling lumbering motions continued for hours, the pungent smell and damp-ness added to the fevered pitch of the voices of the "sane" as they called selected names, the orchestra leader's black box shocking the dancers into convulsions.

"Yes!" I agreed. "Yes, that *was* a dance, a very strange ... even demonic dance."

"See!" said Jeannie, smiling to her roommate. "I told you it was weird. We just kept dancing and dancing, and no one seems to know what the whole thing was for."

"It has something to do with what the staff here has in mind for 'getting us well.' But then, that's *their* plan!" I smiled, mysteriously.

The departure of the ladies going to tell the others about Jeannie's dance left the room suddenly relaxed and almost private. I lay on my back looking at the ceiling and contemplating all the crazy things here. How I wished for some quiet, some sanity for myself, and even for those around me. I was so tired, so fed up, and had so many days to go. I rolled over and curled my legs up near my chin. I wanted to cover up, as I was feeling chilled, but I didn't want to get up for a blanket. I lay there pondering the bleakness of my situation when I was suddenly aroused by another person entering the room. All I wanted was to be alone to empty my mind of rabies, colors, baby murders, dances, lock trying, miracle pregnancies, and on and on. I raised my head to tell the visitor to come another time, and my eyes met Dr. Ashford's.

"What in hell are you doing here, on your bed?" he asked.

For the first time I didn't feel intimidated by him. "I can't think of any place I'd rather be ... at the moment," I said, quite coolly.

"Why aren't you out in the day room, talking to the other patients?" he said sternly.

"*You* go talk to them," I said in disgust. "I've heard all their stories, at least *once*, and I'm tired."

The doctor smiled, "Oh! It's like that, is it?" He seemed to be pleased that I recognized my companions were not quite sane and that I was being so assertive. Hell, I thought, I should have told him how upsetting this place was earlier. Maybe I would be over at the Annex with Dorothy. Dr. Ashford seemed to have read my mind after all; some of the nurses thought that he had this ability.

"I have to keep you here in the main hospital," he said apologetically. "I'd like to have you at the Annex, but you're having so much insulin, we have to watch you carefully for reactions. It can't be done over there. And we need you here, where the house doctor and nursing staff can observe you more closely."

The doctor spoke almost conversationally. He was even showing some acknowledgment of my discomfort. So he *did* know that I was getting a lot of insulin, and they *were* watching me. I told him about the amounts and about Anderson at 200-plus pounds and his 200. Dr. Ashford informed me that the amount, "units," was not related to size or weight. I was just too worried and the adrenaline I produced probably made me need to have larger amounts. He also said that he had administered large dosages—he didn't say *how* large—but his tone and expression conveyed his annoyance at my questioning his medical knowledge and abilities. His immediate disapproval, and discounting of my rights, caused me to rethink my planned appeal and discharged any hope I had for change. I began to feel terribly intimidated by him again. But I needed him on my side, because of his power over me, and I certainly did not want to offend him.

I quickly shifted the conversation by remarking that I had met Thelma. I said that I knew he was Thelma's doctor ... and did he know that Thelma was very frightened by him, so much so that she couldn't tell him things that I had suggested a doctor should know? It bothered me that Dr. Ashford seemed almost childishly pleased that he was threatening to Thelma.

"What kinds of things seem to be bothering Thelma?" he asked casually. I explained the strange associations with color, though I deliberately neglected to tell him that Thelma was afraid of his red face. Still, I related how upset Thelma was with the color "red." I told him about the strange relationships that Thelma made regarding her father's suit and his motives when wearing it, her "wired" car, and the strange concern about the necklace that continued to cause Thelma frustration and worry, how unusual relationships were made in Thelma's mind, connecting her family, boyfriend, and problems with offhanded and irrelevant comments to occurrences here at the hospital.

Dr. Ashford seemed impressed that I could understand Thelma's motivations and some of her reactions. He listened carefully and asked numerous questions. I felt a strange tinge of jealousy. Dr. Ashford had always seemed preoccupied in my sessions with him, before hospitalization, and totally unimpressed—even annoyed by me—since I had been admitted here. I really had never seen this much interest in *my* case, and yet, he was completely absorbed in what was happening with Thelma.

His eyes lit up and he was actually intent, and even smiling at me but all because of the information about Thelma. Why couldn't I provoke this interest? But then, I thought that Thelma was interesting, too. Dr. Ashford asked me to find out several things about Thelma for him. This made me a little distressed. I hadn't felt disloyal at first, as I was trying to assist with information to aid Thelma's treatment. But trying to find out her ideas on purpose sounded like spying, an out-and-out misuse of friendship. But then again, maybe I could help Thelma get well.

"This is important information you've given me," Dr. Ashford said, standing up.

He left the room walking rather stiffly and slowly. His short body was hunched by his shoulders held upward and forward. I hadn't noticed him looking so old and tired before. He hadn't said anything to me, about what I had been up to with the patients or my heckling of the nurses. One nurse had warned me that I would prolong my stay because of what would be charted about me. Maybe my doctor *could* tell what was wrong with a patient just by looking, as the nurses said that he could. Maybe he was wise and competent and could cure me. I certainly hoped so.

* * *

Dr. Ashford walked down the narrow hall to the day room and then stopped at the nurses' station. He was excessively tired today, having been awake a good portion of the night. His coughing seizures had become more intense these past several days and he felt weakened. He gave only perfunctory attention to the charts, but at least he looked at them, which was rare for him. Nothing on Thelma, except signs of withdrawal and depression. Lots on Laurel—nuisance sorts of things. Hmmmm! So Thelma talks with Laurel. Her parents could give him no clues, and she certainly hid herself from him. Some concerns that her mother had from earlier years, they seemed to make more sense now. Thelma was so bright and apparently self-confident. More here, he thought, than I would have guessed. If his anxiety-ridden patient could continue to help, he could unravel some....

His eyes were so tired, and it was a long way to the parking lot. He got out his keys to open the elevator, sighed heavily, and decided to skip the few errands he had planned. Just get home, lie down, and alleviate the pain. He wished he had time to thunder some orders to the staff on the main floor before leaving. This always lifted his spirits. He clanged the elevator doors extra hard on exiting it on the Main Floor, just to let them know he was there ... and in charge.

Chapter Fourteen
Repent!

Sunday morning slipped in quietly. There was little noise on the ward, as no treatments were given on the Day of Rest. Without the hurried staff there was less movement. The patients who were not too distressed to sleep did. I opened my eyes rather slowly and tried to focus. My gaze took in the stark walls and then the screened window, reminding me of where I was. I turned my head and looked toward the other bed in my room. Mickey was staring at the ceiling, her usual preoccupation. Except now her face still held the trace of yesterday's smug smile. I grimaced and buried my nose into the pillow. The pathetic part of all this was that I was beginning to get used to the place. Sleep wouldn't return and, besides, an announcement for breakfast was made by a disgustingly tense little day nurse that I hadn't seen before. Mickey began her constant patter about how wonderful it was that her husband was safe, and that life was good after all. She seemed to exchange her starring at the wall to a phase of continual talking. I escaped to the quiet bathroom.

Not as many patients were around, and the halls were deserted except for the Blonde Lock Tester, who wanted and "deserved" keys; she was trying a back stairway door. When I returned to my room, I dressed hurriedly in a skirt and blouse that Martin had brought on his last visit. I had so few clothes even at home and none of them in very good condition. But now I had some makeup, bubble bath, and several more changes of clothing. I smoothed the skirt and combed my hair. I wanted to look sleek and stunning like Thelma, but none of my clothes were good enough, and my hair was unstyled and thin; the perm I had put in my hair a short time back made it look dry. While Thelma had smooth, shiny, thick hair that curled softly and looked well tended, mine bent in suggestions of curls rather than curling into soft waves; it was a dull brown with almost no luster and had lots of split ends. Oh well. I smoothed it and sprayed on some conditioner, then turned my attention to my makeup.

Mickey had not seen me make this effort before, and eyed me curiously. "You having company today?" she asked me. .

I shrugged. "Probably."

I had wanted my efforts to be unnoticed, and I also did not want to begin a rabies conversation. I inspected my work with little satisfaction. I tried to walk as casually from the room as I could without causing more interrogation.

I wandered past the Blonde Lock Tester again, who was now inspecting the elevator. I noticed that the troubled lady had begun her work early. Would there be no rest on Sunday? I sat rather self-consciously on one of the easy chairs in the day room, very near to the elevator. Breakfast had not yet come up on the dumbwaiter. The floor was still quiet except for the movement of the staff, and they seemed slower this morning. I looked at the tall, arched, unadorned windows. Years of dust had accumulated on their surfaces. They faced east so the early morning sunlight streamed through them, fighting its way past the sparkling, stagnant dust particles in the motionless air and landing in patterns upon the floor near the elevator. I watched the bits of sunlit dust in the light shafts moving aimlessly above me. The dust particles had probably been here as long as the worn carpets, faded paint, and the crooked wooden floors. I watched the patches of daylight on the floor and wondered how long it would take for them to move from their current position, sliding over the ugly brown couch on their way back out of the window. It was nice to be able to focus on these things, rather than the swelling of my extremities or the pounding of my pulse.

Suddenly the elevator banged onto the floor and the gates clanged, as one of the psychiatrists rather pompously emerged. I recognized him from his earlier visits. Dorothy had told me that he put many patients in here; he treated most of the local Catholic community and gave all of his patients electroshock. He wore a very expensive light blue suit, probably silk, I supposed. His hair was silver and very thick. He was immaculately groomed. I thought he would have looked well on Thelma's arm. I had an impulse to run to him sobbing, and crying out for help and understanding, decrying my unworthiness and hapless state at the same time deliberately crushing his perfectly pressed jacket, smearing my inadequate makeup on his shirt, and dampening whatever I could with tears, maybe even grasping at and mussing his smoothed wavy hair. I smiled at my fantasy as our eyes met.

"Well, you certainly look bright this morning!" he smiled condescendingly. "I'll bet that you are about ready to go home!"

I smiled a little more brightly and remarked with great superiority, "No, as a matter of fact, doctor, I've only just recently arrived. I'm hoping that I'll really enjoy my stay."

It was rewarding to see one of the most self-satisfied "shrinks" uncomfortable. I continued smiling pleasantly as he hurried on down the hall. The floor nurse in charge had entered the day room and had heard me. She glared at me and remarked with hostility. "Dr. Broussard is very nice man and cares about all of his patients."

"I hope so," I said. "I think he seems overly concerned for himself. I'm glad he's not *my* doctor."

Annoyed, the nurse started to counter with a nasty comment, but just then Martha entered the day room and began an argument with poor senile Mae, who was in the hallway.

Breakfast came in with two orderlies and lots of noise. Patients took their trays from the three-tiered serving cart and either sat down with them on their laps or carried them back to their rooms. I looked around. Because of the insulin treatments, I hadn't had a hospital breakfast before. I didn't want to eat in my room where Mickey was, and I hadn't seen Thelma. The other lock-trying patient, the one with the long, very black hair, noticed me holding my tray and looking about hesitantly.

"Want to come down and eat in my room?" she asked pleasantly.

I had not heard or seen her converse before. I remembered what the nurse in the garden had said about her having lost her child. In spite of the probability of having to hear one more story, I nodded and followed the lock-trying lady to her room.

Millie (of the locks) dwelled in the far west end of Third South. I had never been back there. In fact, I had no idea that the hospital extended that far; I had been in the hallway only as far as Cheryl's room. (I hadn't heard Cheryl crying for a few days but hadn't gone to investigate.) Millie's room was past Cheryl's and through a door, which I had incorrectly assumed was a single room. In fact it was a whole new section of rooms, or suites. There was one large room with two beds and lots of space and its own private bathroom, and Millie's room, which also had two beds, lots of room, closets, and a private bath.

"Wow!" I remarked, not hiding my pleasure. "This is sumptuous for a mental hospital, I mean!"

Millie smiled. "These rooms aren't *too* bad."

"Have you seen the others? This must be the presidential suite ... if *he* ever needs it. And you have your own bath. I'd give anything for that kind of privacy."

I walked to the bath and looked in. "It doesn't even look institutional!" I continued.

"You're welcome to come back here and use it ... if you like." responded Millie, rather pleased that she might have found a friend.

We both sat at a table and ate breakfast, feeling a little self-conscious with each other. Millie gave little information, only how long she had been here, that she was receiving electroshock, and that her husband was coming today for the first time. I named my treatments, length of stay, and said that I thought my husband was coming, also.

"Sunday visitors day at the mental hospital!" I remarked and Millie smiled again.

After taking Millie's and my trays back to the cart in the day room, I sat in the day room again. I was restless and supposed I should go get my embroidery. A young patient with faint blue eyes and long braided hair walked over and sat at the old upright piano. The piano chords were loud and unpleasant and familiar. Church hymns. Of course, it *was* Sunday. Now was a good time to get embroidery! Mae stopped me to tell me that this talented girl was her daughter, of whom she was so proud. I almost ran to my room. Thank God, Mickey was gone! The music was loud even in here. I dived onto my bed and covered my ears with the pillow.

A few minutes later, Lanny, a male nurse, with whom I had spoken a few times in the insulin rooms, burst suddenly into the room. He was carrying the daily dosages of medicines for the floor and smiled when he saw me. He nodded toward the noisy music and shook his head.

"Yeah!" I said. "It's another one of Mae's daughters. I thought I was in church ... and now that you are here to pass the sacrament, I'm convinced."

Lanny was more than appreciative. He got right into the mood and covered his ears with Mickey's pillow. We laughed about how to continue the "Sunday services" for the patients.

"Mae has never tried to claim *me*," I said, with affected sadness. "Guess I have no talent. But wait till she sees my embroidered pillowcases."

"Gorgeous!" remarked Lanny with dramatic feminine hand movements.

He had set the medicine tray down on Mickey's bed table and was taking a conversation break, as the nurse in charge entered angrily.

"I've been looking for you," she said accusingly. "I need help with Bertha. You're not supposed to be fraternizing with the patients anyway."

"Repent!" I hissed under my breath as he passed me while following the nurse from the room. He tittered and received an angry over-the-shoulder glare.

I began my embroidery to calm my restlessness that was again turning to anxiety. Mickey entered with several other patients who were all talking at once, telling her how easy it was to take the insulin and how much better they were feeling since they had come here and had this done to them. I looked skeptically at them and then continued my handiwork.

"What are you making?" asked Jeannie.

This was the one who thought that she had danced all morning in the insulin room. *She* must be feeling better. She couldn't have gotten much worse!

"Pillowcases," I replied. "Have you done yours yet?"

The ladies frowned as Mickey remarked, "That's a different pattern than you had before, isn't it?" (Very observant, Mickey, I thought. You won't know those things after a few shock treatments.) Aloud I said,

"Yes, this is my second pair. You *do* know that you have to embroider two pairs to be released, don't you?"

The ladies shook their heads and frowned again in disbelief.

"Are you sure?" asked Jeannie.

"Of course," I said confidently. "I hate embroidery. Why else would I do this? I go to OT every day just to make sure that I can get out of here. You see me go, don't you, Mickey? Tell them!"

"Yeah!" said Mickey, not sure of anything.

"They don't *tell* you," I continued. "It's kind of an unspoken rule, but if you are able to concentrate ... to be productive ... they put *that* in the charts that your doctor reads. It helps them to see you as more normal ... even recovered ... that you are able to be so practical. Two pillowcase sets are sort of the standard. Dorothy told me and she's been here before, several times, and *she* always gets out. I suppose that she knows the ropes."

The ladies looked at one another, and then they all started exiting the room probably to discuss pillowcases and OT. I was glad, as now I could be alone.

I didn't know that any visitors besides spouses were permitted. But my Aunt Babette appeared just before the groups were taken out to the garden. Babette was a very short lady with large breasts and tummy, and pretty little legs that ended with small feet, and gorgeously thin ankles. She had large myopic eyes with glasses, a family trait, and she had been married a number of times, also a family trait. Babette was my only "blood" aunt, and was not very friendly with her sister, my mother. She accused my mother of my placement here and suggested that she should have known better. Babette wanted to know about the treatments, the care, the patients, and *mostly* the doctor. Why would he have done this? I didn't seem mentally ill. She asked numerous questions, all the time watching me very carefully. Her eyes never left mine. I thought some of her questions were very strange, almost as if she were trying to catch me with something I should know but didn't. All the while, she stared deeply into my eyes.

How do you entertain visitors in the mental hospital, I wondered. Should you take them on a tour of the treatment rooms, the garden, the day rooms? Try to introduce them to all of your nice, wacky, new friends, show them to the staff, or point out all the interesting locked areas? I didn't have to worry very long. Babette's bulgy pale blue eyes narrowed as she noted the time and nervously watched the other patients who had come back into the room. Babette had reassured me that I, Laurel, was sane and that she, Babette, could "tell" these things though she did not seem so sure of the others around her. She then left rather swiftly.

Chapter Fifteen
The Audacity of Roses

Sunday afternoon in the garden was another "treat" for the "mentals." I had checked with Thelma before going out, just to see if she would join me. But she declined. She was too distraught about her father coming. He would probably be wearing that same brown suit that Thelma detested.

"At least it isn't red!" I commented.

"Just about as bad!" stormed Thelma. Thelma was wondering how Dr. Ashford had known about the dashboard of her car. Her father would have told him though Thelma didn't think her father knew *how* it was damaged. Thelma wondered if Ashford could read minds ... or if *he* had someone to spy on her, as she knew her father did. I thought this was a good time to excuse myself for the garden.

I didn't exactly want to go outside. It was hot. My feet were damp and swollen in my loafers, and my fingertips were starting to feel tingly. I sat on the cement step just outside the door, and watched the others head toward the grass and trees. I kicked off my shoes and dug my damp toes into the cement. The scratchy roughness of the cement helped me to feel alive, in at least one portion of my body. As I dug my toes deeper onto the concrete, Scott, one of the orderlies, came over and sat beside me.

"My, you look lovely today." His tone was half sarcastic, half flirtatious.

"Oh, Golly, I bet you say that to all the 'mentals,'" I responded, looking at him with feigned shyness.

"No, just the pretty ones. I'd like to take you away and run off with you to save you!" he continued.

"That would be great," I agreed. "How romantic. Running away from the loony bin ... with a guy in a white coat. *With* me, not *after* me."

"Okay," Scott continued. "Then I'll come back later ... at night ... when I'm all dressed up. We'll elope. I'll bring a ladder. Where is your window?"

"You'd better bring wire cutters. We're all locked in, you know."

"Let's plan this right," said Scott. "Come with me out by the shuffleboard. I've got to keep an eye on some of the patients."

I declined the invitation. "Naw! I'm uncomfortable enough here, and I don't want to watch Wyoming doing her calisthenics, or hear Mae complain."

Scott took a short walk out, checked everything, and returned.

"Mae's talking to several young ladies. Wyoming is staying under the bushes, and Mike has everything under control. We have more help than usual," he reported.

"You know Lanny?" I asked.

He did, so I told him about the "Sunday Services." I could see that he appreciated the story so I related my conversation about pillowcases to him, also. We were both laughing and exchanging more stories, when Martin came up behind us. Martin was never very comfortable, or friendly, at the hospital, so I didn't even try to set him at ease. I did introduce him to Scott, but the conversation was dead after that so I walked out to the yard area with Martin and showed him the enormous fence with the barbed wire, the shuffleboard area, and the few flowers. Martin said how nice the garden was and agreed that I was well secured with the fencing and walls. I told him I appreciated the bubble bath and described the fancy rooms at the back on Third South. As usual, he didn't have time to stay long. There were always errands he *had* to do or the girls to get. He did bring me a new nightgown from my mother. I walked him to the door and then went back to find Scott.

Scott and Mike were on the shuffleboard court and seemed to be enjoying a game. I wished that I were comfortable enough with my jumpy body to try to play a game or even to walk freely about the garden. I sat on a bench and watched others, then talked to Mike and Scott whenever they came back from playing and monitoring the yard. Scott thought that Martin seemed jealous, as he had been so unfriendly earlier.

"I wish he were." I said. But I didn't think he cared enough about what I did to feel anything.

When Dorothy came into the yard to look for me, the two of us joked and laughed with Scott and Mike about the horrid head nurse on

Third North, Wyoming's rhythmic exercises, Mae's daughters, the bad food (part of the orderlies' compensation), and finally, Dorothy's many marriages. We all agreed that her many nuptials alone could qualify her for entrance here.

After Dorothy left to go back to the Annex, Mike went to supervise Wyoming, who had gone over to some further bushes. Scott walked with me over to the other side of the garden to check the patients there. I stopped abruptly, in surprise, at a small yellow rosebush deliciously in bloom.

"Look!" I said, almost breathless. "Can you believe the impudence of this graceful little bush? It has the audacity to defy its surroundings and be so absolutely lovely ... and near to perfection... Doesn't it know where it is? It is so out of context ... and so beautifully defiant."

Scott smiled appreciatively, and our eyes met. My depression and anxiety had slipped suddenly away, I felt easy and so enthused with the beautiful rose. Somehow I understood the rose and its audacity. I wished that I had its impudence.

Mike called to us to come and join him. He was highly amused at some of Wyoming's new calisthenics and the response she was receiving from several patients.

I hated to go back to Third South. I had almost forgotten where I was during the brief and enjoyable time with Dorothy and the orderlies. After my ride up in the elevator, I slowly made my way back to my room on Third hoping I wouldn't run into Penny. But she was on duty and confronted me with a pinched, angry face and a package of cigarettes.

"These are for you," she snapped. "Thelma said to give them to *you*."

I only said thanks, still worried about Penny's possible recognition of me. Thelma was gone from her room, and so were her things. I wondered if she had been sent home, which seemed unlikely, or to another facility.

When Margaret came on duty that night, she also seemed somewhat angry with me. After the others were in bed, Margaret asked me if I had told Thelma that she could get out off the hospital if she quit smoking.

"Oh Lord!" I gasped. I thought back to our conversation and what Martha had said about smoking!

"Maybe," I said defensively. "I'm not so dumb. I got some free cigarettes that way."

Margaret softened and told me that Thelma would believe everything I said to her.

"She thinks you're her only friend, so you must be careful!" she warned.

Thelma, she said, had really flipped out and become violent, was cursing and throwing things. She had been moved to Third North and was being given electroshock treatments. Even though Margaret told me that it happened after talking with her parents, and displaying some anger and confusion with her father, I blamed myself.

I was called to the phone soon after dinner, which surprised me. I had not seen or heard of phone calls going in or out for the patients. I wished this one had not. It was my grandmother. She wanted me out of here and was trying to find some way to get me released. Telling my grandmother that I had come willingly was not enough for her. She was sure that Martin was doing this to me, and she was working on getting me out, as it was no place for me, she said. I was *sane*. My Aunt Babette knew this. She could tell, as she had looked me closely in the eyes. I was definitely all right. Grandmother would work on getting me released. She had started her quest by sending Babette to see what was going on, and Babette had told her that it was a *horrible* place with some very *crazy* people in it, including my roommate, and she would have it all taken care of.

Grandmother and Thelma were good for hours of insomnia.

Chapter Sixteen
Mickey and Me

During the next few insulin treatments I went into comas but was put back in the long room with the green curtains. However, the staff wasn't sure if I was going into a coma and surely didn't want a nosy patient watching others' treatments. I would lie on the hard cot, eyes closed, and watch the strange light-circle that would form in my darkness. The circle would enlarge, develop a hole like a doughnut, and turn a pale green like the curtains. Then, if I continued to watch, unconsciousness would follow.

I was mentally marking off the days that needed to pass for me to become "well." Dr. Jennings was rather amused by me, and even though I was a definite annoyance, he clearly thought I had a clever sense of humor. He was saying this as I was trying to pull my brain free from treatment. I lay on the cot, the room spinning, and the two nurses and doctor a blur. Jennings was laughing at something I had said. I didn't have any recollection of what it was, and the one of the nurses was not amused. I mumbled something about the "friendly, helpful staff," and the doctor laughed again.

"But don't you think it's a defense mechanism with her, Doctor?" the nurse said, her tone academic.

"Of course," he replied impatiently," but she still has a great feeling for the amusing aspects of things."

"Doesn't she?" I mumbled angrily. "Why am I always in the third person? Act like I'm here. Even if you're not sure ... I *know* I'm not so sure. Medical people are so rude."

One morning I found myself sitting on the cot in the long room, as people were filing into the coffee room I was wearing my night-clothes. My sense of time was obliterated. I did not know if treatments were starting or ending until I realized there were exiting procedures going on. My God, I was dressed, insulin pajamas gone, and I didn't know what had preceded this very minute. It was as if I had just landed here from outer space. The nurse opened my curtains completely and told me to hurry.

"Who dressed me?" I accused.

"You did ... now let's go!" was the impatient response. I was sure that one could not put on clothes while asleep although my younger sister had, when she was sleepwalking during her high school years. But *I* don't sleepwalk, I reminded myself as I stupidly followed the nurse to the coffee room. All morning I was haunted by the feeling of suddenly awakening with no prior life experiences. I also had a headache, and my jaw hurt. Then it all made sense. I had listened to the jaw complaints from the electroshock patients.... they had *gotten* me and were trying to make a zombie of *me*, too. I was more than annoyed when Dr. Jennings stopped in my room later that day.

"You gave me a shock with that damned black box, you little dickens!" I jokingly accused him.

"Yes," he admitted. "How did you know?"

"Because my jaw aches. Well, it won't do you any good. I still know my social security number."

And I recited it to prove that I was still thinking. Jennings laughed and remarked that they probably wouldn't do it again.

"That is so sneaky ... to wire someone after you have already rendered them unconscious, with a probable lethal dose of insulin ... and not even let them know what you were planning to do. Does Dr. Ashford know? Did he order it? I really don't want my mind blown *completely*."

I felt my eyes filling with tears, so I turned away. Dr. Jennings told me a funny story about a drunk on Second South to mend my feelings, and then left me alone.

The following day, treatment was given to me in a different small room, off the long room. There were only two beds in there and I was unpleasantly surprised to see that Mickey was in the other one. Mickey was enduring treatments well. She apparently had had no problem in going into comas.

I had been spending much of my time in the back rooms with Millie and the two other ladies, Kaye and Helen, who I secretly referred to as "The Elegant Ladies." I was using the private tubs and staying in their quarters, talking and playing cards. I had lost Thelma to the Back Wards and wanted to avoid Mickey. Mickey saw me as an experienced friend who could help her. She and her friends from across the hall had begun going to OT, just as I had admonished them to do, and she had lots of questions for me. She had also had become more reserved and more serious, if that were possible.

I was finding it hard to wake up to Mickey in the insulin room as well as each morning in our room. Mickey's large bulging eyes seemed to always be staring at me. She also had a perpetual frown on her face that made deep furrows between her heavy brows. Mickey's head seemed large for her very thin, muscular, yet small body; her hair was very thick and wiry and her face long, with a crooked nose under huge eyes and bushy brows. Mickey was aware of her frown lines and had started wearing an adhesive patch taped between her eyes to flatten the wrinkles. She was bent on being a good and *attractive* wife in the new relationship that she planned for herself and her almost lost husband. Mickey's cot was across the tiny room, and we ladies were placed so that the head of one cot was a few feet across from the foot of the other. So after each coma I woke staring into Mickey's enormous and strained eyes. She watched every move I made and followed my lead.

As we went to the coffee room, Mickey was given a light for her cigarette. The staff was running late this morning, and the nurses and orderlies were even more tense than usual. Patients were being rushed from the coffee room without completing their snacks or coffee. The sweet shakes, however, were another story. They *had* to be consumed. I was hurried numerous times, but responded by commenting that if I drank more quickly the nurse could have it *all* back. The nurse snatched the ashtray from Mickey, who was left holding her cigarette. It had been burning without her noticing it, and the ashes were almost an inch long. Mickey turned her large helpless eyes to me. "What do I do now?"

I had seen the nurse take the ashtray away and Mickey's hesitant manner. "Dump the damned thing on the floor," I said.

The nurse turned quickly just in time to see Mickey concentrating on the task, as she deliberately flicked the long ashes in the middle of the bare wooden floor. I smirked but Mickey was confused. She had gotten a smile of approval from me and an angry glare from the nurse

"It's okay. You're doing fine," I encouraged Mickey.

The nurse turned to the group of patients and took a deep breath to control her anger. She then explained that we were going to have to take the elevator, as we would be late for lunch, and please "everyone stay together," as we needed to go through the other door instead of down the stairs as we usually did. Mickey stood in confusion and stared.

"Bring Mickey!" the nurse commanded me.

Why was Mickey my problem? I wondered as we entered what I remembered as the day room for the men on Second Floor. There was a large pool table, and the same enormous arched and undraped windows that were on the floor above. There were a few chairs around the perimeter of the room and a TV set. But the pool table seemed gargantuan. I slowed to look at it. I had been so dazed at my last time through here that I had not observed what the room had held. I had never seen a real pool table and was very impressed with its size. Mickey, since she was following me and because *I* had said, "come on" to her, thought she was supposed to be in my care and she slowed to look at the table also. I walked around the table rather than going directly to the elevator. Mickey followed.

"What are we going to do?" she asked me, with her perpetual frown.

"Guess we're going to play a little pool," I said, smiling impishly at the nurse.

"Get on this elevator, *now*," said the nurse impatiently.

I looked at Mickey and raised one eyebrow.

"*You* can play if you want," I said as I slowly dragged myself to the elevator.

"Mickey! Come!" The nurse's voice got louder and more insistent.

I stepped onto the elevator.

"Should I?" asked Mickey, looking at me for direction.

"Do whatever *you* want!" I answered and I smiled again at the nurse.

"We're late! Get her on this elevator. You are not funny. *You* are responsible if anything happens."

Mickey stood between the elevator and the pool table, waiting for me to make a decision. It could be a problem if the men came into their day room and saw the ladies in their nightgowns still standing there, I thought. The idea was wonderful. The nurse was beside herself. She had an elevator full of electroshocked patients not very aware of the situation, a troublemaker laughing at her, and a confused lady in a hypnotic trance who would do whatever this willful, annoying tormentor said to do.

"Please, Laurel, get Mickey to come onto the elevator. *Now.*" Her voice was becoming louder, more demanding, and full of frustration.

I savored the moment while Mickey awaited my command.

"Okay, Mickey, guess we better go." I sure hated to give up that power.

On Third Floor, Mickey continued to wait for me to tell her what to do. I directed her to get her lunch, go to her room, and eat. I was relieved when Mickey lay down to nap. I was getting ready to go see my friends in the back and have a peaceful bubble bath, when I was aware of Mickey sitting straight up in bed, with her huge eyes looking extremely surprised or shocked.

"Lie down, Mickey," I commanded, partly to help Mickey and partly to see if she still obeyed.

Mickey lay down. The patient from across the hall had come to see Mickey, and she witnessed the command and the resultant compliance.

"What's wrong with Mickey?" asked Jeannie.

"Just not completely out of shock yet. She'll be okay," I explained, hoping I was right.

Mickey shot up again probably from hearing the voices in the room. Her eyes were opened very wide, but were vacant.

"Lie down, Mickey," I repeated, firmly.

Mickey lay back. Jeannie was astonished.

"Will she do whatever you tell her?" asked Jeannie.

"Apparently so," I answered, thinking of the possibilities.

"Tell her to sit up," requested Jeannie.

When I declined, Jeannie tried. Obviously Mickey was only under my influence. Jeannie ran to get her roommate, to show her how Mickey was in a hypnotic trance, and under my power. I would only demonstrate by having Mickey lie down each time she sat up on her own. The other patients were frightened and impressed. After Mickey seemed to be sleeping, I went for my bath.

When I returned to dress so that I could go back to visit the friends in the back, I found I had company. Two male missionaries from my church were sitting in the room. This seemed so inappropriate. I didn't want their company and they surely wouldn't want to have come *here* unless they were curious, like Martin. They introduced themselves, and the awkward situation was increased when Mickey, hearing voices, came to a sitting position like a shot. The men's eyes got as large as Mickey's.

"Lie down!" I commanded her.

Mickey obeyed. As the men tried to talk to me, the noise caused Mickey to rise up several more times. I repeated the demonstration of my power for them, and the uneasiness grew. The missionaries finally excused themselves, saying that they would come at a more convenient time.

I had decided that OT might be a better choice than cards in the back, as I was a little unsettled at how Mickey had "lost her mind." I felt that I needed the security of my friend Dorothy and the comfort of a structured and protected environment.

Dorothy was there, and we talked. I got another paint-by-number set to do in my room. I had finished tooling a belt for myself and was decorating a purse for Karen. There were a few patients from Third South, and I excused myself on the pretext of using the hall bathroom. I was under no restrictions for security, nor was Dorothy, so we both went to the hallway. I told my friend about the pillowcases that had to be embroidered, and we both laughed at the "run" on the OT shop.

"Oh well, we can't have it all to ourselves, anyway," Dorothy lamented. "I'm going to leave in a day or two, and the OT therapist needs the business."

It wasn't good to lose Dorothy, as she'd been the only pleasure I had. I supposed that I would have to start spending all my time in the back rooms where the patients were alert. Dorothy left to go back to the Annex, and I agreed to walk her to the front door.

"Will they wonder where you are?" asked Dorothy.

"I doubt it. No one expects me to break out of here ... I'm too phobic. But I'll have to get someone to let me back upstairs."

We talked for a while near the entrance, and an alert came over the intercom for orderlies to go to Third North. I hoped that it wasn't a hypo for Thelma, whom I hadn't seen in days. I told Dorothy about the cigarettes and Thelma flipping out. We bemoaned the continual use of shock when someone was very upset. From that, the conversation naturally developed into negative discussion of the staff. The secretary at the desk was half listening and half monitoring the telephone and intercom. Dorothy and I looked knowingly at each other, aware of the lady's interest. It had started to rain, and Dorothy mentioned that she did not have one of her many umbrellas with her.

"How many?" I asked. I had lived here all of my life and never owned an umbrella.

"Six," responded Dorothy, proudly. "I only had one, but I decided to buy another, when I went on one of my sprees. I bought five before I could get out of the store. They were all different, and some were very pretty. Boy! Did my husband flip when I came home with five umbrellas."

"Is that why he committed you?" I asked, winking.

We both noticed that the secretary was still tuned to our conversation.

"He thought they were weapons of some sort. He said he saw no need for *five*. Why, everyone should have at least five, don't you think so?"

"If I liked umbrellas, I'd have even more. Whatever someone decides to collect cannot be overdone, even with fear of being incarcerated in a mental hospital for it. I'm sorry your umbrellas got you in here. But you'll be out soon, I'm sure."

The secretary was acting a little uncomfortable, as Dorothy and I were edging closer to the area where she was working. I smiled at the secretary.

"She could sure use one of her umbrellas ... what with all this rain. Oh, dear! ... I guess we'll be stuck here for a while." I smiled again at the secretary.

"What floor are you girls on?" asked the secretary, a little uneasily.

"Oh, she's from the Annex. But I'm on Third North." I thought that "North" would disarm the secretary. It did.

"What are you doing down here?" she asked nervously.

"I'm supposed to be in OT," I said, "But I wanted to see my friend out, so I sneaked away."

The secretary was obviously under stress, and Dorothy was acting very excited.

"Look at all this equipment that she has for her job. Isn't it great? Phones, intercoms, typewriters," expounded Dorothy, as she and I moved closer to the desk area.

"Wow!" I responded. "Which is the intercom? Which buttons do you use?"

"Probably this one ... I saw her push it down earlier."

"You girls shouldn't come back here. What are you doing? You need to get back to your floor," the secretary said, panicking.

"It's okay, They won't miss me.... You know we are ... we're trying to decide what to say over the intercom, huh, Dorothy? Maybe 'fire' or something exciting.... Which button did you say?"

The secretary came out from behind her desk and was nervously looking about for help, while trying to guard the equipment.

"Now, girls, you wouldn't want to do anything like that. You would frighten everyone, and it could cause a lot of difficulties for the whole hospital. Please move away from the phones or I'll have to call someone.... Come on! You need to leave. I need to do my work and you don't want to cause problems for yourselves, do you?"

Dorothy and I smiled at each other and shook our heads obediently, just as two orderlies came in from the garden area.

"You best leave now," demanded the secretary, glancing in relief at the men in white. I walked to the door with Dorothy, and then headed toward the OT room.

Chapter Seventeen
The Elegant Ladies

Third South was quiet. Patients were either sleeping off shock or out in the garden. I wandered back to see the Elegant Ladies. From my few conversations and observations, I had come to realize that they were from wealthy families and were not here on "company hospitalization," as were most of the patients. Kaye and Helen had both been committed here by their husbands, and both were very angry with their husbands, their doctors, and the hospital. When Helen told me her last name, I recognized it as one of the prominent families in the city. Several city structures bore this name, and the family was frequently mentioned in the arts section and the social section of the local papers. The ladies seemed to know a lot about each other, and I didn't know if this came from sharing their room or from prior social friendship outside. With Millie, the group was large enough to play various card games. The other three had begun trying to teach me to play bridge.

The four of us passed the rest of the afternoon, and when dinner came, I noticed that instead of going to the day room to get their dinner trays, that nurses brought the trays to them. Kaye told the nurse to bring a tray for me. Money surely had its privileges *here*. I had begun to realize that mentioning of Dr. Ashford's name had also brought more cooperation and respect.

Millie had changed after a number of her shock treatments. She had stopped trying the locks and had begun talking more. Not just a little more, but almost as continually as Martha had done, and it was loud. Millie shared that she had spent all of her time, before coming to the hospital, traveling to and from the cemetery and sitting at her seven-year-old son's graveside, sobbing. She couldn't break the grieving cycle. The family had brought her to Mountain View out of desperation. She had received a number of electroshocks, she had no idea how many. But her depression was obviously better. Along with her loud voice, she had an annoying twangy New York accent. Kaye and Helen had made some comments about her "gabbiness" in a friendly but pointed way. They were talking about the change in her behavior, and I was *very* amused, because Millie had become more and more whiny about her surroundings. Her voice got louder and more annoying, and finally Kaye became more direct and issued a sharp "shut up." I laughed.

"I remember when you just went around trying locks. You didn't talk at all," I said.

"That would be nice!" Kaye commented snidely.

Millie laughed, a little self-consciously.

I had gone to my room in case Dr. Ashford came to see me. I was a little uncomfortable about being so friendly with this elite crowd, as the nurses were very hostile about them, and I was afraid that Dr. Ashford would be concerned about the negativity there. When the door to their suite was closed, the ladies were much worse about the staff than Dorothy or I had ever been. And none of it was said with humor.

When Dr. Ashford came to see me, he was unwilling to give me any information about Thelma. Only that she was being "treated" and that she would improve. He was also very annoyed that I had a "paint-by-number" set. It didn't fit with my talent or mentality, according to him. Didn't he know that just trying to fill in areas with predetermined colors was enough of a challenge when your hands were shaky and your mind helter-skelter? Sure, I would *like* to paint the Sistine Chapel, but that had been done, and I needed to wait for a better time to be creative. After telling him about my visitors, and my embarrassment in both situations, I asked if he could stop everyone from coming except Martin.

"Yes, I'll do that. They shouldn't have been admitted anyway. The staff is out of line. I'd like to stop your damned husband, too. I understand that he comes at the end of visiting time, and only stays a minute or two."

I confirmed that this was true about his visits, and Dr. Ashford's face turned very red, just as Thelma said it did.

"I told him several times *not* to try to come every day, and just run in and out ... too time consuming ... running back and forth across town for ten minutes! I'd rather see him come for a nice long visit, once or twice a week," Dr. Ashford growled.

I wondered how Martin could handle a long visit. Mickey would really freak him out.

"This isn't such a great place to entertain," I remarked in defense of Martin's noncompliance.

"You can meet with him on the main floor, in the visitors' rooms," he snapped. "That's what they're here for."

I followed Dr. Ashford out of the room, and said goodbye near the elevator. He was somewhat pleased with this and smiled all the way down in the elevator. I was going to go back to the card games, but when I glanced at the clock I saw it was late. I supposed the others might be getting ready for bed soon. I picked up a magazine and decided to wait for Margaret since it was her night on duty. Mae and Bertha, the senile pair, were both sitting and pretending to watch the television program. Mae's "daughter" was eyeing the piano but decided to pace the halls instead. Mickey and Jeannie were talking together across the room, and another lady was embroidering something in her lap. Several other patients and visitors, whom I did not know, were sitting around the day room. I attended to the television show and wondered if Martin would dare run in and out again tonight. He didn't. Margaret showed up after a while, and most everyone went off to bed.

Mae sat there on the old brown couch staring at me. The nurse had asked Mae several times to go to bed, but she had only shaken her head. The nurse returned and requested Mae to leave, again a little more emphatically.

"Why doesn't *she* have to go to bed?" Mae asked, indicating me, with an angry glance.

The nurse came over and asked me if I would mind going to bed, so that she could get Mae to cooperate. I just looked at the nurse and made no comment. I wanted to watch this TV show and didn't think it necessary that I humor Mae to help the staff. This nurse had not been around much, and she and I were not acquainted because, of late, I had spent so much time in the back rooms. I counted on the nurse not knowing much about my condition and hoped that she would assume I was not even processing the conversation. Mae was asked again and refused the nurse even more angrily. She even tossed a magazine. The nurse stomped off to the station, and Margaret came in.

"Laurel, please help us, I know it's not your problem, but Mae is reacting to you for some reason. Just *pretend* to go to bed. You can come back out after she leaves."

I wondered why the other nurse hadn't asked me in that manner. I also wondered what the nurses would do if I did not help. It was so tempting to find out. I wished Dorothy were here, and then I reluctantly told Margaret goodnight and exited dramatically for Mae's benefit. Mae was obediently following Margaret, as I turned the corner to my room. I did not return to talk with Margaret. Mickey was sleeping heavily and, as I undressed for bed in the half-light from the hallway, I could hear faint cries of distress from the alcoholics, as the sounds echoed across the lighted courtyard below.

Chapter Eighteen
Wyoming Remembers

My reaction to the treatments was changing. I seemed to be perspiring more from the insulin. I would awaken from the coma completely soaked and would start to chill and shake. An orderly or nurse would bring me a blanket, and then another, and often three or four. The blankets were old, like everything else in the ancient building, and they were very scratchy. They bore the same imperceptible coloring as the sheeting and the pajamas, a dirty shade of ecru. But I was grateful to have them, as I felt cold to the bone.

When I would first awaken I would feel clammy and wet. I would reach for the straps of torn sheeting that tied my hands and feet and, when untied, slip my wet pajamas off under the covers and shake until the staff had brought enough blankets to warm me. I couldn't remember when I started being tied down during treatment. I dismissed the possibilities of my thrashing about while in coma; that scenario belonged to the Lady from Wyoming in the weird small room. That sight had moved into the back of my mind, like that of a bad dream. I accepted that many patients were tied and perhaps *I* just slept quietly.

I hadn't worried about the excessive sweating. It seemed to have built up gradually or maybe it was just suddenly there. I didn't remember. The first time I had become so chilled, a nurse had said to take off the wet pajamas as they made me cold. And so it had become a routine. I would awaken, struggle to get some slack for one arm or the other and, with poor coordination and concentration, untie the knotted strips of cloth from my hands, dizzily bend down and untie my feet, wait to get my strength, and then remove the soggy insulin pajamas. I would drop them on the floor beside me and call for someone to come get me a blanket. Sometimes the blanket was already over me when I awoke.

One morning as I awoke, the blanket was there and so was someone. I tried to focus my eyes on the body standing over me and was suddenly aware of something more. The nurse was startled at seeing me open my eyes this soon.

"Lie still! It's okay! Don't move. You'll be all right! I'll just take this out! Lie real still."

There were hoses, or *a* hose, coming from my nose. I didn't know which. The anxious voice of the nurse frightened me more than the hoses, as I was too confused to understand what was going on. The nurse yanked suddenly and there was a painful ripping sensation in my nose and throat as the hose flew out and lashed about above my face. The nurse grabbed her paraphernalia and scurried frantically from the room. It took a few minutes for me to realize what was happening, but I was still too dull to react. A few minutes later Dr. Jennings came in and injected a colorless liquid into the back of my hand. He had tried unsuccessfully to find a vein in my arm and, in frustration, had settled for my hand. I just frowned in confusion while Mickey awoke and stared, unable to process any of this.

Later, in my room waiting for lunch to come, I pieced together the events. I was first frightened and then depressed. I felt mentally and physically logy. I decided to wait till after lunch to bathe and dress. Mickey did her sitting up and lying down on command. I was suddenly concerned about what could be happening to Thelma. She was still in the back rooms on Third North and was probably locked in. I hadn't seen her in the day room even to pick up a tray.

I wandered to the day room and then on around the corner past the nursing station toward the back locked rooms. Lunch trays were just now coming up on the dumbwaiter in that hallway. With the noise and confusion for lunch, maybe I could slip back far enough to see if I could find Thelma.

I had only gotten as far as the bend past the nursing station, when Wyoming's roommate came to the hallway and began pulling at my arm. "Come help! Madelyn is upset ... she's talking ... and she's very upset!"

I stuck my head in the room and gazed at Wyoming. She was a little wild-eyed but not as vacant-looking as she had been. She sat in a heap on the bed. Her usual rigid posture was gone, along with her tense, unfeeling face.

"Where am I?" She looked at me pleadingly, "Where am I? I'm not at home. Where is this?"

I supposed that the truth was probably the best answer.

"You are not in Wyoming anymore," I said. "Your family brought you here to Mountain View. You are in a hospital."

Wyoming was confused and extremely frightened. "What am I doing in a hospital? What is wrong? What kind of hospital is this?"

I decided that the staff should be dealing with Wyoming and answering her questions. I didn't know what I was supposed to say or how much to say. I darted from the room and went from one nurse to another. I pleaded with them, telling them that Wyoming was awakening from her amnesia and asking questions, and said that someone needed to counsel with her. The nurses were not only impatient but out-and-out rude. They told me to get out of the way, that they were busy with lunches, and that it would be "taken care of ... later." But wasn't it the priority of a mental hospital to deal with the mental problems? I couldn't understand the lack of concern for the distraught lady who had lost her family. Wyoming's roommate was back at my elbow trying to get my help again.

"She wants to know where she is and what happened ... She knows her name now. Come help me! I don't know what to tell her."

"I guess we should tell her the truth. If she asks, she must be remembering anyway," I responded as I followed the roommate back to Wyoming.

"There was a lot of water!" Wyoming remembered, frowning, "and a boat. There was an accident, wasn't there?"

"Yes," I assured her, feeling apprehensive about what she might remember and if she would react violently.

"There was an accident with a boat on the lake. Someone was killed, weren't they?" Pain was coming across the face that had been stoic for so long. "Who was killed? Was everyone killed?"

"No, *you* were saved. You were very lucky. You are still alive," I reassured her afraid that she might mistake this hospital, and/or treatments, for death and hell.

"My husband! Is my husband okay?"

This was hard and I stepped to the hall, and tried again to gain a nurse's assistance, but was again brushed past and dismissed. Wyoming repeated her question as I stepped back into the room.

"No, your husband didn't survive. They couldn't reach him in time," I answered hesitantly.

"How about my son ... and the baby? Are they all right?

Wyoming was bent on getting all the information that I was now sorry that I knew.

"Your older son was also drowned. But you saved your baby boy. You were able to swim ... and you were able to reach the baby. The baby is all right.... He is with your family. And you ... you are all right. You forgot everything with the shock ... and so you are in a hospital, to help you remember, and deal with the accident."

Wyoming began to whimper softly. Then her tears grew more intense. Her body began to shake as she wrestled with her anguish. I put my hand on the woman's shoulder and patted her feeling very uncomfortable in this role.

"You will be all right. A nurse will talk to you, soon. And your doctor will be here."

"Who is my doctor?" Wyoming asked helplessly.

I didn't know, and again looked into the hall for help. I was near tears myself and certainly felt unable to handle Wyoming's grief. The roommate was just standing and staring at the two of us. The nurse entered with a lunch tray, and I approached her again. The nurse was visibly annoyed with the whole situation and I was angered by this.

"Madelyn knows who she is," I said emphatically. "She knows what happened to her, and that there were deaths in her family. She needs to talk with someone."

"So you said," responded the nurse tersely. "And I told you it would have to wait. We have lunches to take care of!"

"Well, excuse me. I thought that talking with her ... and helping her ... was part of your job.... It's certainly not mine. And besides, she needs someone to help her *now* ... not when it's convenient." I stopped short of saying that I would have to mention this to Dr. Ashford.

"We'll take care of it," said the nurse angrily, and then feigned concern as she handed Wyoming her tray.

"Are you hungry, dear? You need your strength. And someone will come and talk with you a little later."

At these condescending remarks, I angrily stomped off for my own room.

Mickey was eating lunch and someone had left a tray in the room for me. I picked at the food and then lay down on my bed and turned my head to the wall. Feelings of anxiety, dizziness, and depression were all muddled together in my mind. Panic was building so I concentrated on relaxing and trying to sleep until my noon dosage of tranquilizers could take hold. I had no idea how much time had passed when Dr. Jennings' voice brought me from my despair to reality. Mickey had eaten and gone into her drugged sleep. When Dr. Jennings opened the door that I had used to shut out the world, Mickey did her "bounce up into sitting position" act. Dr. Jennings said, "Lie down" in the same commanding voice that I had used, and I turned quickly to see if the command worked. It did.

Dr. Jennings talked a little to me about my treatments, telling me they were going well, and tried to reassure me about the hoses. I said I had read about how the glucose was put into patients, but the sudden reality of the experience was quite distressing. He took my hand, which was now swollen from the morning injection.

"What happened here?" He seemed genuinely ignorant of its cause.

"Oh, some ham-fisted doctor tried to put some glucose in me ... and missed, I guess."

I examined the hand and wondered why I hadn't noticed it before. It was quite deformed from the swelling, and it was painful when touched. I must have been asleep without knowing it. The doctor apologized, saying that he should have been more careful and was too rushed. He seemed a little embarrassed as he rubbed the swollen area near my wrist and informed me that he would send someone to check it again, later. And then he said that I should probably have some more orange juice with sucrose to make sure that I didn't have an insulin reaction.

I told him about Wyoming's ordeal and the insensitive nurses who would not help her. He made excuses for them and assured me that someone would talk with Wyoming. I wished it would be him, as he was the kindest one in this nasty place. When Mickey sat up again, I ordered her down.

"She does that a lot." I remarked to Dr. Jennings. "Is it okay? ... Like normal ... for the 'abnormal'"?

"Everyone reacts differently with treatments," he responded kindly.

So I told him about the cigarettes and the pool table. When he laughed, I asked him about Thelma, hoping that the ice breaking would give me an edge for information.

"She's coming along pretty well ... I think you'll be seeing her soon. She's much more cooperative, and I've been talking with her."

I wondered why "cooperative" was equated with "better." That would certainly make my friends in the back of Third South in for a long stay.

I made a brief trip to the OT shop and said a sad goodbye to Dorothy, who would be going home with her husband that evening. We had exchanged addresses and promised to keep in touch, although I'm sure that we both wondered why anyone would want to keep a friend who would be a reminder of these times.

I had gotten quite dizzy in OT and the nurse who had taken me down to the shop noticed that I seemed woozy, so she was staying for a while to watch me and to keep an eye on the Third Floor patients. The nurse and I left to go to the kitchen entrance down the hallway to get the sugary juice for me. The intercom had announced a need for orderlies on Third North, and I was concerned that Wyoming was out of control. Everyone's problems seemed larger than my own, and I felt stupid and unable to cope. The nurse was being friendly, but I hated her, the occupational therapist, Dr. Jennings, the whole staff, and probably my family. I decided that maybe a trip to the garden could help my attitude.

Chapter Nineteen
Mae Throws a Party

The garden was more of a distraction than I had hoped for. The weather was changing, and the sudden dark clouds and cooler temperatures appeared to be affecting the patients. I was talking with Mike and Scott; the friendly nurse, who usually worked on Second, was out also. All the ladies seemed a little more agitated than usual. I told the staff about Wyoming's remembering. Wyoming had naturally not come to the garden that day, but there were two rather active men who were just as much in need of supervision. There was also a rather hyperactive redhead with whom I had shared insulin therapy. She had completed her treatments and was staying at the Annex, and had come over for a visit to the garden and to see her former roommate. She spoke loudly and excitedly and walked with long athletic strides. A tall, thin lady, she was lanky in her movements. Her red hair shone radiantly in the sunshine and her strange narrow face, with the long pointed chin, looked almost beautiful. She seemed to be ever on the move and was talking incessantly.

I supposed that the treatments had done this. The treatments had quieted Martha. They had awakened both Wyoming and Millie from muteness. What would they do to Thelma, and how would they change me? I asked Mike about the others. He was there supervising the patients, but he never had any serious conversations; he acted like it would be a professional betrayal to tell me anything of this nature. Or maybe he didn't know. I asked the friendly nurse, whose name I learned was Jennifer. Jennifer knew my name, but I did not try to learn names for the staff. Naming them would have made everything here seem more permanent. Jennifer was patient and explained that the treatments had different effects on different people, depending on their personalities and their problems. She didn't know what Thelma's might be like, as she had never met her and didn't know her problems. I wanted to explain Thelma to Jennifer but sensed that she wasn't interested. Also, the staff had more to worry about today because of the excited patients and weather.

The sun was in and out of the clouds, and some very dark clouds were building up out toward the west. Changes in the sunshine seemed to be agitating everyone. I had not felt as phobic and anxious as I had previously for a number of days now. I suspected that the treatments were helping or possibly it was due to the new medication they had started using with me. But today I was feeling somewhat excitable. It didn't seem to be the usual anxiety with pending panic. It was more an anticipation of something. I had no feel for whether it was for a positive or negative event. There was also a slight breeze, which seemed to cool my usually sticky skin, and my hands and feet did not feel puffy and swollen as they usually did.

I felt good enough to try a little shuffleboard with Mike and Scott although a very loud lady patient was playing with them. She was from the Annex and was conversing loudly about "the place," calling it "a hotel." She expounded on the food, which was certainly not as tasty as food prepared at better hotels where she had stayed in the past. I exchanged knowing smiles with Mike and Scott. Scott was ornery enough to ask the lady how she happened to be at the hotel.

Her family was traveling, but she did not like to travel. In fact, she could not travel for health reasons. So her family had found this hotel where she could stay until they returned. The lady seemed to be about Martha's age, maybe fiftyish. She didn't explain her health problem but was hoping that her family would return soon and take her home.

"Bet they don't," Mike whispered to me as he went past to take his turn at the shuffleboard

"At least, " the Loud Lady continued, "the food is better over at the other building than it is in this one. But this garden is really nice. They haven't a garden across the street."

"I wonder how she got over to the Annex," Scott commented quietly to me.

"Think she might wander off?" I asked. He nodded.

The sky was cloudy again and I stood against a small tree nearby. Mae came over and smiled sweetly at me, which was very unusual for Mae, who was usually negative, and even competitive, toward me for attention from the staff.

"Isn't it a lovely day?" she said, very properly.

"Oh, yes!" I replied, in the same affected tone.

"This is certainly a lovely party, isn't it?" Mae continued.

"Very lovely," I agreed pleasantly.

"I do think that they are all enjoying themselves, don't you?" Mae asked.

"They seem to be, but I'm a little concerned about the weather. Do you think we might have rain?" I smiled at Mae politely without a hint of sarcasm.

"I surely hope not. It could spoil everything we've worked for," responded Mae.

"Your turn!" Mike called to Scott from the shuffleboard court.

Another, louder request for Scott came from the Loud Lady.

Mae walked up to the Loud Lady and asked her to keep her voice down. "You are not very ladylike," she remarked critically.

Scott looked at me and smiled again. An angry retort from the lady, and several angry comments from Mae helped to break up the game.

The weather seemed to threaten rain, and Jennifer, Scott, and Mike began discussing the possibility of taking everyone in early. I walked over near the flowers and a picnic table. I was feeling a lot freer in my movements today. Maybe the anticipation was good for me. I wandered further all the way to the edge of the lawn and stood all alone with no one having to walk with me! I was so pleased with myself, to have walked so far away from the security of the building walls. I was able to get a very good view of the tall fencing and noticed several layers of barbed wire across the top and also across the large gate, which was secured with a large chain. The gate could swing out and allow the ambulance entry

For the first time I felt confined, even "jailed," rather than protected. I shivered a little at the thought of being locked up in a "mental hospital," and the stigma this inflicted. I wandered slowly back to the area with the flowers and the picnic table, where Mae approached me again. Today there had been lemonade and cookies in the garden. The staff had done this on other days, but I had always been too nervous to have any. Today I had helped myself to a drink and was enjoying it as Mae asked me about the refreshments.

"They're just perfect," I had told her, continuing the charade.

"Well, how much do you think we should charge them?" Mae asked me, nodding toward the other patients.

"Oh, not too much ... want them to enjoy themselves and not feel put upon." I responded in my best society voice. "Let's say, maybe ... a quarter? Do you think that is appropriate?"

Mae smiled. "That sounds about right."

Mae turned and headed toward a group of three ladies. I wished that I could hear the responses to Mae's request for a quarter.

A few drops of rain had begun to fall, and the staff made the decision to take everyone in. Mae had gone to scold the Loud Lady again. She then took the lady by the hand and led her over to me.

"You need to lower your voice," Mae was saying. "You need to talk more softly. Now look at her." Mae indicated me. "She speaks softly and is very refined. Watch her and see if *you* can't act more ladylike. And keep your skirt down ... and your legs together."

The Loud Lady pulled her hand from Mae, frowned at me, and mumbled something as she walked away.

"I don't believe that I should invite *her* again," remarked Mae, disdainfully to me, and she tilted her chin in a defiant and superior manner.

Mike had taken a group of patients up on the elevator, and Scott had gathered another group at the entrance. Jennifer had been called into the building, and one of the unfriendly, even hostile, nurses from Third South had come to help take "the crazies" in from the rain. Scott took his group up, but Mike had not yet returned. The nurse had two full loads of patients to get into the building alone, and the rain was now coming down lightly. She asked me to please keep my eye on Mae and three of the ladies, while she either went to get help or took the others on up.

"Hey, I'm not getting paid," I commented, not smiling.

"I just want to know if you'll help me. Will you?"

The nurse was anxious as it was starting to rain a little heavier. I smiled and nodded.

"I mean it ..." pleaded the nurse. "Will you watch them? Can I trust you?"

"As well as you can trust anyone *here*," I laughed.

The nurse decided to take her chances and left me with Mae and the other ladies, while she took her group up. I grew nervous, wondering if everything would be all right till she returned and at the same time wanting things to be disruptive. But I couldn't think of anything to do to upset the nurse, as I had so little notice to be creative. The nurse returned, obviously relieved that things were still in order. She loaded the last group on the elevator and started up. The clanging elevator was the only noise as the group ascended. Mae glanced at me appreciatively and in respect of our collusion.

"Well, we all enjoyed ourselves, didn't we? We thank you all for coming ... to say nothing of your nickels and dimes." Mae giggled slightly and nudged me. "Isn't that so?" she asked.

I nodded.

"What are you up to?" asked the nurse.

"Mae, I always enjoy your garden parties," I smiled, sweetly.

That night The Elegant Ladies and I ate dinner in the back. When I told them about Mae the ladies were not too amused about the "garden party." In fact, they were completely disdainful of my associating with the others in the garden.

"Why don't you stay up here with us, instead of being directed about like part of a herd of cattle? It is so demeaning to be treated like that," Kaye pointed out.

"Well, it is nice to get fresh air," I attempted as an excuse.

"Not at the expense of such degradation. We can open a window, you know. Stay away from the stupid staff ... and all the crazy patients," Helen chided.

After dinner they played cards, complained about husbands who wanted them confined, and berated the staff. The nurse who came to remove the trays seemed very uncomfortable, since the laughter and talking ceased as she entered. Kaye had been given permission to have a television, and so the ladies watched a late show in their quarters. Millie walked back down the hall with me as I went to my room; she wanted something for her upset stomach from the nurses' station. I decided that Millie was getting to be very annoying, with her constant complaints. She told me that she had mentioned to her doctor that I had said she was too talkative and that I had said, "He should have quit while he was ahead." Millie was smiling and seemed to think the doctor had been amused.

"You've never said why *you* are here," Millie mentioned with a frown. "Why did you come? Did Martin put you in? The two of you *seem* friendly ... I mean like you are getting along well enough."

"Oh no, I came on my own. I'm here willingly. I even *wanted* to come actually ... I'm ... writing a book."

It was said as a joke but Millie seemed impressed and, even better, convinced. I decided to correct the misconception at a later time and bask in the respect given me for now. It would take a while, and some embarrassment, to explain myself to Millie. Millie wanted to know if she would be in my book. When she was assured of her place in such doubtful history, Millie insisted that the two of us exchange addresses so I could send her a copy of the book.

I felt no shame. In fact, I felt a little pleased. Besides, the Elegant Ladies were all so full of their own self-importance, and I needed some for *my*self. Millie didn't share a lot with the other two, and I suspected that even if she did tell them about my being an author, they would have either thought it was so or that Millie and I were fools or crazy. I didn't care.

Chapter Twenty
Seduction and Escape

My late nights with the Elegant Ladies made it hard for me to wake up in the mornings for treatments. I had begun sleeping a little better, but the sleep did not refresh me. I felt logy and drugged most of the time, and I had even stopped making any effort to sleep, except for escape, in the daytime. Double dosages of insulin had been discontinued for me, and Dr. Jennings had let me know that I was going into coma now with only 225 units rather than the original 450! He was puzzled that I didn't seem pleased or relieved. I was only making, as I said to myself, "the worst of the worst situation." My sometimes hostile and impudent behaviors did not come to my doctor's attention often, as he still was not reading charts, and the nurses were reluctant to openly appear negative toward his patient.

I would never have told him myself about my rebelliousness but I had told him about Wyoming, hoping that he could change some procedures or attitudes here in dealing with the hapless sufferers. He did seem concerned, but there was a pervasive attitude, among the staff *and* the doctors, that patients were somewhat less than real people, so I supposed that even *he* had no empathy.

Days went by slowly but I was more than halfway through my "morning tortures" in the insulin ward and I was still alive. Some days being alive didn't seem that important either. I only vaguely remembered how terrified I had been coming here, how I had feared the treatments, and how I had prayed frantically each morning that I might be saved from death and even be made well. Nothing seemed very worthwhile now. Despite the diminishing of my absolute terror, I still had some concern for my safety. But I was not sure about a recovery, going home, and having a good life. Seeing others leave with some improvement should have reassured me but how could the obvious incompetence of the staff and the fallible characters of the doctors promise me much hope? If they were actually curing people, it must be partially by chance or due to the new drugs I was reluctantly taking on the chance they would work for me.

My earlier infantile belief that I had come here to be cured in a few days, through the great wisdom and superior skill of the esteemed Dr. Ashford, had gradually yielded to amused skepticism and a feeling of being betrayed by everyone concerned. Dorothy and I had often remarked that we could do whatever pleased us because we were "crazy;" it was expected and, after all, what were the consequences? We could be sent to Third North! Well, we'd both been *there*. If we were still incorrigible, what could the staff do? Shock us? We had been there, too.

I was becoming more defiant and less impressed with the capabilities of my keepers. I was also feeling alienated from my husband and the rest of my family. Dorothy was gone and I didn't know what they had done with Thelma. The Elegant Ladies were not actually friends and, besides, they couldn't conquer the system either or they would not be here. Margaret was sweet and Dr. Jennings was okay. Scott, Lanny, and Mike were funny, but fools. Everyone else was either cruel or crazy.

I lay on the insulin cot looking across at Mickey and decided that there was nothing to do but wait it out. Mickey had closed her eyes and gone off to Coma Land. I closed my eyes and tried to see the pale green donut, so I could let it hypnotize me into a coma.

When I awoke some time later I was drenched with insulin sweat. I blinked my eyes several times and noticed Mickey's large eyes looking back at me.

"Oh, shit!" I thought. "Another day in the coma ward of the loony bin."

My hands had been tied more securely than usual, and I had a real struggle trying to get them loose. I wondered if all the patients untied themselves. When I got my hands free, I reached for my ankles. A chill was starting to creep over me, and I was impatient and felt nauseous. My skin crawled. As I sat up, Mickey raised her strong eyebrows quizzically. I ignored her and tried to undo my legs. Mickey whispered to me. "Are you tied down?"

"Yes, I'm tied down," I answered sarcastically, but also in a whisper.

"What shall we do?" another whisper.

I continued the conversation in a more melodramatic whisper, and Mickey replied in kind.

"Are you untying yourself?" Mickey persisted.

God, *yes I* thought, what did you think … jerk! But I only said, still in a whisper, "Yes, I'm untying myself. You should probably try to untie yourself. You need to hurry."

"Why? What are we going to do?"

Some question! I didn't pause long before I answered. "Escape! We are going to escape from this God-forsaken-hole. *Now.*"

Despite my dramatics for Mickey's sake, I shivered and wished for another blanket.

"Nurse?" I called out, hoping that I would be heard through the closed door.

Mickey jumped and the frown line between her eyes deepened, as she tried to quiet me. "Shhhhhh! We don't want to let them find out we're … they can't know! Don't alert them!" she cautioned in an angry and more audible voice.

"I'm not. I just need a blanket. Get yourself free."

An orderly bounced in and placed another blanket over me, as I held my covers around my neck and shivered. I had recognized him as Doug, one of the regulars. He bounced back out just as quickly as he had come. Mickey had untied her hands and was working on her feet. I wiggled out of the wet pajamas and kicked them out from under the sheets and onto the floor, and then continued to shiver.

"If we are going to get out of here you need to help me," Mickey whispered to me again. "Let's get this window open."

I glanced up and saw that Mickey was on her knees on her cot. She had reached high above her and was prying frantically at the dirty, curtainless window at the foot of her cot.

"No! No! It's okay. Let the window alone!" I whispered loudly.

"Shhhhhhh!" whispered Mickey angrily. "They're going to hear you. You'll give us away … They'll be here … We need to escape!"

I assumed that the window had the same heavy screening on it that I had seen throughout the building, but I wasn't sure because the viney coverage concealed the view and the dirt. Mickey had pried up the window partway and was now standing up on her cot. Now I've done it, I thought. Margaret had tried to tell me not to tease or confuse the other patients. Now Mickey could hurt herself trying to get out of the window. I was feeling too chilled and woozy to get up, and I was naked besides. I made a quick decision to call for help. Doug was the last Keeper-Person I had seen, so I called out his name. Alarmed, Mickey plunked herself down on the cot just as Doug entered the room.

"What's wrong?" There was annoyance in his voice.

I looked at Mickey. I couldn't explain this while she listened. Mickey was obviously very confused and excited. I pulled one hand from the covers and motioned to Doug, with my index finger, to come closer so that I could quietly tell him what Mickey was trying to do. He frowned. I motioned again, and he took a few steps toward me. Just then the ridiculousness of the situation struck me. I smiled and tried to stifle a laugh as he bent over my bed. Suddenly his eyes opened wide and he looked aghast, then he hastily fled from the room. Mickey started to climb up again. I cried out again for assistance. Mickey crashed back down on her cot, looking totally astonished.

This time a nurse entered our room and glared at me. From my bare shoulders she could tell that my pajamas were gone.

"What are you doing with your clothes off? Here, put these on."

She handed me my pajamas and my robe, picked up my wet clothing from the floor, and turned to Mickey, who was sitting innocently on her cot. Her anger suddenly made sense to me, and I began laughing uncontrollably. Doug had seen my bare shoulder sticking out from the blankets when I withdrew my arm to motion to him. He realized that I was naked under the covers. I had been smiling at him and trying to get him to come closer to speak to him, but he had thought I was trying to seduce him!

I tried to explain to the angry nurse, who could only see a nude, sex-hungry, lunatic and a confused shock patient, and the need to get us both dressed and out of the room. I laughed and stammered something about the window, needing help, and Doug. The nurse was very short-tempered and did not even try to hear my explanation.

I tried to feel embarrassed but that didn't work. I kept smiling and chuckling a little every now and then as I went through the coffee room rituals. Mickey continued frowning. The staff accepted that this was another strange reaction to insulin shock. They probably thought I had a suppressed libido. Poor Doug. The situation was priceless to me and probably no one would ever believe me. Maybe Dr. Jennings would think it was funny, but he would have heard another version before I ever had an opportunity to tell him my version. Now I could imagine that this staff-perceived behavior could earn me more time here. But, unknown to me, the medical insurance was more definitive when it came to the length of my stay. God! How I wished that Dorothy were still here. She would have really appreciated this.

Dr. Jennings did come by at lunchtime. I told him what really happened in insulin treatment. He was somewhat amused, but I was now feeling a tinge of embarrassment, and I wondered if he really believed my side of the story. I found later that he had, but he was so overwhelmed with the pressures of too many new patients this day, he didn't respond as appreciatively as usual to my "crazy-happenings-at-the-funny-farm" stories. I took his reaction as disbelief and my embarrassment grew. I was now afraid the staff would make sure that my doctor knew that I was trying to seduce that poor orderly. I didn't want to try to explain to Ashford, who had *no* sense of the ridiculous. He was so Freudian that sex would *have* to be the answer.

Chapter Twenty-One
Got a Cigarette?

When I was taking my tray back to the cart, I stopped near Thelma's old room; the door was open and someone was inside. The return of my friend would be very welcome news. I walked closer and looked in. It wasn't Thelma. One of the new patients, who had Jennings so concerned, looked back at me. She was very young, only in her late teens, and she was perched on the bed wearing faded, worn jeans and a wrinkled long-sleeved shirt. Her knees were pulled to her chest and her arms wrapped securely about her knees. Since this was my "high anxiety" position I assumed she was very distressed. She had slightly mussed dark hair that tumbled in wavy strands about her shoulders. Her face was rather nondescript, except for her eyes. They were deeply set, under almost indecently long lashes, and were the most vibrant blue I had ever seen. She stared back at me, with her cerulean eyes, and absolutely no trace of a smile. I was suddenly aware that I had been rudely staring at this creature.

"Hi!" I said, shifting my foot uncomfortably in my embarrassment.

"Hi! Do you have a cigarette?" the girl asked flatly.

"I can get one for you," I offered, trying to be helpful.

I left for my room to find the cigarettes bequeathed to me by Thelma, after which it took a while for me to find someone smoking and get a light from her. Like most patients, I bothered the staff as little as possible, and everyone was happier for it.

"Here!" I said, offering my gift to the quiet girl, who was still perched in her same position. "I had to light it for you. No one is allowed matches."

"I know. Great trust, huh?"

The blue eyes were like satin and very arresting and, although the patient seemed aware of their impact, she was clearly annoyed at me for continuing to stare. She introduced herself to me as Marcie but gave little information about herself or her circumstances, except to say that she was here on a court order. I too gave information rather selectively,

160

as I'd been in error before in my estimation of how much reality a patient had in operation. Marcie was appreciative of the comments to help her know what was expected and where things were. She was very tense, and her flat voice seemed to be covering the trembling inside her. She did not seem surprised about the cigarettes and had none of her own. I brought her several more before going to see the Elegant Ladies in the back.

The ladies weren't interested in the new arrivals and made no comments except for a remark from Helen that it was sad for someone as young as Marcie to be in a mental hospital at her tender age.

"Hell, she's probably better able to handle it than we are," responded Kaye, wasting no compassion. Millie was the most concerned. She had expressed how sorry she felt for Cheryl when I related *her* story, which was one that the Elegant Ladies had not heard before. Like Kay, Helen had little sympathy and was simply glad that Cheryl was gone. She had read the accounts in the newspaper and was sure that Cheryl was culpable, even after my repeated explanation of the circumstances and even after hearing the reported results of the autopsy.

"I think she was a child-killer and if I'd known she was in this building, I would not have let them put me anywhere near her," Helen said adamantly.

"Where would you have had them put you?" I asked. "The Annex isn't locked and Second Floor is full of male alcoholics. The only other space is clear around on the North Wing ... and that place is beyond hell. Did you know that those rooms are locked, the beds are bolted to the floor, and there is nothing ... and I mean *nothing* in the rooms, except the bed ... not even a lamp? I've seen it."

Helen was unperturbed. "Well *we're* not that disturbed," Helen remarked smugly, "and if they tried to do that to me I would sue them. In fact I *am* suing the doctor, the hospital, and my God-dammed husband. He'll be so sorry he accepted this stupid idea from that idiot doctor. What men won't do to protect their money ... and he'll lose even *more* this way."

Helen's husband had not been to visit (not surprising, I thought). Her doctor had tried twice to see her, but Helen would not talk to him. Her behavior was such that he dared not try treatments; she'd already threatened him about that. She had a friend who had been admitted here against *her* will, and she had given Helen some advice. The court order to get her in was about all that could be done for now. No treatments had been authorized, as Helen's husband was reluctant to anger her further. Kaye hadn't had treatments either, but if it hadn't been for Helen's influence, her doctor and her husband could have convinced her that it was the right thing to do. They had been verging on that acceptance when Helen had appeared. Now Kaye was angry with her husband and refused to allow him to control what happened to her. Kaye's doctor was the silver-haired, immaculately dressed shrink I had goaded. Since he was also very diplomatic, he was trying to achieve results with Kaye's approval. He was frustrated with Helen and planned to talk with Helen's doctor at the next staff meeting. Millie, in contrast, the third member of the Elegant Ladies accepted her doctor's directions and was grateful that her husband and children had forced her entry here. Of course, Millie was in such a state on her entry that she really didn't know what was happening to her, nor did she care.

Looking around me at the spacious quarters I wondered what would have happened if these Elegant Ladies had been placed in the room where I had been at the time of my admittance. They surely would not have tolerated the noise of the dumbwaiter, the scary, strange bathroom without stall doors, the abuse of the nurses, and most of all the insulin therapy. I understood that they probably paid more for their "accommodations," but were they really that much less crazy? Millie was very much like the others here, but with Kaye and Helen it was difficult to tell. They were so private.

I was invited to watch television with the ladies after we had our dinner in their quarters. Millie went to her own room when her husband arrived. I sat there, enjoying my escape from the rest of the hospital. In these quarters, one rarely saw the nurses, no one bothered us, and noises were shut out, as were the wandering patients. It was very secluded, and this area did seem much like a hotel, what with the privacy, nicer furnishings, and even our own television set. I almost forgot where I was again, until a nurse came and told me that Martin was waiting in my room.

Martin had come earlier this evening, as Dr. Ashford had asked, but he didn't stay much longer than usual. As always, he seemed uncomfortable, continually watching the door as patients went past. Mickey was a little disconcerting to him, and she would have bothered him even more if I had related "the escape attempt," or if he had seen her when she was spaced out and following commands. Nevertheless, Martin liked to hear bizarre details about the place and had acted as if I were in the company of celebrities when Cheryl was there. He told me he had bragged to his family that he had seen Cheryl; he had described her, and given intimate details about the other patients. But I had long since decided not to share much more information with him about my own experience and others here because he seemed to associate me with their crazy world, and he was almost arrogant in his affected superiority. So we did not have much about which to converse.

He gave me news of home, the kids, our family, and neighborhood. I asked about my flowerbeds. In moments of severe depression, I often felt obsessed by the asters that I had planted. They were almost ready to bloom, which is what had happened last summer during my incarceration. The perfectly organized flowerbed had been left with half-grown asters. I had not been home to tend them and, upon my release into the sane world, I found them almost waist-high, twice as thick as I had expected, and the blooms, in multi-shades of pink and violet, seemed to greet me scoffingly when I came up my walk. The asters seemed to have developed a group personality of disrespect for their gardener. They had defiantly survived in spite of me and were angry at their abandonment.

I blinked and suddenly shut down these ideas in my mind, realizing that I was beginning to sound like Thelma. Martin had stopped talking and was studying me. I smiled at him with no emotion. He remarked that I seemed preoccupied. I nodded slightly. He commented that we could go out for coffee or a snack if I weren't on such heavy dosages of insulin. "As soon as your treatments are over," he promised.

"How about I just go home, then?" I asked. "Why just out for a treat? How long did you plan on my being here, anyway?"

After listening to my Elegant Ladies, I was angry and suspicious of him. We were both feeling uncomfortable, and Martin found an excuse to leave. I wasn't enjoying his company and who was to say how sane *he* was? Maybe I could commit him someday and watch *him* cope with this insult to one's humanity. I walked him to the elevator, without even trying to gain any physical contact with him, which appeared to be something of a surprise for Martin. Then I went around the corner to check on Marcie, the new patient.

Marcie's room was empty! There was no evidence at all of a tenant. The bed had been stripped and not remade. The iron bed and the stained mattress, along with a metal closet and ugly night table, were all that were left in the windowless room. I asked about Marcie at the nursing station, although I didn't expect to learn anything and I didn't.

Margaret was on duty that night. She did not know Marcie but said she would try to find out anything she could. I noticed that Margaret wasn't as friendly as she had been before I started visiting the Elegant Ladies. She disapproved of Kaye and Helen, and had cautioned me about getting too involved, saying that it could cause me big trouble.

"They don't get along well ... with *anyone*. They're rude to the staff ... and act like they're *superior* to everybody. They're both under court orders ... and seem to want to be left alone."

"They *invite* me back to their rooms," I said in my defense. "Others in here are under court order, too. Besides, it's more comfortable back there ... less institutional."

"Well I just know there's a lot of talk about them. Millie is okay, but the other two are upsetting to the staff. You're best advised to stay out of it," Margaret admonished.

I didn't think people should be judged by the company they kept in a *mental hospital.* That seemed the ultimate injustice.

Chapter Twenty-Two
Confrontation

Several days passed with insulin mornings going as usual. I spent my free time in the back rooms with the Ladies, I still went to the OT shop in the afternoons, and I had the usual brief visits from Martin in the evenings. At the OT shop I had produced a tooled belt, a purse for Karen, a picture for Sissy, a small coin purse for someone-yet-to-be-decided, three paint-by-numbers, two embroidered sets of pillowcases, an embroidered cloth for an end table, and a braided key chain. These, it seemed to me, were probably the sole profits of my stay.

To Martin, the objects were of monetary concern. He was unsure if our insurance would pay for the cost, and when he asked me the prices I was flippant and annoyed. I had tried to make him feel guilty for being concerned about finances, when lack of entertainment, my sanity, and well-being were at stake. The hospital OT shop charged dearly for materials, and Martin offered to try to find some "handiwork" for me on the outside that would not be so costly. Insulted and hurt, I continued my daily trek to the OT room since it was a place to go and something to take up the time when I wasn't in the exclusive back rooms that housed the Elegant Ladies. Also, I took some slight pleasure in annoying Martin.

Granted, the paint-by-number pictures were of no real value. They would certainly not be useful for gifts; they were an artistic insult to anyone I knew. But I was intrigued by the blending of the areas of color into forms that took shape when you held the picture up at a distance. The premixed colors were also fascinating. What unusual muted colors, yet clean and unmuddied! I had difficulty blending my own oil paints without sullying the tones. I examined the premixed paints carefully and tried to determine what raw colors had been used along with the obvious white. It amazed me to see how the shadows in the picture were created by using a different color in a strange, unexpected shape. I, as an artist, hadn't learned to see objects in shapes and tones, and wondered at the invention of this rather strange "paint-by-number" craft. The pictures were of landscapes, and their rather meager size allowed me to stash them away from Dr. Ashford's disapproving sight. I knew he was upset that I was not creating my own work with oils, but he never mentioned my other busywork.

It seemed that everyone had come and gone from the hospital while I stayed on and on. Wyoming was scheduled to go home one morning, and several patients had gathered in her room to perform the social pleasantries that existed even here. I gave Wyoming a rather stiff hug, not knowing exactly what to say or do on such an occasion. Wyoming was going to continue having "therapy" in the form of counseling from a doctor in her hometown. I had mentioned this follow-up of treatment to Dr. Ashford, asking if this were because Wyoming could not stay longer. Dr. Ashford was surprised at my naiveté and impatiently remarked that "probably all patients here would receive therapy from their doctors following hospitalization." He asked why I had not followed up with him after my last stay.

"Since you didn't follow up, I wasn't surprised when you called and had to be readmitted. You never took care of the problem."

My mouth fell open. I had thought that the shock treatment *was* the cure. I hadn't known that he wanted to see me. My menopausal neighbor across the street had had shock treatments and that was the end of it. She overcame her depression (mostly) and continued her life as usual. I was unaware of her having had any "counseling" afterward. Dr. Ashford's face reddened and his voice rose.

"The treatments break up the depression cycle ... and behavioral deviances. They open the patient up for acceptance of counseling. Why the hell didn't you continue with your therapy ... and get in for counseling?"

I was embarrassed to admit that I didn't know, that I hadn't been told.

"I told that son-of-a-bitch to get you into my office!" Dr. Ashford stammered, his face getting redder.

He started to cough and I was frightened. His coughing attacks had alarmed me in the past, but this was the first one I had observed at the hospital. He left the room and went, choking, to the nurses' station, where he pulled an inhaler from his pocket and waited for the attack to subside.

* * *

How can a doctor expect to treat adequately when there is absolutely no cooperation? Dr. Ashford growled to himself. Laurel seemed stupid and naive. Martin was either stupid ... or connivingly vicious. And he ... he must not let himself get so upset. It triggered an attack. His lungs were getting worse. The malignancy (which was his own secret) was winning, and he probably wouldn't live long enough to help Laurel or Thelma. He took great pleasure in counting his successes and was hoping to have several more to add to his latest report for the annual convention. Damn! The tiredness was setting in and with the exhaustion that would follow, he might have trouble getting home.

* * *

He, of course, did not go back to my room, and only checked with the nurses on Thelma's progress with the electroshock. I saw him walk hesitantly and weakly to the elevator, shakily unlock the door, and leave. His head was lowered in pain and weariness, and he was unaware of the nurses and me watching him.

Back in the ward, Millie talked incessantly of going home, which seemed to annoy everyone. She reminded me, on several occasions, about the promise to be included in "the book" and repeated that she *must* be given a copy. For a second time, she insisted that we needed to exchange addresses to "keep in touch." I smiled wryly. I envisioned having Mickey, Millie, and others staying "in touch" ... and perhaps having regular reunions. Maybe the other two Elegant Ladies would want to be a part of the exclusive lunatic graduation club?

Days had passed and Thelma had still not reappeared. Margaret reported that she was still having electroshock in her lockup. And whenever the parade of orderlies, accompanied by Dr. Jennings (with his black box and rubber hose), debarked the elevator or passed me in the hallway, I cringed. Margaret had reported that Marcie had to be put in the locked, seclusion area because she was self-destructive. She was unable, or unwilling, to give more information.

Marcie did come back a day or two after her disappearance. She was put back in the same room, and was still wearing the jeans and the same wrinkled shirt. Her hair still appeared uncoiffed. Her reddened eyes were still beautifully hypnotic, even in their reddened condition. I smiled hesitantly as I passed Marcie's partially opened door. Marcie called out to me and then asked me in. In the sparse conversation that followed, I learned that Marcie was still in high school. She had been brought in by her parents who had totally lost control of her. Marcie didn't seem too concerned that she was in Mountain View. She had been in several other mental hospitals, and her attitude relayed an acceptance of this as a natural way of life. I watched as Marcie picked at a round sore on her hand. It was raw and bleeding slightly.

"What did you do?" I questioned, expecting that her treatment in the locked rooms had something to do with her injury.

"It's a burn." Marcie's face showed no emotion. "I burn myself when I'm upset. I don't know why," she said flatly as she shrugged her shoulders.

That must have been what Margaret meant by "self-destructive," but why would they put her in the secluded rooms where they shock patients regularly. They must have known about this burning behavior and with such control and supervision there was no way for her to set fires *here!* A nurse walked by just then and turned back when she saw me.

"You remember now," she said firmly to Marcie. "No smoking unless a staff member is with you."

Marcie nodded.

"Oh God!" I thought. "Thelma's cigarettes that I gave to her ... she used them to burn herself."

As we talked, I noticed a number of circular scars on Marcie's hands and wrists.

"Oh, yeah!" Marcie said, slightly defiantly. "You're looking at my burn scars ... Here, I have lots of them." She rolled up her shirtsleeve and exposed numerous round marks on her lower arm. "Both arms," she explained, "and on my legs, too. I've tried to quit. They try to stop me. Nothing works." She shrugged again and tears welled in her eyes.

"I bet you'll get over it *here,* "I said politely but without conviction.

Marcie's head just shook slightly, and I crossed and uncrossed my legs self-consciously. Dinner came conveniently, allowing me to escape.

Chapter Twenty-Three
An Interrupted Party

Mickey and I both ate in our room. Mickey was becoming more out-going and was also becoming quite social and businesslike in her inter-actions. This was an aggravation to me, as Mickey always had patients coming to the room and visiting, and she always appeared annoyingly busy and officious. When I was in my room, I wanted quiet and seclu-sion, and lately that was not to be found around Mickey. Mickey was also chatting much more, not just about her husband, but her children, her plans for the future, the other patients, the hospital, and even on occasion, something from television. With all this happening around her, she still always wore the heavy scowl on her face, her brow deeply furrowed. She also still wore the tape on the bridge of her nose to erase the strong, deep crevice in the center. The large wrinkle remained even when Mickey was smiling. More than once Mickey commented that she and I, and our families, *must* get together ... perhaps for a barbecue. I nodded and took back both dinner trays.

In the hallway, one of the patients told me that Millie was look-ing for me and had said to send me back to her room. She wanted to see me right away; it was *very* important! I stopped in my own room, picked up a magazine that I wanted to share with the Elegant Ladies, and headed for the back rooms.

Kaye and Helen were watching TV and only nodded as I went on past them to Millie's room. Millie had company. It wasn't her husband; I had met him. As the man turned to look at me, Millie smiled pleas-antly.

"Laurel, I want you to meet my doctor ... Dr. Guardierre, this is my friend, Laurel, that I've told you about."

The doctor extended his hand to me. Even with his smile, he appeared rather stern.

"Laurel is writing a book!" Millie continued. "It's about the hospi-tal. She's here to get information ... she wanted to research the topic. She's going to put *me* in as one of the characters."

Millie was obviously pleased and enthusiastic about the book. The doctor looked intensely into my eyes.

"Shit!" I thought, while outwardly remaining impassive. "Millie's big mouth!" While I tried to think what to do, the doctor continued to look deep into my eyes much as my aunt Babette had done to determine if I still had my sanity.

"So ... you're writing a book, are you? About this hospital and the patients?"

I would have appreciated a twinkle in his calculating and intense eyes. None was there. I swallowed almost imperceptibly and calmly met his gaze. Trying hard not to reveal anything but only to show matter-of-fact confidence, I smiled slightly.

"Yes," I responded. "I'm writing a book. Millie has asked for, and will receive, a copy when it's completed."

Several seconds passed as our eyes locked, both of us determined to refrain from revealing any attitude about the veracity of my authorship. I was relieved when the doctor finally spoke, his eyes still searching mine.

"That is very nice ... that you are writing. I wish you good luck in your endeavor."

I returned his polite half-smile. "Why, thank you. That is very kind."

I smiled confidently at Millie. "Thank you for introducing us."

I turned to the doctor. "It was very nice meeting you. Millie speaks so highly of you, and you *have* done such a great job with her. It has been a pleasure."

It was my turn to offer my hand. I made my exit slowly and deliberately, trying to maintain the facade of composure and self-confidence. I could feel him still staring at my back, as I stepped carefully out of the room, and then I wondered what he would say about "the book" to Millie. I hurried on past Kaye and Helen and on down the hall to the group bathroom. I closed the door behind me and heaved a sigh of relief, not knowing whether to explode in hysterical laughter or collapse in tearful embarrassment. The worst part was there was no one with whom to share this.

I gained my composure and then slipped furtively up the hall, passed the nursing station, and stopped to see Marcie, thinking that Dr. Guardierre would never see me there. I didn't know that Dr. Guardierre was also Marcie's physician and the Fates had been on my side that day since he had visited Marcie first! I waited a very long time before going back to visit the Ladies. I wanted to make sure that Millie no longer had company. I wondered if the doctor was convinced that I truly thought that I was researching a book and that this was my insanity or if he knew the truth. Only Dr. Jennings and Margaret would have been able to enlighten him since they knew me. Not even Dr. Ashford would be sure. I would probably never know what he thought and it worried me.

That evening the back room was especially full of levity. Millie was leaving in the morning, Kaye was agreeing to work with her doctor, and Helen had seen her lawyer and was feeling full of power. The three residents of the back rooms had tried on several occasions to start bridge game instructions for me, but something had always interrupted us. I really wasn't that interested, and they had gotten only some initial strategies across to me. I knew how the "hands" were dealt and had been given a little instruction in the "bidding." Always after the attempts, and then the interruptions, we ladies would resort to a game that all four could play. Tonight there was an air of celebration for Millie's goodbye. Kaye had brought out some chocolate, Helen had gotten out some cookies that she had received from her sister, and Millie rounded up four water glasses. Water glasses were only to be found in these Elegant Rooms, and *they* were plastic.

The Ladies were sitting around the table eating, drinking, playing cards, and pretending to have a real party when Nurse Penny came in. She accused our group of being too loud and suggested that we needed our rest. Helen was very pointed in letting her know that her presence was not needed. The rest of us ignored Penny and continued playing. Penny left in a huff but I knew she was resolved to win at the situation. I slipped back to my room to dress in my pajamas, as we all decided to be ready for bed and perhaps partially defuse another possible confrontation.

I slipped on my robe, shut out my light, and exited, ever so quietly, from my room. Mickey's light was already out, as she almost always went to bed by ten for a good night's rest before her good long day's rest. She was *so* annoyingly dedicated to the treatment procedures. I saw no need to get to bed early. If the whole morning was a period of unconsciousness, I figured that should be enough rest for anyone.

The hall was quiet and since I had no watch—who needed one *here?*—I could only guess that it was a little after eleven as it was Penny's shift. The Ladies started the party again, more quietly this time. As the evening grew later, the noise increased and Penny came back again, this time with another nurse. She walked to the table and suggested that I needed to go to my own room.

"Mind your own damn business!" said Helen in a low, threatening voice. "This is our room and we've invited her here."

Helen then turned to talk with Millie while Penny stood there waiting. I felt that I should go, in order not to cause problems, but I did not want Penny to succeed in intimidating everyone, as always.

"You need to go to your room." Penny stared firmly at me with her narrowed green eyes. "You are keeping others awake. You are all being too noisy ... and it's very late."

"Did my *doctor* order a bedtime?" responded Kaye with an edge of sarcasm. "We're back here where we won't bother anyone ... *and* ... where *we* won't be bothered ... Laurel stays."

Penny looked at the other nurse, who was very uncomfortable but was waiting for Penny to make the move. After a long silence, she did. "I suppose that you want us to call the orderlies to make everyone get to bed?" she questioned.

No one answered and Helen began dealing another hand of cards. Penny started to pick up the cards as they were being dealt. Helen stood up threateningly. She was much taller than the little redheaded nurse, and she looked down at her with complete disrespect and disdain.

"I would appreciate it if you would get out of our room and go about your duties. We do *not* need you *here*." Helen bit off each word as she spoke.

Penny ignored her. "Help me pick up this table," she commanded the other nurse.

* * *

Everyone was now standing, and Kaye also moved toward Penny. The other nurse was edging toward the door. She did not know whether to call for help or to aggressively support Penny. She knew that she did not want to try to fold up the table. She wished that Penny had just left the situation alone. After all, what did it matter if they didn't go to bed? They were clear back away from the others, and she really didn't believe anyone could hear them. It had just gotten to be a matter of principle with Penny. She had a real need to control. And she knew that Penny absolutely hated Helen. The nurse was always a little discomforted about sharing a shift with Penny.

* * *

Penny and Helen were squared off now. The other nurse was in the doorway, and Millie and Kaye were also approaching Penny.

"Best you leave!" said Kaye in a low but commanding tone.

"I'm not going to leave until Laurel is out of here, Millie goes to her own room, and you two get to bed."

Penny was bent on standing her ground. I started toward the door, but Millie was in my way. Penny made the mistake of touching Helen's arm. Helen pushed her arm off and muttered something under her breath. Penny reached over to grab the card table. This was enough for Helen. She took the card table and shoved it into Penny's firmly planted legs, almost knocking her over.

"If you want the damn table ... then you *take* it!"

The anger in Helen's face was as strong as the resolve in Penny's. Penny shoved the table out of the way, and it fell against the wall. Penny stood her ground, and Helen came toward her and lifted her foot high. She kicked Penny in the stomach and yelled, her eyes flashing and her face contorted, "Get out of here, *you* ... you ... *bitch!*"

The other nurse pivoted out of the door and ran down the hallway. I moved past Millie with a frantic desire to get to my room before the orderlies could arrive. Millie and Kaye eyed each other as Penny grabbed her stomach in pain. Seeing that she was so outnumbered and had not been able to frighten this group into submission, Penny walked haltingly from the room, uttering threats as she went. Kaye was completely unintimidated and even laughed at her as she went on down the long hall.

Back in my room, with the light out, I heard the "Orderlies to Third South!" call come over the intercom. A few moments later I heard the rushing of footsteps and Penny's voice as Penny went back toward the scene of the crime with her men-in-white-coats. I lay frightened and frozen in the dark, waiting for the inevitable return of the commandos. I had turned my head to the wall and listened as Penny opened my door and stared in with the orderlies at each side of her.

"Guess she's decided to do as directed ... we'll take care of this in the morning."

This was a strange threat. What would Penny do? See that I had a particularly bad insulin treatment? Could she have some influence in seeing to it that I received another horrendous electroshock *with* my insulin?

Things seemed quiet down the back hallway. I wondered what Penny had done to my friends. I didn't dare go to see. I just lay there listening to Mickey's heavy breathing.

Chapter Twenty-Four
Escape

As soon as the stirrings for a new day's preparation began on the ward, I was awake. Before I could sneak down to check on my friends, there was a young man in white requesting blood from Mickey and me.

"Are you some kind of deviant vampire?" I asked without smiling.

"Just a technician following doctors' orders," he responded without smiling. He was tall and thin, and carried himself with an apologetic slump. He looked uncomfortable doing his job in this particular environment. No explanation was given why the blood was to be taken. I was disgusted. The hospital staff had waited this long and had never given me any kind of tests for my protection. It was a little late now if I had any preexisting condition. The fact that Mickey's blood was being taken was a slight relief from an edging paranoia that perhaps the blood thing had to do with last night's brouhaha.

"Are you taking blood from everyone?" I persisted, glaring at him from behind sleep-clouded eyes.

"Depends on your medications," he said a little shakily. Mickey did get the same black and green capsule that Dr. Ashford had prescribed for me. A fine thing, I thought, give dosages of an unproven medicine for a while, and then test to see what damage has been done. I shook my head in disbelief and gave him my arm, after he completed with the more compliant Mickey. By now, the nurse had arrived to usher us both to the insulin torture chamber, and there was no opportunity to check with my ladies in the back. Besides, the nursing shift had not gone through their changing of the guard. Communications would have to be on hold until after my morning treatment. I was resigned to eating lunch in the back room and reviewing the situation then. Millie would be gone, but the goodbyes were implicit in our "party." I reluctantly followed the escort nurse. Mickey hurried along almost eagerly.

The past few treatments had brought the house doctor and several nurses to my treatment room, at my awakening. This was puzzling to me. I wondered if the tubes to my stomach had met with disaster or possible obstructions. It definitely had to do with me; they paid no attention to Mickey except to occasionally assist her with strap untying. They were always wearing wide smiles, and their amusement was unsettling. It had started with just a nurse being amused. The following treatment I had awakened to the doctor and a nurse smiling down at me. This had blossomed into a group of three visibly frivolous staff members. If I had had a problem, they shouldn't have seemed so happy.

This morning the group had exploded into a veritable convention; the doctor, two nurses, and two orderlies. I was aware of speaking to them while still not quite awake, something about the "damned, evil-eyed, thin-lipped night nurse." I seemed to have no control over my mouth and wondered who had said that. I focused the blur into Dr. Jennings' face just as he was asking me something about who I thought had a "radical brain transplant." I frowned and then raised my eyebrows quizzically. The smiles melted and the group dispersed. I wondered what they were doing to me in my unwanted unconsciousness.

Mickey had begun to be more independent even in treatment. She usually managed to awaken first, untie herself, and lead the way to the coffee room. This was fine with me I could use someone to lean on. I followed Mickey to get coffee. Mickey had coffee and a sweet roll. I was still getting the nauseating "shakes." Everyone sat in their usual silence until the nurse came and ordered us into groups to return to our floors. The few men were led through a door on one side. The women were grouped according to who had completed their snacks and taken from the room, through another door, to climb the steps to Third Floor. I got up with Mickey and waited by the doorway, incredulous that Mickey seemed so eager to do everything that was expected. The nurse stopped me.

"You are not going back to Third," she said tersely and with no explanation.

I looked around me in confusion. Were they planning on doing something else to me today? Was it in retribution for my actions the night before? Another nurse took me by the arm almost gently.

"You have been moved to Second Floor. You'll be down here now."

She unlocked and opened the third door, which I had only seen opened once at the beginning of my stay. This floor must have very disturbed patients, possibly worse than the Third North did. I had often heard the orderlies called to Second North. The kinder nurse went with me into the hallway. There were several rooms on either side, and all the doors were closed. I was shown into the second room on the left. My few belongings were lying on the bed. The nurse showed me which door contained the bathroom, and suggested that I get ready for lunch. So this was to be the consequence of last evening's defiance!

After bathing and dressing, I wandered again into the hallway but saw no one about. The nurse came back and opened the "coffee room" again. This time leaving the door unlocked and indicating that lunch would be served in that room. How disappointing. I would be spending all of my time in the insulin quarters. The room didn't appear any more comfortable with the patient zombies and the coffee gone, except that I noticed a television set in the corner that I had been unaware of before. The door to the men's day room opened, and an orderly wheeled in a cart carrying five lunch trays. At least I had not been placed in isolation as I was beginning to fear.

The nurse took two of the trays to the rooms down the hallway and knocked impatiently on the two other doors, announcing that it was lunchtime. A tiny quiet woman with frightened eyes, thin arms, and birdlike hands came, took her tray, and sat across from me. Had she smiled, I would have initiated a conversation, but she only looked out of the corners of her eyes at me and started picking at her food. Then a lady about my age came into the room and looked directly at me.

"You going to be here on our floor? Did you just come in?"

She was not shy but pleasantly open and although not smiling she exuded an air of friendliness or curiosity, I wasn't sure which. The nurse unlocked the stairwell door, exited, and relocked it from the other side.

"Well," I said, "I guess she doesn't want us to leave."

The woman laughed a little tensely. She had chin-length, dishwater blonde hair and blue eyes. She was quite attractive, even perky-looking and acting. She had quick, controlled movements that seemed a little nervous but also full of energy. One might even call her vivacious. She was wearing a hospital gown over bra and panties and was very obviously pregnant. Across the bridge of her nose was a medium-sized Band-aid. I wondered if her injury had been sustained at the hands of the staff.

"I'm Alice," she said, rather directly to me.

"Hi, I'm Laurel. I've been here a while but on the Third Floor ... I just got moved down here today."

"Great!" was the response. "I ... we could use some company."

Alice looked tellingly toward the tiny lady. "That's Esther," she indicated.

Esther didn't even look up from her food picking.

"I've been here about two weeks ... and I'll be leaving as soon as I can possibly get out of here," Alice explained.

Alice was obviously restless and distressed. She moved about incessantly and sat only long enough to eat quickly. She made several trips to the hallway, to her room, and to the bathroom. She constantly shifted her eyes toward the locked hallway door.

"Do they come to take you to the garden or to OT?" I questioned.

"They take the old ladies, from down the hall, to the garden ... and Esther, when she wants to go. I can't leave this floor," Alice answered with no further explanation.

Esther finished her lunch and went to her room. She still had not spoken.

"Does Esther talk?" I wanted to know. I wondered if Esther were suffering from amnesia, as Wyoming had been.

"If she wants to, which isn't often," came the reply. "The ladies down the hall are pretty old. They talk but don't know too much ... My husband thinks that they're probably senile. I haven't tried to find out. Don't really care ... just want to get home so I can call my doctor. It's his fault I'm here."

Great, I thought, here comes another fantastic story ... maybe "the book" was a good idea. There was certainly enough material. But Alice didn't volunteer further and I didn't choose to know ... for now.

I could go either to the garden with the old ladies or to the OT shop. I could not do both, as the nurse hadn't enough time to run me about. Esther had chosen to stay in her room, with the door closed. Alice had to stay on the floor and she said she intended to nap.

OT had four other clients: Marilyn, a new patient from Third North, who I had not met before; one of Mickey's buddies, who I already knew, and two ladies from the Annex. Mickey's buddies were there to do their "two pillowcases." There was not much conversation from anyone, and I was bored. I moved over to the table where Marilyn sat and began talking to her.

Within an hour or so Marilyn and I had become quite friendly. Mutual distrust and anger toward our confinement brought us close. We talked in hushed voices and disguised the actual content, with occasional "craft-related," more audible remarks. But the occupational therapist kept glancing over at us. Marilyn was barefoot. The nursing staff had rendered her so to prevent her from trying to get away, since the OT shop was on the first floor. One of the regular nurses from Third had brought Marilyn down and came back and forth periodically to check on her. The occupational therapist was also watching her and none too subtly. Marilyn and I exchanged smiles whenever the therapist responded nervously to movement from either of us or to our getting up from our chairs.

Marilyn had been locked up without any prior knowledge of what was going to occur. She had a young son about whom she was desperately concerned. Her family had not let her talk to him even to say goodbye. She had been denied use of the phones here and had had no visitors. She told me that she really wanted just a few minutes on the phone with her boy. That certainly did not seem so unreasonable to me.

"So they're watching you so you don't run away?" I asked quietly.

"I did try several times but they always grabbed me before I could get through the outside doors. Now they take my shoes away whenever I'm on the First Floor near the unlocked doors ... and they keep a constant eye on me."

I looked down at Marilyn's long bony feet. I wondered if my shoes would fit Marilyn. My feet were short and sturdy, not fat, but certainly not bony.

"What size shoe do you wear?"

I was not whispering. The therapist looked up quickly and then moved over toward us. Marilyn was drawing a design on paper for leather tooling. She carefully wrote a numeral seven, and pointed at it when I looked at her again.

"Oh, darn," I said, with feigned concern, "I made this *six* and *one-half* instead of *seven* ... oh well, I think that it will work."

Marilyn understood the agreement that, even though my feet were smaller, I would loan my shoes.

When the nurse from Third dropped in again, expecting to escort her patients back to the ward, Marilyn announced an urgent need to use the bathroom. Knowingly, I smiled, slipped off my shoes under the table, and with as little movement as possible, scooted them close to Marilyn. I elaborated upon the plan by walking a little dizzily and seeming to be confused as we all started to exit the room. I knew this nurse, which made my scheme easier.

"I feel real weak and shaky," I said, looking pathetically helpless and staring into the therapist's face.

The therapist was already insecure from dealing with Marilyn the past several hours, and she looked anxiously at the nurse for assistance.

"Come with us," said the nurse.

Her voice was emotionless but her facial expression exhibited some irritation. To the more timid therapist, she ordered, "Call Second and tell them that I'll bring Laurel up."

When they reached the hallway, I stumbled a little.

"Boy!" I managed to sound shaky. "I think I must be having an insulin reaction. I feel very weak and ... strange."

I blinked my eyes several times. Because the nurse was familiar with my treatments, she also knew what to do.

"Guess we better stop and get you some orange juice before we go up."

The irritation was gone, as she saw herself presented with the opportunity to become an angel of mercy. Neither of the attendants had noticed the feet of their charges. The nurse stopped a little way down the hall at the kitchen entrance. We had just passed the women's restroom on the opposite side of the hall. Marilyn and I exchanged glances as the nurse knocked on the kitchen door. I maneuvered the other patient, who was completely self-absorbed and unaware of anything, in between Marilyn and myself. Then I staggered a little and swayed into the open doorway. The nurse steadied me, while requesting some orange juice from one of the kitchen attendants. I managed to hold the nurse's attention long enough for Marilyn to pivot quickly and move noiselessly back down the hallway, past the OT room, and head for the side exterior door at the end of the hall. I gratefully, but hesitantly, drank the juice, while the nurse watched protectively. When I seemed to be taking too long, the nurse lost her focus on me and noticed Marilyn's absence.

"Where is Marilyn?" came the startled question.

I looked quizzically at the other patient, who stared blankly.

"Oh," I said, with relief. "I think she must have gone on into the restroom instead of waiting for us. Didn't she?"

I directed the question toward the other patient. The nurse looked from that patient to me and back again.

"Are you sure?"

"Yes," I confirmed. "I'm sure I saw her go across the hallway into the restroom."

"Wait here!" the nurse ordered quickly, as she glanced from the bathroom to the hallway, and then called to an orderly, standing near the admissions desk a short distance up the hall.

Marilyn was no longer visible. The orderly arrived at the nurse's side, awaiting her orders.

"Watch them!" she commanded as she ran across the hall to check the restroom. She was back in seconds and angrily confronted me I tried to seem confused about all the commotion.

"Where did she go?" she demanded, and then she noticed my bare feet. "Your shoes! Where are your shoes? Did you give your shoes to Marilyn?" she accused.

I had trouble stopping the guilty smile that was trying to force its way at the corner of my mouth. So I frowned, looked toward the restroom, and unconvincingly asked, "Are you sure she's not in there?"

The nurse lost no time in getting the orderly to pursue Marilyn. I could not believe their efficiency. An excited call was already coming over the intercom for orderlies, and the nurse hadn't even left her post.

"Her feet were hurting and they were cold." I started to explain, ... "from the hard cement floor in OT. She asked if she could borrow my shoes. She was barefoot. I didn't know. Did I do something wrong?"

"You knew what you were doing." The nurse cut me off.

I still maintained my wide-eyed, confused expression. To myself I said, "I'm crazy ... What the hell do you expect? ... I'm certainly not going to be accountable."

The Third Floor nurse came to my floor and returned my shoes to me before dinner. Alice and I were in the insulin coffee room/Second Floor day room when the nurse burst through the stairwell door, stalked over to me, and stared into my eyes as she thrust the shoes into my face. "Here are your shoes!" she nearly shouted at me.

She was probably expecting an explanation, but I only looked at her blankly, took the shoes, and said thank you, with a tone of mild appreciation and no guilt. Of course, I couldn't ask about Marilyn's escape, and the shoes hadn't returned on their own. The presentation of the shoes seemed like a victorious announcement that the "crazies" had not prevailed. Since expressing any interest in Marilyn might make me seem more culpable, I returned the continuing stare with a look of puzzlement and shook my head slightly, as if the whole escapade was beyond *my* understanding. The nurse wheeled about in frustration and slammed the door in her exit.

"What was that all about?" queried Alice.

"I have no idea," I responded, in feigned ignorance.

The Second Floor nurse had come in and was carefully observing us two patients. I did not know how long she had been there or whether or not the nurses had shared any information. I never again mentioned the shoe incident to either Alice or the Second Floor nurse.

After dinner I was at last made privy to Alice's "story." Alice was waiting for her husband to arrive and her restlessness had increased.

"He doesn't help me and he could," she complained to me. "He has use of the phones, and he should demand that my doctor do something. He should sue him and least confront him and try to get something done."

"What do you want done?"

The question was naive, as I knew that it introduced, and gave permission to relate, her problems. It was probably the most interesting tale yet encountered.

"I had an operation ..." Alice began her explanation. "I had plastic surgery. I thought that my nose was too large. It looked too long. I wanted it shortened. He did a terrible job. I mean ... the nose isn't deformed or anything ... it's just not right ... too small, doesn't look right. Ohhhhh." Alice covered her face in despair. "I don't look like *me* anymore. He got a court order to try and stop me from calling. I don't care. I *have* to talk to him. I have to get my nose fixed. This is driving me crazy."

Hearing Alice's story, I decide that the "drive" was obviously over and that Alice had arrived.

Chapter Twenty-Five
Alice's Nose

In the several days that followed, I developed a real liking for Alice. I was amazed that the inept system would allow that Alice be given treatment, particularly electroshock. But they had and were. Alice was seven months pregnant, and they were connecting that damn black box to her and jolting the hell out of her and her baby. Alice's husband was a gentle, rather nice, but inadequate man, who seemed completely baffled regarding what to do for Alice. He talked as if he were supportive but did nothing for her in regard to the plastic surgeon. He seemed to be deceived by the psychiatric conspiracy here and unable, or unwilling, to help his wife.

Alice and Ben had been married only five years and had four children. The small children were very noisy and exhausting, She was engulfed in laundry, housework, and cooking and when she found that she was pregnant again, she felt overcome. She began feeling old, dowdy, fat, and very unattractive. She had never liked her rather long nose, and imagined the only slightly visible bone in its bridge to be a large, irregular, and ugly hump. Each time she looked into the mirror, that long, bulbous nose glared back at her. She was not yet beginning to show her pregnancy, but she certainly felt it.

Alice desperately feared for Ben's loss of love for her. She asked him regularly, and he always assured her of his undying devotion. He tried to reassure her that she was still "pretty" and that he always loved her when she was pregnant. He made the mistake of describing her as always pregnant, and she had dissolved into tears.

She grew more and more unhappy with her appearance, and when she was finally able to pinpoint the problem as a need for her to improve her looks with plastic surgery, Ben was more than delighted to find a tangible, although expensive, solution to her unhappiness. Alice had mentioned wanting a "nose-job" early in their relationship while they were both still in high school. Ben had told her then that he loved her the way she was. This had assuaged her worries then, but Ben couldn't get it to work for him now. She was persistent in wanting to "be prettier." They made the arrangements and Alice's mother came to help them while Alice had her nose operation.

Ben was mistaken in thinking that the problems would get better. He now had his mother-in-law for an extenuated visit, and the kids were upset and acted frightened that their mother looked so different. And Alice ... it turned out that Alice could not cope with the change. Each time she looked into the mirror, she cried. She constantly called the plastic surgeon's office, first asking, then pleading, finally begging him to help her. She called Ben at work and although he had junior-partnership in the small firm, he was seeing his job slide into jeopardy. The plastic surgeon told Ben that he needed to take his wife to a psychiatrist, that she was becoming "unbalanced" about the operation. When Alice's calls to the plastic surgeon's office persisted, he had threatened a court order to restrain her from bothering him further.

Ben was a very nice guy. He never liked any sort of trouble. He had taken Alice to a psychiatrist who had seen her three or four times and had not been able to ease her fears about her nose. In fact, it seemed to make the situation worse. The psychiatrist was focusing on her feelings about herself. Alice's feelings about her nose *were* her feelings about herself, and she became more irrational about getting her nose changed. She began going to the surgeon's office whenever she could get away from home. Ben had seen to it that she had no car and no cab money so she walked the long distance, at both ends of the bus route, to the surgeon's office. Ben tried keeping money from her, so that she didn't even have bus fare. She borrowed from helpful neighbors or stole from her mother. In desperation, Ben followed the psychiatrist's counsel and admitted Alice to Mountain View.

No one seemed to question the professional wisdom of the surgeon in performing this type of operation on a discontented housewife and one who was pregnant. Had Ben been more assertive in dealing with the situation, and more analytical in his thinking, he might have been able to reverse the threats for legal action. Instead, Ben was dealing with another questionable medical procedure, that of giving shock therapy to his pregnant wife. He did what was recommended by those with the knowledge in their field because Ben was such a nice, trusting guy.

Martin was a nice guy, too, and the nice guys enjoyed each other's company. They had met during visiting hours with Alice and me and enjoyed being able to share their frustrations at dealing with their "unbalanced" wives. For the first time, Martin felt comfortable at my hospital. He had finally met someone who was easy to talk with, had mutual concerns, and was a nice guy. He was also relieved that I was not on the floor with the crazier and louder patients. The old ladies he understood. Esther was refined, and Alice was a little flighty and overly concerned about her nose operation, but otherwise she was not so bad off mentally. With the Band-aid on her nose, she didn't talk much about her looks, as if no one else could see the difference. Also, the smaller population on Second Floor was less threatening to an outsider. I was pleased that Martin was approving of Alice and Ben. Martin's visits were much longer when Ben was there, and after their second visit, the two nice guys left together and went for a beer.

At Martin's next visit, after I realized that I would never see the Grand Ladies on Third South again, I divulged the fact that Helen Temple was a patient and "under court order."

"What?" Martin declared in shock and great interest. "Not one of *the* Temples! The society Temples!"

"Yes," I responded, feeling the guilt of betrayal overcoming me. "She had a room clear at the back of the South Hall. A very large, well-appointed, almost beautiful room, and with its own bath. I guess they save those rooms for the wealthy or important patients."

"Well, she is certainly both ... Damn! That's really hard to believe."

"Why?" I asked in irritation. "Didn't you think that rich people, important people could go berserk, too? ... Cripes! Martin, it could even happen to you."

I wished at times that it would. Him *and* Ben. I was relieved when he left with Ben. I lay awake accurately imagining him telling his family and few friends what he knew about the Temples.

During the next visit to OT, I was relieved to find Marilyn. She was again barefoot. The two of us exchanged slight smiles and waited discreetly for an opportunity to speak. When I changed activities, I moved to the worktable with Marilyn. We continued to work but didn't speak. The therapist began giving leather-tooling instructions to a male patient, and during her discussions with him, I spoke softly. "Did you make it to the phone?"

Marilyn spoke just as softly and tried not to have any telling inflections in her voice. "Just barely. But I didn't get my call through. I ran down the street and turned at the corner, in case someone was following. I only went about a block and one-half. There was a day care center there ... lots of kids. I asked at the desk for a phone, but then I had to ask for some change for it ... the woman pointed me to a pay phone. I was dialing ... just got to the last number ... when a hand took the phone from me. I looked around and there they were ... the men in the white coats. Thanks for the shoes, anyway."

"Well, shall we try it again ... or plan another move?" I asked, smiling. "I can just see the situation ... you and the orderlies. Did they drag you back?"

"Naw, I came willingly ... I knew the jig was up. It's happened before ... them grabbing me, I mean. It doesn't help to fight."

I was smiling. "How about the woman at the day care. Was she shocked?"

"That was odd," Marilyn responded. "She just looked at me. She didn't seem the least bit concerned. I wondered if they had had escaped mental patients drop in there before ... being so close to the hospital and all."

"They should be a little more accommodating," I snickered, breaking the disguise of the conversation. "They should install a regular phone, closer to the door, or at least put out change for us."

The therapist was trying to hear the conversation, but she had tuned in too late to have anything of substance to relay.

"We do have phones here," she intervened. "But you need to ask your doctors for permission to use them."

If the therapist were trying to get information, she didn't succeed.

"See!" I said to Marilyn, adopting a condescending tone. "There *are* phones here. I thought so. I guess the nurses hide them. I wonder if I could get permission to call. Do you have permission?"

"I really don't need it," smiled Marilyn. "My mother came to visit and we called my son from the phone by the office. I have a planned conversation for tonight, again. There's really no one else I even want to talk with."

"Well, I guess that takes care of the shoe question," I whispered.

"I wish I could do something for *you*," Marilyn said, almost audibly.

"I just hope we both get out of here before winter ... or that you get your shoes back," I laughed.

"What about shoes?" asked the therapist.

"Marilyn ... she doesn't have any shoes. Did you notice? It's hot out, now. But fall will be here before we know it. I didn't want her feet to be cold. Do they feel okay now?"

"They're fine ... I'm okay," came the stoic response.

I looked at the therapist. "I don't think that it's okay," I said. "It seems cruel that she has no shoes. What a sadistic hospital, punishing a patient by making her walk on this hard, cold floor with her bare feet. I'm going to ask my doctor about it."

"There are good reasons for everything that we do," said the therapist, indignantly. "If she didn't try to get away, she could have her shoes."

"Who would want to try to get away? Why, Marilyn, they are just trying to *help* you here ... Don't you want their help?" I tried to sound ingenuous.

"I do. I do now. I really *want* their help ... even the shock treatments ... that they want to give me. I think that it will be a real *blessing*." Marilyn didn't even smile as she said this.

She is *good*. I smiled to myself. She is an even better actress than I am. Too bad we aren't on the same floor, but they would just have to move one of us. I never saw Marilyn in OT again.

Chapter Twenty-Six
The Dance

The first Saturday night I was on Second, Scott burst into the doorway from the men's ward.

"Hey," he said to me, "what are you doing here? ... Thought you would have been moved to the Annex by now. Your friend Thelma is over there."

"I get to go when my treatments are completed ... which is this coming week. How is Thelma?"

"But I didn't know her before ... only from what you said. She never came out to the garden, and I do garden duty and work the Annex. I'm just filling in here tonight. Thelma looks good ... seems okay. She is rather quiet."

"She is pretty reserved. ... Doesn't go about trying to make conversation," I responded.

"You're coming to the dance tonight, aren't you?" Scott asked with a huge smile.

"You are kidding ... What dance?"

"Right here! ... I mean *here!*" Scott indicated with a swoop of his hand toward the insulin room."

As I stood with my mouth open, Scott unlocked the door to the insulin room.

"What are you doing?" The surprise in my voice pleased Scott, who started folding cots and moving them to one end of the long room.

I started laughing. "I know you must be joking. No one could ever conceive of anything as bizarre as a dance in a mental hospital. That would be the ultimate in social pleasures. A Grand Ball at the loony bin."

"No, I'm not kidding ... isn't it a great idea?" he laughed. "Want to help me set up?"

"This is too crazy. I can't handle *this* ... Everything else pales at the idea of an actual dance in Mountain View. And in the *insulin* ward."

I laughingly reminded him of the story I had told him about

Jeannie, from Third South, who described her treatment "dance." He nodded. "Well, *we* are going to have a real one. Just watch!"

He went back into the men's ward and returned a few minutes later with a small, and very old record player, with built-in speakers. With another trip he produced a box with some old LPs and brought along a nurse who joined him in arranging the room. I stared for a few minutes, and then started helping with the cots. The nurse looked inquisitively at Scott, and he nodded reassuringly. I was the only patient around, as the old ladies had gone to bed early, and Alice was with Ben in her room. Martin would not be coming again until tomorrow. The Second Floor nurse came and helped in the room setup. It seemed strange to assist "the enemy," and I knew that my help was uncomfortable for the nurses also. But Scott kept encouraging me. All the cots were stacked in Mickey's and my private little coma room, which was at the end near the coffee room exit. I decided that the room must have been an over-sized closet in its previous life. All the thin green drapes were pulled all the way back on their runners, till they were almost flush with the wall. The record player was set up just outside my insulin "closet." The group stood back and admired their work.

"Needs something." I remarked. "How about the medicine counter ... can't you change it into a bar? ... That sounds fitting ... Aren't you having refreshments? ... What kind of a dance is this?"

Scott laughed, but the Second Floor nurse only managed a smile.

"Great idea," said Scott. "You should have been on the dance committee. If this one works, next time we'll include refreshments. Cookies and punch ... at the insulin counter. Yeah!"

He nodded and was obviously pleased. Scott was always enthusiastic ... he liked his job. The nurses disappeared. My nurse to check on her charges, the other one to gather some guests.

"Who's invited?" I asked. "Where did you get your guest list? ... *It* must be very interesting."

Scott looked serious.

"That's a problem," he agreed. "This thing is my idea, and I'm still working out the bugs."

"Nice choice of words," I smiled. "We have several nice old ladies, plus a mute, and a charming, pretty young lady ... who just happens to be seven months pregnant. Better try Third Floor," I told him help-fully.

"Guess *you'll* have to come," he said. "I have some guys from Second Floor, and Sylvia went up to get some of the Third Floor patients."

"You'd do better to change it to a staff party ... but then, there is the problem of leaving the patients unattended ... *that* could be *very* interesting. And it could be entertaining ... the staff dancing while the patients were left to do unspeakable, weird things ... an unusual Saturday night extravaganza. But a dance, Scott? A dance? You're not going to find any group with a poorer sense of social skills than here. Were you trying for a challenge? I don't think it's safe to even watch."

"Hey give it a chance ... nothing is going to happen. We'll have staff here. I just want to see them have a little fun."

"Fun? Who?" I frowned accusingly. "The staff or the patients?"

Scott was aware that, because of the jokes we shared, I had reason to be sensitive and question his motives.

"Really!" he assured me. "It might be of some benefit ... get them up ... away from TV."

I shook my head. "Scott, most of them won't even know that they're being entertained. Most are so zapped that they can't maneuver on their feet. This is pathetic."

"Give it a chance," he repeated in a low, unsure voice. Then he picked up his enthusiasm that I had ground into the ugly tile floor. "Stay and at least watch ... Save *me* a dance ... I'll be your partner ... This will be *fun*."

Scott went to get his guests and I looked around me. A long, old, and faded asphalt tile room, with periodic tufts of extremely cheap curtains against the wall, three or four very high windows barren of decoration, a long, worn, wood-paneled counter with ugly dark brown Formica on its top. This could pass for a church or small-community party setup but it was the tackiest dance environment that I had ever seen. I wondered if the insulin room smell was gone. I had such poor olfactory senses that it could well be very present. My concerns were confirmed as another Third Floor nurse appeared, nodded only slightly at me, and proceeded to spray a Lysol can from one end of the long room to the other. "This will be a lovely, romantic, and unforgettable evening for everyone involved," I thought, only somewhat amused.

The other nurse, Sylvia, returned with her "selected guests." The ten or so ladies were barely familiar to me. I had seen several of them either in OT or the insulin room, but I had no speaking relationship with them. They all stood there awkwardly. There didn't seem to be too much change in their demeanor from either lining up for trays or waiting to go back from insulin shock. They all showed a noticeable lack of anticipation for the "pleasure" that was to follow. I wondered if any understood they were coming to a dance. If any had combed their hair, bathed, changed clothes, tried to fix their faces with make-up. I looked carefully at each one. They didn't seem aware of my gaze. None of them looked as if they had taken any pains with their appearance, but how could I tell? I hadn't seen them earlier. Maybe they had had no notice of the big event or maybe they were no more excited than I was. They just stood, seeming too unaware of their environment to be uncomfortable, just awkward. I hoped that Scott and the other staff were sincere in being helpful and that this was not the ultimate in cruelty, that they were not going to observe these sad individuals in their most desperate circumstances with derision.

Scott came in with his group of seven tortured-looking men. All their pride was stricken from their faces. What little they had coming to the hospital had disappeared for most of them after the first few hours of incarceration here. Most of the male patients were alcoholics who were not examples of social grace even prior to their admittance. Without the alcohol to cover their inadequacies, and to give them false courage, they were even more socially inept. They stood, awkward. Those who were not so medicated were even somewhat self-conscious. The nurses and orderlies had to help them to find partners so they could start some dancing. A short wiry little man, with a partially bald head, looked about him with some slight interest. Scott walked him over to an even shorter lady, with a tightly permed hairdo, glasses, and too wide eyes. They didn't even smile, just eyed each other with suspicion. Scott had to remind them to get into dance position. He even gave them a little push for a jumpstart. They moved hesitantly to the center of the floor.

A tall thin lady with large breasts and pigeon toes walked with the nurse over to a man she had selected herself. He was very cowboyish-looking, even sporting some Western boots. The nurse appeared to be introducing them. This lady even smiled a little, but her partner looked very stern. They took off almost at a gallop. The other nurse found a likely pair, as did the second orderly. The staff exchanged "pleased-with-themselves" smiles, and then, after pairing several others apiece, they each took a partner for themselves to get the dance rolling.

The staff was efficient in helping to get some interaction going at this event. It wasn't as though the "ice needed to be broken." There was no ice. The patients were not really shy, or "cold"; they were just hesitant and confused. It was the hesitancy that needed to be broken. Their confusion the staff could not fix. The vinyl record selection was not bad for this population. It was the "oldies" that had lasted, and most of the music was slow enough for the delayed reaction of the shocked and dulled. It was a marvel. The couples actually moved together about the floor, and most even in time to the music. Dancing must be automatic, like riding a bicycle, I thought.

I watched from the doorway, thinking how sad it was that the staff was trying to help these people enjoy themselves when there was no delight left in them. It was almost ready to push me into tears, when Scott bounded up to me and swept me in onto the dance floor.

"This is my dance!" he said enthusiastically. Then he said quietly into my ear, "See, it's working. I knew it could. I think they're having a good time."

Scott was having a good time. He was feeling useful and maybe getting some sadistic pleasure in watching them. I looked at his face it was hard to tell. Scott was a good dancer, but I was inhibited from moving very gracefully myself. Just like most of the others, my body did not feel or act much like my own. I tried to switch it into neutral; that worked better. Scott was chatting about the evening, the dance, his ideas for improving entertainment here, and I was more than self-conscious about the circumstances.

"You dance well," complimented Scott. "Maybe we should leave this place and go to a real dance?"

The music had changed to a faster pace and he swooped me

dramatically across the floor. One of the nurses looked over at us and smiled broadly at Scott's silliness.

"I know," he said laughingly. "Let's slip out of here and go some-where that is really fun ... maybe even romantic."

"Hey, I waited weeks ... for you to come to my window ... for our elopement," I remarked, starting to laugh also. "I stayed awake late at nights, waiting. You never showed up," I accused.

"Okay. It's *now* ... are you ready?" He made several more large swoops down the long room and toward the door at the far end.

"Is that an exit?" I asked.

Scott nodded.

"Well, if you have the keys, I have the time," I joked.

Scott jangled his keys out of his pocket with one hand, while mov-ing me into a spin with the other arm. He came within inches of the door. No one was dancing this far down toward the end of the long room, and for a minute I was a bit frightened. I didn't know how far Scott would take this game. I did not want any trouble from the rest of the staff. I looked at Scott anxiously.

"I think we'd better dance down to the other end of the room ... we're getting some looks." I wanted to tell him about the shoes and Marilyn so he would know why the nurses might be watching me. But I was not that trusting of his friendship. Instead, I talked to him about Alice and her nose as we returned to the middle of the floor. It took another dance to relay the story of what had caused me to get moved to the Second Floor.

"Maybe your doctor just wanted you in a quieter place. Did he know about Penny being kicked?" Scott tried to reassure me.

"I don't know. I never mentioned it. Dr. Jennings never said any-thing," I puzzled.

"They wouldn't talk about it, unless you did ... I don't think," Scott said in a rare, serious moment. He had heard, he said, in the hospital gossip about Penny being kicked but he reassured me that my own name was not mentioned.

The evening ended early. The enthusiasm, except for Scott's, had remained low. I heard the staff members talking at the cleanup. They all seemed to think it had been a good thing. I knew it was at least memorable for me. I told Scott this, in hearing range of the others, as I was leaving. "A wonderful dance, great company, terrific ambience, fine band. I don't remember ever going to one in a mental hospital before. I shall always remember this one as the *first*." Then sensing that he was a little hurt, I added, "But, *actually*, Scott, you did a good job ... and a good thing."

He smiled appreciatively and went on about the cleanup. I lay awake for a long time pondering the pathos.

Chapter Twenty-Seven
Treatment Plan for Alice

While I was entertaining the staff with my treatments, Alice spent the mornings fretting about her nose. She flinched each time she walked near the mirror in her room or the bathroom.

The rooms on this floor were better furnished than Third South, excluding the back Elegant Quarters. These rooms had bureaus with dressers and mirrors. There were closets in each one, making the floor look more like an old, cheap hotel than a hospital. The old ladies were semi-permanent residents, rather like Mae and Maude, upstairs, except that they needed less care and observation. They caused little or no trouble. The tiny little "bird-lady" was not receiving treatment; she was suffering from a very deep menopausal depression but had not seemed to be suicidal. It seemed I was put here to be in a more subdued atmosphere and to break up the clique of nonconformists upstairs.

I learned that Dr. Ashford had been advised that I was unduly influenced by the discontented patients, and he decided that a more controlled environment would be best for me until I finished the last few treatments. He hadn't discussed the move with Martin, as he felt Martin was not cooperative or actively supportive of my condition. He waited for me to mention it, or ask questions; since I didn't, he must have dismissed it from his mind. He said he was even a little pleased with the upheaval on Third South, as he had noticed more assertiveness on his patient's part, and from my conversations, he doubted that I was too easily influenced. Secretly I think he hoped that *I* was doing the "influencing." Helen Temple's doctor seemed to annoy him, as Ashford had noticed that he had a disproportionate number of his patients admitted under duress. This case, he said almost with delight, had the potential of exploding in the doctor's face. He didn't want any of *his* patients associated in any way. He had always smiled smugly to himself about what a good analyst he was, and he knew how well both Thelma and I were doing.

Alice was the only Second Floor problem. She was very agitated and had to be watched. She had started in the Annex, with very serious reminders about no contact with her surgeon. She had secretly used the pay phone on several occasions and had left without telling anyone where she was going. She had gotten within several blocks of her plastic surgeon's office, when Ben, her husband, who had been alerted, caught up to her. She was then placed at the main building on Third South for security reasons, and in spite of her pregnancy. She had run away once, was moved to Second Floor where the area was more secure with no outlet to the elevator, and yet had gotten loose again.

Second Floor duty was an easy, and almost boring, shift for the nurses. Little care was needed for the elderly ladies and Esther. Most of the time was spent just keeping an eye on Alice. The nurse was even able to leave the floor from time to time to run errands. Vera, the nurse who usually had Second North in the daytime, wasn't too concerned about the possibility of fire, should she leave the ward for too long, although there was no way for anyone to get out unless there was someone there with keys. Vera felt sorry for Alice and worried about the shock treatments' effect on the unborn baby. She liked Ben and Martin. She wasn't sure about me. Some of the nurses had said that I could be trouble.

One evening Vera sat across from me in the day room/coffee room. Alice had her husband there and was pleading as usual that he take her home. I was pretending to read a magazine, while also half watching the TV set. I liked Vera. She was a nurse who had soft, lightly starched dresses, unlike Penny, who liked her uniform very starched. Vera's shoes were worn, and not so neatly polished as Penny's new shoes, which had not a mark on them. I had observed that, when the nurses were more relaxed in their uniforms, they were more relaxed in their roles.

"I bet Helen relaxed Penny a little!" I smirked to myself. Vera brought knitting to do on her shift when things were slow. She had some trouble with a complicated pattern one evening and, when she uttered a groan in frustration, I offered to help her. Vera was surprised to see a patient interacting as much as I did. The "dance" situation had surprised her, also. Scott had told Vera, later, that I was "okay" although Vera was withholding judgment. She and I glanced back and forth at each other suspiciously, waiting for Ben to leave. Vera wanted to do her knitting and couldn't relax until she let Ben out and secured the door. I wanted to talk with Alice.

After Ben left, Alice asked me to come to her room. She had told me that her own nose was much like mine, before her operation. This was not very complimentary for me to hear, as Alice had been going on and on about how badly she had wanted to change her long, ugly nose. I had reassured Alice many times that the new nose was nice. Alice had even removed the Band-aid for me to look at it closely. The band-aid, Alice conceded, was only there to stop the shock that resulted from noticing her new, strange image in the mirrors. Alice kept insisting that she just did not look like herself. She kept her nose covered and ruminated over the surgery, her changed appearance, and the uncooperativeness of her doctors. I liked Alice's looks. The new nose was small and perky, and gave the active Alice a vivacious personality. I could not envision Alice with a long nose. Alice had asked Ben to bring a high school graduation picture for her to share with me. Ben had done so on this particular evening. I couldn't wait to see from what Alice had been transformed.

Alice was right; her old nose was long, rather severe, and somewhat similar to mine. My mother had said things like "elegant," dignified," and "distinguished" when correcting my own descriptions of my nose as "large," "long," or "pointed." Alice had had the same experience. Her old nose had given Alice a completely different look.

"You look quiet and reserved ... and very serious in this picture," I stated. "Were you?"

"I think so," agreed Alice. "I think that your appearance affects your personality. That's why I want my old nose back. I look in the mirror and I don't know who I am ... or how I am!" Tears were building in Alice's eyes.

I spent days trying to convince Alice that she was fine the way she was, with her new nose. I hardly noticed my own anxieties, in my worrying for Alice and her shock treatments. They came for Alice while I was in insulin, and Alice was back by the time I was conscious again.

The cute perky nose fit the energetic, enthusiastic, and childlike charm that was Alice. In our long talks, I learned that Alice had run away from the Annex and had headed for the surgeon's office. She was going to force him to see her. She didn't know *how*, but she wasn't taking "no" for an answer. Alice said that she *wanted* to do what Ben asked of her, but that she couldn't be the "new" Alice with the tiny nose. Her friends didn't recognize her, and her children were upset. She could only stand *herself* with her nose bandaged up. When they put her in the main building, she knew that she had to find a way out. Just like she had to find a way out now. She had escaped, she said, by taking the bandage off her nose, acting "normal" and pretending to know a pair of visitors near the elevator. She was new to the Third Floor and the nurses didn't know her. She talked with the man and woman, who were leaving, pretending to be with them, and was able to board the elevator with them, nodding and saying "thank you" to the nurse. When she got to the main floor, she just exited with the other visitors. She got clear home before anyone had even missed her. She was brought back and put on Second North.

When the staff took the patients from her ward to the garden, she escaped again. She got out of the garden by pretending to be a visitor and going in the back door, again thanking the staff. She got all the way home the second time. Alice guessed that her pregnancy and her acting made her believable as a visitor.

Now, Alice was not given her "outer" clothing to wear. They kept her in a hospital gown. She could not go to the garden and was never allowed to go to the OT shop. She was kept more secured on Second North, as there was no elevator, and there were fewer patients, so she could be more closely watched. There were three exits for Second North; one to the insulin room, which had an outside door that was never unlocked; one to the men's day room, which could give her access to a locked elevator that went to the main floor; and one more exit that went to the back stairwell. Alice spent much of her time thinking about how to get out, and even more time thinking about her nose. When she was not talking about escape or noses, I thought that Alice seemed quite normal. I was not surprised that she had been able to trick the staff.

It seemed the only way that Alice could get out would be to adjust to her nose. If she kept it covered all the time, she could not gain her acceptance of the change. I kept talking to her about how well it suited the "new" Alice and told her to try to learn to like the change at least long enough to get out. Alice couldn't reconcile to this. The only other approach was to *pretend* to be okay with the nose. Some way must be found to get them to stop shocking Alice. I feared so for the baby!

I talked Alice into removing the Band-aid for a while each day and was working on helping Alice to lengthen the times that the Band-aid remained off. The nurse had noticed the difference and had commented. We two cohorts felt that we were making good progress. Alice confided in me that, she really hadn't changed her underlying attitudes, and *would* get in touch with the doctor again, just as soon as she got out. She *had* to have her old face back. But I believed that there really was some slight adjusting taking place. Alice seemed more comfortable about her looks and didn't mind the nurse and me looking at her. There was only one serious problem. Time was running out as I now had only one treatment to go. I would undoubtedly be moving to the Annex. I was determined to discuss this with Dr. Ashford.

Chapter Twenty-Eight
The Girls Come to Visit

I lay awake ruminating over Alice's problems. Dr. Ashford would probably not see me before my last treatment, and I had such ambivalence about moving to the Annex. It would be nice to see Thelma, but I wasn't certain my friend would even remember me. There were so many patients who forgot everything especially those receiving electroshock, as Thelma was. Martin had told me that Dr. Ashford thought the insulin therapy was better for me, one of the reasons being that it did not have as much effect on the memory. Mickey's memory seemed to be fairly well intact, but her personality had really shifted from one bizarre manifestation to another. Basically, she was probably the same, a take-charge person with another focus. Thelma was enigmatic and her below-surface self was hidden by an almost imperceptible smile. I thought this made her dramatic and extremely interesting. I wondered about Thelma's deepest thoughts.

On Sunday Martin had brought our children with him, for their first visit. I met them in one of the conference rooms on the main floor. I was not very communicative with the girls because my feelings of disappointing and deserting them were so strong that I had difficulty even making eye contact. I had asked Martin not to bring the children to this place, and I was on the verge of tears. It haunted me that they should have to visit their mother in such a confinement. Martin didn't understand my desire to wait to see them until I was home. But then, *he* didn't carry the stigma, nor did he believe that they were aware and a part of my shame. These thoughts were very private and, if I looked at Karen long enough, I knew that she might unveil them. She was so perceptive, I feared that she could read insanity in her mother's countenance.

My "baby," Sissy, was nearing a year and a half. Her eyes were troubled for one so young. She was walking but still sucking on a bottle that Martin had let her bring along. Everyone at home seemed to feel that she still needed it to replace parental nurturing. Sissy seemed to remember me, and fluctuated from clinging to my legs to almost hiding from me behind her sister.

I tried to act normal, and this was probably what made both children so uncomfortable. Karen's eyes watched me incessantly. The tooled purse that I had labored over in OT was presented to Karen, a small picture of little animals was given to Sissy. Karen kept staring but smiled slightly, and lovingly held the purse very close to her the entire visit.

The visit seemed painfully long. I assured them both that I would be home very soon. Luckily there was too much feeling for the tears that I had dreaded, both mine and the children's. Karen was distressed and very pensive, and looked as if she were starting to cry when they were exiting the front door. I stood back in the hallway and turned so that I couldn't see.

While struggling to maintain my composure, I bumped into Dr. Guardierre, Millie's doctor. He smiled wryly. I pretended indifference, giving a very slight nod that meant *possible* recognition. A whole cadre of psychiatrists was gathered near the front exit, still conversing importantly as they continued to emerge from a conference room behind the admissions area. I noticed Dr. Ashford, who signaled me to wait. I hadn't had a nurse stay with me during my last few visits to the Main Floor. I believed that I was trusted because everyone knew that I was too frightened to even step out into the street. I wondered what they would do if I defied all suppositions and ran triumphantly out the door, down the sidewalks, and then the miles to my own home. I was so impressed with Alice and *her* independence and valor. Why did my own terror imprison me, and how was this obsession any different from Alice's preoccupation with her nose?

Dr. Ashford's colleagues appeared to treat him with great respect. He seemed to be held almost in awe by the men standing about. I wondered if this were *my* interpretation, or if they were more concerned about his powerful position than they were "expressing respect." Dr. Ashford walked, with great stateliness, into the small conference room that I had recently vacated and I followed behind him. Still unsmiling, he closed the door and motioned me to a chair. I was stiff. He was still swelled with his dignity, enhanced by the loftiness of his treatment.

"Well," he began in a very professional tone, "how did the visit go?"

"It was okay."

He didn't like my unenthusiastic tone.

"Weren't you glad to see them? How did Martin act?"

I was very hesitant.

"The girls are fine. They seem sad ... or upset. I didn't want to see them *here*. I will be home soon ... won't I?'

"Yes, but they should probably see their mother in the meantime. Martin tells me that they've been asking to see you. And, yes, you will be home soon. How did you get along with your husband? How did Martin act?" he asked again.

I was confused. Martin didn't act any specific way ... ever ... he just *was*.

"The same as usual ... rather unexcited, unconcerned, a little distant. I guess. I think that the hospital makes him nervous. He seems annoyed that I'm sick." I started to bite my lip.

"Well, he's not all innocent of all this himself," Dr. Ashford was grumbling a little and his face had started to redden. "I warned him about a pregnancy ... he didn't listen."

"That was both our faults." I defended him.

"No! I told him specifically, *no more* children. He deliberately defied my orders. What about the abortion?" His face was very red now.

I was in utter shock. "No one said anything ... *you* never said anything about abortion!" My eyes were wide, and the doctor was so angry that he did not respond to my reaction to this revelation.

"I told that damn-fool husband of yours that you should *not* have the baby. It was all arranged. Dr. Holmes and I had it all worked out."

I didn't process anything else while he continued to grumble. In my shock, I was trying to maintain my impassive face and continue trying to glue my shakiness together and find an appropriate moment to remove myself from his presence. Dr. Ashford could read that I was uncomfortable, but I hoped that my expression buried the depth of my distress. I even managed to smile at him as we left the room. He had said something about the Annex and the preparations for home. I nodded, not attending to the actual words. There was something about "trips" home, but I really didn't care.

The next several nights I had gone over and over the conversations that I had had with Martin during my pregnancy. Martin hadn't *really* betrayed me. He knew me so well that it was very obvious to him that I would never have an abortion. I had wanted another child for quite a while, clear up until I started having my panic attacks in full force. Martin had told me that the doctors said that I would be fine. That I would be better after the baby was born. He wasn't lying. He was trying to save me from a decision that I could never have made. I supposed that I would confirm the story with Martin but not for a while. I had to get over the shock first. This played on my mind constantly. Now I had another obsession to cover.

When I was awakened for my last treatment, I had slept only a few hours and was very tired. My eyes burned. I tried to talk to the Second Floor nurse, to let her know I wasn't sure about the Annex and to have her tell Dr. Ashford to see me *before* he made a transfer. The nurse did the customary nodding and discounting of what any patient had to say, especially if it were a request. I had almost decided that it would be best to stay and help Alice. The Annex stay was not so important to me. I would be leaving before long, and I was almost comfortable on Second South. I watched my green light-donut form and felt relieved that I only needed to live through this last insulin coma. I had even smiled at Mickey when we both took our places on the cots. I was getting very adept at going unconscious; it now took me very little time. Relax. Watch the green circle form in the blackness. It would develop a hole and then swell....

The light was coming in through my partially opened lids. There they were, the entire group. Once again they were all laughing, and I had the same vague sense that I had been telling them all "something." The laughter diminished and they glanced knowingly at each other. I didn't like the joke being on me. Dr. Jennings smiled right at me and said, with sincerity, "We are all going to miss you here, Laurel."

I frowned and in lucid speech that seemed to proceed without my conscious decision, I spoke to them all in sarcasm and oration.

"Why, thank you! I wish that I could say that I have enjoyed taking these treatments as much as you all have *obviously* enjoyed giving them to me."

Another chorus of laughter ensued and, since I apparently seemed confused and a little sad, Dr. Jennings stayed for a few brief seconds to let me know that he would be around "if I needed him."

"A cold day in hell!" my inside head said, but I smiled and thanked him for his concern.

Looking around me in the coffee room, I tried to remember the first impressions I had had as a new patient. I felt a little confident that I had changed some. I was not nearly so fearful, and my nervousness had diminished but my rational thoughts reminded me that everyone gets used to their environment no matter how desperate those circumstances might be. The population had changed from day to day in the treatment room, but the behavior remained consistent. For the most part, they all acted stunned and out of their bodies. "Actually," I thought, "it's more their heads that they are out of. The bodies walk around with no real persons directing them." How would the doctor put these partial human beings back together? Maybe that was the point. No one liked them "together" so they were all going to be redone.

It must be hard to remake a personality. Alice got hers done by plastic surgery, but there had been a real flaw in the procedure. Now someone had to reorganize the entire structure. Mickey?... "Re-done" on her was strange. I often wondered if she were now her "old self" before the rabies scare. If these doctors were going to restructure people, they needed better plans. No one seemed to be a sterling example of psychiatric recreation. Maybe they all left while still under construction.

That was it! Take myself, for example. I felt a lot like Alice but who was *I?* My kids seemed confused and doubtful of me. Martin wouldn't have noticed if I completely changed personalities. He would just give me his blank stare. Perhaps my Aunt Babette would know the difference. And was "different" necessarily "craziness" or "well adjusted." Dr. Ashford was *very* different and it made him wise, profound, even brilliant, to others. I wondered if he had had his head altered while studying Freud in Europe.

A nurse nudged me and told me it was time to go back to my

room. The coffee room was almost emptied, and the staff was clearing the table.

"My God!" I thought, in alarm. "I forgot to mention the Annex to Dr. Jennings ... or to try and find Dr. Ashford. I need to work on the transfer." I jumped up and almost fell from the room in my dizzy staggering. When I found the floor nurse, I asked if Dr. Ashford would be coming in.

"He isn't regular with his visits. We never know. I think he *likes* it that way."

There was a hint of disparagement in her voice, and I looked at her severely. The nurse seemed uncomfortable. I felt pleased. There was a strange sense of power coming over me, now that I was not to be debased by insulin confinement any longer. I smiled, almost with superiority, toward the puzzled nurse.

After my bath and lunch, I settled into the now day room with Alice. We ate, ignored Esther, and talked about Alice's nose some more. Alice had not worn the band-aid at all, for over two days now. She still was not looking into the mirror, and she did seem more relaxed.

"You're doing great!" I encouraged. "Now just don't talk about it ... in front of the staff ... that is. When they see the change, they'll send you home."

I hoped that the pretended change would affect Alice more deeply and that her obsession would gradually diminish. It seemed like a clever plan. Maybe I should think about going into the business. From my observations, there didn't seem to be much superior competition. I warned Alice that I might be leaving, if I couldn't convince my doctor otherwise. Alice didn't like the idea and was even a little frightened.

"It's going to be all right either way," I encouraged her. "You know what to do ... or rather what *not* to do. Just stay away from the mirror, leave the bandage off, and don't discuss it."

The orderlies came to get Alice for her treatment that had been put off till the afternoon. I waited for her return impatiently. I was worrying and hoping that Alice's improvement had been noticed and that they would not jeopardize her further with their voltage. When Alice returned she was a little stunned looking and very pale. I had not seen the electroshock patients right after treatments as I was always in the insulin room. (Those who received unscheduled treatments were always back in the lockup area; *no one* saw *them*.) But I could see the signs in Alice. She lay on her bed for a while and slept a little. When she got up again and walked hesitantly into the day room to join me, she had the Band-aid back over her nose.

"Alice!" I reproached her urgently. "Get that off! Remember what we are doing ... the plan?"

Alice looked confused but was adamant in her refusal to remove it. I tried to be quiet, so that the floor nurse didn't hear. Alice seemed to start to remember the problem and the solution we were working on, but nevertheless kept repeating that she could not take it off, that she had to get the surgeon to fix her nose. I was in despair. All my work with Alice had been destroyed, with the small part of her brain that they had blasted. I was very disheartened as I watched Alice start her pacing and ruminating. I just sat, numb. Alice went to her room for a while apparently to think things over. She looked concerned that I seemed angry.

When Alice came back she started talking very quietly to me, explaining a plan that she had just derived. "You see, I *have* to get out of here. I don't have any clothes. Will you loan me some? We could both escape at the same time. If we work together it will be easy."

Poor Alice, she had forgotten that I wouldn't, actually couldn't, run away. I was entrapped not by the hospital so much as by my phobia. I just shook my head.

"I can't leave," I said flatly. "But I could loan you my clothes."

There seemed no point in trying to continue the previous plan to get Alice out of here. The shock therapy had spoiled it all. There was only one other option, and that was for Alice to escape again. I listened to Alice's idea.

"You see, they come out of the hallway door to bring medicine, change shifts, and such. We need to watch and wait. When the nurse comes through he door, one of us will hit her. You hit her ... I'll grab her keys ... or *I'll* hit and *you* grab the keys ...we run down the stairs and get out the back door."

I shook my head. The back door went into the garden, at least, that's what I thought. How could anyone get out of that secured garden?

"Alice, I can't leave. I can loan you my clothes, but I will not hit anyone. I might distract them for you ... but you're on your own with any violence. I can't afford to have trouble now; I'm to be released soon. I can only loan you some clothes."

I warned her about the garden security and worried for Alice's safety. Alice seemed to understand and was grateful for the small help that I could offer.

We walked casually to my room, and I gave Alice a slip and my faded blue dress that I hated to wear anyway. There was no assurance that I would have my belongings returned, even though Alice insisted that she would see that it happened. I was pretending to read in the day room, when Alice emerged with the slip and dress on under her pale green hospital gown. The gown was a little longer than the dress, but from the back anyone could have seen the difference. The gown had three ties and between these were not-so-slight gapes. I was always a little embarrassed for Alice when she wore the gown, as her bra and panties were visible from the back along with her pregnant nakedness. Few people had been there to notice, and Alice had always seemed unconcerned about her lack of privacy. I fastened the ties again for Alice as tightly as I could. The dress was still obvious. Alice sat in the day room, apparently waiting her chance.

The floor nurse took a phone call and then told me that I needed to get my things together, as they were transferring me over to the Annex before dinner. I argued that I wanted to talk with Dr. Ashford first, but to no avail.

"It has already been arranged," said the nurse with finality.

I packed up my few belongings, and a nurse from the Annex came to take me to my new quarters. I looked at Alice nervously. I wondered when Alice would try to make her move. Alice just looked back, divulging nothing in her stares at the nurses and me. Maybe Alice thought that two nurses were too much, and she was waiting till she was alone with one small and rather weak one. I hoped that it would not be Vera.

The nurse and I exited through the men's ward and went on to the elevator, out the main door, and started to the Annex. This would not have been a good way for Alice to try her escape; too many junctures and staff members along the way. But the fence was in the other direction, that tall hulking fence with the wicked barbed wire. I had been hesitant to say goodbye to Alice, as I was afraid that in calling attention to my friend, the nurses might notice the obvious dress bulging under the usually thin and revealing green gown.

Chapter Twenty-Nine
The Annex

The nurse took me down the locked elevator and onto the street. The outside world appeared strange. It was brighter and clearer than I remembered, almost as if it were being viewed through a new eyeglass prescription. It was comforting to have a nurse at my elbow, and I wondered if I would have had the courage to walk to the Annex on my own. The nurse was, as most of the staff, business-like and disinterested. It occurred to me to begin a conversation, and then I wondered why it had not occurred to my keeper. I walked quickly, to keep up the pace being set by the nurse, and I was busy breathing in the outside and noticing how blue the sky was and how green the trees. The sounds from the traffic were almost piercing, and even the movement of the leaves was a little startling. Colors and sounds seemed more intense in my freedom than ever they did in the closed-off garden.

The Annex was across the street and into the middle of the next block. I remembered this from my last year's lockup. I looked anxiously for the old, white, wooden, three-story house that looked as if it had been on loan from a movie set. It had been set back into a large yard with many lovely trees. It had been badly in need of paint but such character! There was a porch that surrounded three sides and a wooden railing that spanned the entire porch. The main floor had a living room and a dining room, and areas converted into a medicine storage and a nursing station. There was still enough house left for a bath and a couple of patient rooms on the main floor. The second floor had only patients' quarters. The third floor was used for the housing of several orderlies. This had puzzled me. I wondered if they needed to be housed at the hospital for emergencies, if they were students of some kind, or if their room and board were part of their pay. They did take meals with the patients, even when they were not on duty.

I looked now for the familiar old house like searching for an old friend. I didn't see it, and the nurse was turning into a walkway beside an apartment building, lodged between several large private homes.

"What is this?" I asked in alarm.

"The Annex," the nurse stated automatically.

"But I was here last year, and I remember that it was a large, old white house." I was wondering if I had lost more of my senses.

The nurse smiled and chuckled slightly, pleased that she could be informative. "That was the *old* Annex. It has been torn down and replaced by our new building. So, you were here last year?'

"Yes." I tried to hide my embarrassment. I had vowed not to let anyone else know that I was a repeater. The staff seemed to hold "repeaters" in even more disdain than the new entries. I didn't say anything more, and the short conversation remained dead.

The "improvement" was much colder than the old house, which had so much distinction. This building was almost hidden from passers-by. Perhaps that was the intent. It was placed lengthwise back into the lot, and its flat modern surfaces were also white but made of cement. There was a short stairway at the side that entered a nondescript doorway. Windows that could have graced the long sides of the building were too small, square, and totally unimaginative. The front of the building was quite narrow and had no windows.

"Ugly!" I thought. "I hope this isn't Dr. Ashford's taste. It's so cold and clinical. It could even pass for a very low-rent apartment building."

Inside, it appeared more like a cheap college dormitory. There was an elevator right inside that accessed the garden-level cafeteria and kitchen, which were on the lowest level. On the main level, right inside the doorway, was a long counter, behind which was a nurses' office and a nursing station. To the right, at the front of the building, was a large day room. A big picture window at the end would have been nice here. But the windows were, instead, on both sides of the room, which was decorated in drab masculine stripes with tans, oranges, and browns. The sun, from the windows, was the only accessory that added a note of cheerfulness. Upstairs, on the second, third, and fourth floors were single and double patient rooms each with its own bath.

Checking in was very unceremonious. We just stopped briefly at the desk. It was strange how the keepers felt that mental inmates do not deserve any introduction. My name was stated as if I were not really present, and the nurse at the counter nodded and busily checked a chart, and then told her colleague a room number. The nurse helped me find my room on the second floor, told me when dinner was served in the cafeteria, and then left. It felt so odd to be standing there, with no one watching and the doors all unlocked. I took my small suitcase and went into my room to settle in. This was pure luxury for me! I had my own room, as no one had been assigned to the other bed, and the bathroom was mine, all mine.

I went to the hall and looked—no one there. I peered into the bathroom—*my* bathroom. No one! With outstretched arms and palms open, I swung about the narrow room, chuckling ever so softly, just in case someone could hear. I hung my few clothes in my side of the long closet that reached all the way across one end of the room. I walked in and out of the bathroom several times, caressing the sink and the tub edges with my fingers and smiling at myself in the mirror. My own place!

My own place *in a mental hospital*. My smile dissolved. I looked into the empty hallway again. I had no watch and wouldn't know when to go to dinner. Everything was too quiet and too empty. An odd feeling of being alone and unsafe stole over me. Shouldn't I be guarded or at least watched occasionally? I had an urgency to feel more a part of something, to not be in such strange isolation. I pushed the button for the elevator and was relieved to find another patient inside. Perhaps the lack of concern for the patients was really a positive, deliberate thing to help them learn to fend for themselves, to show a little independence, figure things out, be sociable. A nice try but not true for the staff I knew.

On the main floor, I went in and sat down, looking hesitantly around me. All the ladies there were occupied either in conversation or at card tables with puzzles or games. What a change! Patients were actually entertaining themselves. I watched and listened. They were conversing, even quite normally. The nurse remained in the reception area and no staff was there to observe, chart, or harass the patients. The group increased as dinnertime neared, and I was approached by a pleasant lady in her thirties who introduced herself, and a friend with her, to me. They asked me to join them in the cafeteria for dinner.

In the elevator, on the way down, they continued to ask questions to get acquainted.

"So, are you married? Do you have any children?" the one lady asked.

I said that I had. I had two.

"You look so young!" the woman said. "Doesn't she look too young, Barbara?"

"She is just a baby herself. Doesn't even look old enough to be married, much less have children!" agreed Barbara, who felt a good deal older.

I smiled. I had supposed that the trauma of this stay would have aged me beyond recognition. Another short, older lady was scowling at me. She was obviously annoyed by me for some reason, and this made me feel uneasy and eager to alight from the elevator.

Nevertheless, I couldn't help smiling. This was such a nice change to be free to be acting on one's own. The smile turned into chuckles. Everything pleased me—getting my own tray, selecting my own portions, being treated normally by fellow humans. And especially no one watching—the continual, *suspicious* watching.

The ladies with me were smiling and pleasant, and seemed very impressed with me. They had come from out of town and were having regular consultations with their doctors. Based on my last few weeks of experience, these women seemed relatively sane. I wondered if they weren't there following a current fad looking more deeply into themselves, discovering a better self. They were dressed as if they might have the financial ability to pursue that. While the three ladies were making jokes about dinner and selecting food in the line, the disgusted lady from the elevator was watching us all and appearing to become angrier and angrier with me.

I learned that the life of this lady, too, was not a happy one. She had no family left but a sister, with whom she did not get along. Numerous bouts of depression had made her less and less pleased with what life had given to her. She had never married and envied her friend and her sister, both of whom had married. Life had passed this woman by. She certainly would not have her family now.

Looking at me, she might have thought that I did look too young to have a family. And since I was laughing, appearing to enjoy my stay here, she might also have thought I wasn't concerned about them. As we all turned to seek a table, the old lady lashed out at me. "So, you're off enjoying *yourself*. What about your children? You just ran off and left them?"

Stunned, I responded with an air of flippancy. "You don't have to run off ... if you wait long enough, and get crazy enough, someone will come and throw a net over you and *take* you away."

"You make me sick," the old lady said, amid the rather self-conscious chuckling of those within earshot. She took herself to a table as far from me as she could get. She seemed to feel I had embarrassed her. She probably thought, "The stupid girl deserves to be here."

I was a little embarrassed, as I realized that the patients here were not completely shocked out of their social sensibilities and that cordial niceties were well accepted, even expected. I looked about and spotted Thelma at the far side of the small cafeteria. I caught Thelma's eye and smiled. Thelma returned a smile, but it was difficult to tell if it contained recognition or just a pleasant response to friendliness.

Most of the dinner group reassembled into the day room upstairs while a few patients went directly to their rooms. I looked about anxiously for Thelma. She was standing near the counter and was exchanging messages with the nurse on duty. I walked over and called her name. Thelma's green eyes were again twinkling with a hidden knowledge that was, at the same time, both appealing and disconcerting, though it was still difficult to tell if Thelma really knew me.

"You look great! How have you been?" I said

Thelma's confident-appearing smile was impenetrable. "Fine! You look good yourself. Want to sit in here and talk?" Thelma said.

"Sure! How long have you been here ... I mean, at the Annex?" I pursued.

"Not very long ... a few days anyway. I don't know. You know how it is here," Thelma said, with a continued pleasant, yet nondisclosing, partial smile.

"I heard that you had come over here. I hoped I would see you again, before you went home," I tried again ... a little more daringly.

"Well, you did. It's good to see you, too. That other building is really something ... isn't it? Did you have treatments?"

Thelma's conversation seemed a little forced, and I was almost sure that she didn't know me. Then a strange squint came into Thelma's eyes, and her smile broadened. "Oh yes, *you* have my doctor also. You met my parents. We were together over there with that awful Penny. Do you remember her? I *detested* Penny!"

"Yes! ... Me too." I smiled with relief and excitement. She actually remembered at least some things! They hadn't blown her brain completely.

Thelma was very excited, also. The two of us had been almost like sisters to each other in this awful place. She couldn't remember my name but she remembered that we thought alike, had the same likes and dislikes. There was something about high school. Did we go to school together? Anyway, she remembered that we were friends and that I could be trusted, but my name ... she could not recall my name. She would listen and find out.

It was a while before anyone said my name, and it was when the nurse came to announce to both of us that Dr. Ashford wanted to see us.

Down the hall, a short way from the counter was a small conference room where the doctor visited with us, talking with Thelma first. When she emerged from the room with him, both were smiling as I started toward them to take my turn. In passing, Thelma said softly, "Still red." This indication that their relationship was still intact was also a little upsetting. Did it mean that Thelma was still obsessed with color meanings? Was this just her way of laughing off the past? I did not mention the comment to Dr. Ashford. He was pleased that we had remembered each other and we were getting along so well. It seemed to him a good idea for both of us.

In the conference room, Dr. Ashford looked intently at me. He is trying to read my mind, I thought, uncomfortably. He smiled a little, realizing that he had intimidated me.

"You are going to stay here only a few more days. But you have some work to do. You have to get out ... outside. I want you to walk ... around the neighborhood. I also want you to take a couple of trips home and back, before I release you. You have to be able to get around better. You are going to need to come to see me. Do you understand? You need to get to my office when you get out."

He watched my face and saw the expected anxiety well up in my eyes. The thought of walks was a little scary, the drives home a little scarier. *But* trips to his office? I hoped that the treatments had done *that much* for me. I nodded my intention to follow his directives, and he continued with how he would pass this information on to Martin and talk with me again in a day or so.

* * *

Dr. Ashford was unpredictable. He came at different times to visit. Margaret had said that he could tell more about the patients if he saw them in different situations, and at different times. Dr. Ashford got to the hospital when he could, when he had time, and when his lungs were not distressing him too much. In the past, he was accustomed to visiting daily, but now, this was not always possible. Often he would call and check on his patients by phone. He was a very concerned doctor and had even taken on a young partner, and briefed him on all of his current patients. He had mentioned a "possible retirement" to the young man but had not shared the knowledge of the cancer that was encroaching.

* * *

Annex patients made good use of their day room. There was actual television viewing going on, and a number of ladies involved themselves in regular games of Scrabble, including a very large lady who came from across the state to visit daily, for a period of several weeks, with her doctor. Thelma and I wondered why she didn't get a doctor closer to home, and the nurses seemed to have a secret about her. The large lady's name was Arlene. She was mammoth. Her broad shoulders attempted to help camouflage enormous breasts and wide hips. Her thighs and legs were heavy also and were supported by thick ankles and wide feet. She was wearing shoes with only a stub of a high heel. She was not really fat, just heavy, sturdy, and large. She was taller than most everyone there, and her vastness was not held in just her physical being, but in the personal dominance that she exercised over the patients and staff. She loved Scrabble. It was hers. She won every time, and the other ladies either didn't mind or thought that it was hers to win and that they would help her. Thelma and I watched her, and the group that she dominated, while we sat nearby and caught up on our time apart. I pointed out the angry old lady who wanted me to be home taking care of my kids. She was doing a jigsaw puzzle at a corner table with another grumpy person. Several groups of ladies came and went. Four ladies came in and described their excursion to a local cinema, and a few patients returned with friends or family, from the evening out.

"It's much like a boarding house, or college dorm ... only with a nurse in charge." I decided.

"I guess so. I hadn't really thought of it that positively. But it *is* much better than that awful main building," agreed Thelma.

A nurse from the main building came in, walked across the day room, and stood directly above me. She was holding my old blue dress and my slip.

"Are these yours?" she asked, knowing the answer.

I nodded and reached to take them.

"Alice had them," the nurse said accusingly.

Silence.

"How did Alice get them?" the nurse asked, coldly.

"I really don't know," I said, feigning confusion and disbelief. "I didn't miss them. I was on her floor. Perhaps ..."

"I know you were ... I can't believe you didn't know. She could have been badly harmed. You should be ashamed," the nurse admonished and then walked away to talk to the nurse at the desk.

"I'm *not* ashamed," I said, in annoyance to Thelma. "They are the ones who should be ashamed. They were giving Alice shock therapy and she ... "

I looked at Thelma. I wanted to tell her the whole story, but I didn't know about Thelma's thinking processes. She *must* be all right, I thought. She's at the Annex now. They all seemed all right over here. But I stopped, remembering the cigarette story.

"Oh, you know how the staff over there can be," I finished innocuously.

Later, when Thelma's mother came to visit, Thelma asked me to accompany them upstairs so that she could show me which room was hers. Thelma was on the fourth floor, near the front of the building. She had a double room and was the only occupant.

Thelma opened the long closet and exposed more clothes than I had ever owned. They were all neatly pressed and hung. They were many beautiful colors, except for red. There were dresses, pantsuits, robes, gowns, a veritable feast for my eyes. Thelma's mother had brought more clothes. It seemed that this is what this mother did best. I self-consciously excused myself, promising to come back up and visit before bed.

I got the very slightest bit of a thrill in calling for the elevator by myself and riding all the way down alone. In the day room I found Scott. He was circulating about and entertaining the ladies. This job seemed to suit him well. The patients liked him and he enjoyed their attention. He looked up when I entered, and then ushered me over to the corner to talk. I commented on how Scott appeared to be in his element here, interacting with patients, and yet apparently, observing, evaluating ...

"You really like your job, don't you? No one else around here seems that concerned," I complimented.

"Well, I'm studying ... *here*, too." he smiled. "You did know that I was in school ... part time?"

"Yeah ... I heard you were working on your pre-med degree."

"Well, I graduated in a related field ... biology ... but I really want to be a doctor, so ... I'm working on it."

"What area of medicine? Have you decided?"

"Psychiatry ... that's why I say I'm *studying* here."

"That explains your positive interest ... and I *would* say 'compassion' but that does not appear to be a quality necessary in your field. Or, perhaps they all start with it ... and lose it later? What do you think?"

"Oh, Laurel, you find that in every profession, ... some dedicated, some compassionate in their service, and those who are just in it for money, prestige, and whatever other interests they may have. Also, seeing so much and not being able to help, does make some of them cynical. Someday, I hope to make a difference ... find some new ... better ... approaches ... procedures ... I'm still an idealist."

I nodded as I looked at him. "One of the *few* ... but it's nice to have *you* around.... So much of this ... treatment here seems so hit and miss. I know *I'm* getting cynical."

Scott looked a little concerned and then changed the conversation abruptly.

"Did you hear about Alice?" He looked at me very seriously.

My heart jumped. "Is she all right?" I asked anxiously.

"Yes, but I'm surprised." He was watching my expression. "Did you give her your clothes?" he questioned, a little casually.

"Well, she had them," I answered cautiously.

Scott smiled his acceptance of my vague answer.

"She got out. She actually got out ... *and* all the way home."

I was too delighted to cover my feelings. "All the way home!" I marveled.

"Yes. She got some keys away from a nurse, and got out to the backyard. She climbed over that damned tall fence. It has barbed wire on the top, you know."

I nodded, still smiling.

"An eight-foot fence ...with barbed wire! How ... "

"I *knew* she could do it ... she was so determined!" I interrupted him, enthusiastically.

"Did she tell you she was going to?" There was concern in his voice.

"She said she *wanted* to," I corrected. "Did they bring her back?"

"Of course," Scott was frowning. "What else are they going to do with her?"

"Well, certainly not give her electric shocks ... when she's pregnant."

"Yeah, I'm not sure that's such a good idea. But she's back safely on Second. Her husband was sure surprised when she showed up at the door ... it was night. I guess he had a hard time convincing her to come back. They had to send the ambulance for her ... she had to be sedated."

"She wanted to talk to her plastic surgeon," I volunteered, trying to find out more.

"I guess she did make a few calls." Scott acknowledged with a smile.

At least *she* got through, I thought, remembering Marilyn's failed phone calls. So strange. I could only help others who were desperate to escape. I was too afraid to go myself. And they even had to *force me* to leave. I tried to imagine forcing myself to get home by myself.

The next evening after work, Martin came to take me for a drive home. According to regulations, you had to sign a sheet at the desk, stating your designation and expected return time. My handwriting was shaky, just like the tremor that ran from the back of my neck all the way to the base of my spine. I had gone back upstairs to get a sweater, even though it was an extremely warm evening. Beside my name, under "destination" I had written, "moon." Martin had to check everything that I did, as always, and he frowned at my notation.

"Well, it feels that way to *me*," I said, defensively.

He wrote in "home" *for* me and escorted me out the door.

It was already starting to get dark, which was a relief to me. Earlier in the afternoon I had tried to take my walk and had walked with hesitant steps all the way to the main building, with no one at my side. I had felt strange, unreal, and a little nervous. I walked all the way to the end of the block and turned, feeling the anxiety start to build, and then walked, a little more rapidly, back the block and a half to the Annex. My breathing had become quite shallow, and I took in a large breath in relief as I stepped onto the walk belonging to my building. Tomorrow I would walk further, several blocks, maybe even around a block.

I got in the car with Martin and sat stiffly very near to the window. He was talking about work and the traffic, and I wasn't listening. I asked him to turn some music on the car radio, feeling the need for distraction. Martin obliged and even hummed along for a little time. He seemed totally unaware of any discomfort that I might feel. I was determined that I would show him how easy this was, how "well" I had become. I relaxed back into the seat and even smiled. After a couple of miles, while we were still in the residential area, I began talking a bit. Martin lowered the radio, and our rather stiff conversation continued. At a red light, I felt my body tense in anticipation of the old fear. It didn't come. I relaxed again. Things went pretty well until we neared the tall apartment area on the fringe of the downtown district. There were more cars on the streets here. I took a few deep breaths as the anxiety started to seep into my thoughts.

"Just stay calm," I told myself. "You are fine. This is no problem. You will be home before you know it." Aloud, I said in a tiny voice. "Martin, I'm having some trouble, the buildings ... they are too tall ... I'm getting nervous."

The traffic was increasing and the city lights were beginning to come up and outline the enormous structures ahead.

"You're fine," Martin said, not hiding his impatience very well. "Just don't look at them. Look down at the floor. You're doing okay."

I breathed deeply, curled my toes, and stared at the floor.

"Hurry!" I pleaded weakly.

The car jerked to a quick stop. Martin hadn't been watching closely and almost missed a red light. The abrupt stop caused me to glance up suddenly. We were right at the main intersection of the downtown area where the two major streets crossed. Up in front of the car loomed several of the city's tallest buildings.

"Oh, my God!" I whimpered. "I can't do this. Get me out of *here*. Take me back." My anxiety had grown into near panic.

"Shhh! You'll be all right. We'll be out of here in a few minutes. Relax!" Martin's impatience was quickly turning to anger. The anger made my emergent panic swell into terror. I clutched my arm and dug my nails into the soft underside to still the fear. I started to cry more audibly and then began pleading.

"Please ...take me out of here ... *Now* ... take me back. I *need* to go back!"

I was now sobbing, clenching my toes, digging my arm, and scooting up into my old fetal position on the seat. My thoughts were racing uncontrolled and incomplete.

"All right, damn it ... We're *going* back ... just let me turn the damn car around.... Damn it!"

Martin turned at the next light and headed back to the hospital. I was able to breathe a little more easily after the traffic was gone and the lights were no longer defining the tall buildings. I took several breaths. Martin glanced sidelong at me, not even trying to hide the disgust on his face When I could think clearly again, I realized the consequences. I had to get home or the doctor wouldn't release me. Hadn't the treatments worked? They had. I *felt* that I had changed, but here was the old fear again. I looked at Martin. He was frowning and intent on his driving.

"Maybe we should try again?" I asked hesitantly. "Maybe go a different route?"

I didn't want the failure there.

"Hell, it's too late now. We'll have to wait till tomorrow. We don't have time. I have to get you back."

He didn't talk to me all the way back to the hospital. When I asked if he was angry, he reassured me that it was just disappointment. I didn't believe that *his* disappointment could come near to measuring up to my own.

Chapter Thirty
Practicing Home

Determined to conquer my fear of getting about, I began with a walk right after breakfast. I did not see Thelma in the cafeteria, but I had learned that not everyone got up for breakfast. I had spent very little time with Thelma the night before; I wasn't feeling very sociable after failing my trip home. I had gone to my room, soaked in a bubble bath to soothe my despair, and then lain awake for hours, worrying about preparing to go home and face life. It seemed that my major problem was coping with my fear and since I felt stronger than when I had come, I must practice doing whatever was still giving me some discomfort and overcome it.

Using OT as an excuse to take a very short walk, I stopped in briefly at the main building to get something to do. The walk over was a little easier, but hovering in the back of my thoughts was the memory of the looming buildings downtown. I was pleasant, almost friendly to the therapist in the shop to her surprise as she was so accustomed to my badgering or taunting her. The therapist responded in kind but was a little suspicious. I looked over some embroidery and finally selected a dresser scarf. On leaving OT, I felt a sudden flurry of sadness at the past month and my puzzlement over what had occurred on my drive with Martin. Tears crept into my eyes, and I headed toward the restroom to relieve the sadness in private. With head lowered, I bumped into Dr. Jennings.

"Hi!" he said, startled by my running into him. "Are you okay, Laurel? Is there anything wrong?"

"I'll be all right. Just bring on the lobotomy!" My forced cynicism pushed back the tears.

"Things can't be all that bad. You mean, you didn't like our treatments?" He tried to joke with me.

"Well, I'm supposed to go home soon ... and I'm sure not ready. If the insulin therapy didn't work ... I thought maybe a lobotomy could be done, as sort of a last resort. Do you do those, too?"

I pinched my fingernails into the palm of my hand to stop the tears that were building again.

"Come in here for a minute ... can you? We need to talk."

Dr. Jennings led me into the conference room a few doors away. It was very uncomfortable for me to tell him much. Our relationship had been one of casual joking, and I did not see him as very supportive of the patients' emotional needs, just businesslike and amusing from time to time about the hospital humor. I eyed him cautiously when he asked why I was so upset. I explained that I didn't want to go home. I was afraid of having to turn around and come right back, and I surely would never want those horrible treatments again. I told him briefly about not getting home the previous night, and my fear that I was not "cured." And then my recurring doubts that Dr. Ashford would not send me home, that he would not feel "finished " with me and would detain me longer.

Dr. Jennings studied me carefully. I think it was difficult for him to understand how I could be so naive, and at the same time so cleverly cynical. I didn't realize that insurance and money were the main factors in how long a patient stayed here. There was no way that my doctor would repeat the treatments. Most medical policies stipulated a thirty-day hospitalization as a maximum. I had not learned this as yet. And Dr. Jennings no doubt wondered why I was still laboring under the illusion that the treatments could "cure" patients. He probably thought he needed to clarify some of this and yet not interfere with what Dr. Ashford might have said or implied.

"Laurel, you will not be given any more insulin. You are considerably improved ... look how well you've been doing. You will need to follow Dr. Ashford's orders *precisely* when you get out. I'm sure, while everything is not perfect now, that you will continue to improve. You will not have any more insulin therapy."

This he could count on, as I had no financial ability! He said he hoped that my doctor had recommended therapy sessions but money, again, could be a problem. "Things will work out fine for you, I'm sure." (I don't believe he was sure, I *had* been here before but he seemed to be trying to appear confident.)

I tried to smile. "I'm just so afraid that it won't. I don't want to come back again and again ... like some of the patients that I've seen here."

"You won't be back," he assured me. This was true, at least for a year, until insurance claims could again be effective. He put his hand on my shoulder, and told me to discuss this fear with Dr. Ashford. Then, to lift my spirits, he changed the tenor of the conversation with, "Hey, you remember Madelyn .. the Lady from Wyoming ... the one from insulin ... how she screamed during treatment?"

"Yeah," I smiled.

"Well, one day ... her last treatment ... she was sitting up and screaming, as usual, and ... you know how patients are not supposed to hear you when they're in coma?" I nodded. "Well, I said, 'Lie down, Madelyn! Be still!' and she just plunked down suddenly on her cot ... and with her eyes wide open and said, 'Okay.' ... But they're not supposed to be able to communicate!" he explained again.

"That's hysterical!" I laughed appreciatively, but underneath I felt a tinge of anger that sport was being made of someone in that condition. Just as they had done with me when I was coming out of unconsciousness. They had never explained why I was so funny to them. The picture in my mind of the situation was both funny *and* pathetic.

I thanked him for taking time to talk with me and tried to smile as he reminded me again to talk with Dr. Ashford. Talking *with* Dr. Ashford was not so easy, I mused. He talked *to* you and didn't expect discussion. He frightened me almost as much as he did Thelma.

I decided that, rather than to go directly back to the Annex, I would practice getting around more. I headed the opposite direction from the hospital with the intent of circling the block. I walked to the end of the block, hesitated, and looked back down the street toward the Annex. The Annex was not actually in my view, but I could see its general location. I made the decision that walking in a straight line would be better for "early" practice, as I could still look back and see the hospital, and know that the Annex was just beyond; it would be hidden from me by the large trees on the other side of the block.

I got to the second corner with some difficulty. I was breathing shallowly and feeling dizzy. I turned at the corner, took a deep breath, and tried to walk slowly the two and a half blocks to the Annex. The hospital in between gave me some security. As I neared my destination, I picked up my pace so that I was walking very rapidly by the time I was in front of the Annex. I assessed my attempt as encouraging but certainly not great.

My work warranted me a rest, I thought, as I headed on up to my room. On the elevator was a nurse with a very young patient. The girl was just a teenager. She was being encouraged by the nurse to stay calm. The nurse reminded the girl how she had not had "any problems" now for a week. I got off the elevator wondering what her "problems" were.

* * *

Dr. Ashford made an appointment for Thelma at the Annex and one with Laurel at the main building. He wanted to be assured that Laurel did at least this small walk today although, ironically, the walk was too much for him. Today his weakness was apparently overtaking him. he would meet Laurel, go to the parking lot, and then drive the half block to meet with Thelma. No one would notice. He would not have to explain this lack of energy. They probably wouldn't pay that much attention to what he was doing or where his car was parked. It was also hard for Laurel to get from one building to the other, he reminded himself. He was inhibited with pain and physical weakness, she with fear and emotional weakness. He felt he could empathize with her.

* * *

I was almost happy to turn around and make another trip to the Annex, as I wanted more practice. In fact, I felt compulsive about making more trials. This trip was almost easy. My mind had been distracted by thoughts of what I could tell Dr. Ashford about my drive with Martin. How I could make excuses for myself and my failure. I really wanted his approval and felt a strong need to please him. I hardly noticed the small amount of anxiety that grew on my way down the street. I did notice Dr. Ashford's car in the parking lot. I was feeling a little more confident when I entered the conference room where he was waiting. He rose politely and offered me a chair opposite him.

"Well, how did it go?" he asked directly.

I squirmed a little in my chair.

"I didn't make it," I said a little above a whisper and feeling like a disobedient child.

"What do you mean, you didn't make it?" His voice seemed angry and almost thundering. "Tell me what went wrong."

I tried to sound more adult, and held back my tears. "I was doing fair .. some ... a little ... nervousness ... but okay. ... until we got to Main and Broadway. I don't know what happened ... I'm sorry! I just freaked out."

Dr. Ashford's face turned a very deep red, and his voice *did* thunder. "What in hell were you doing *there?*" he demanded, not even trying to hide his displeasure.

"Trying to get home," I pleaded pathetically.

"Not *that* way. Damn it! You were not to go *that* way! I told that son-of-a-bitch to skirt the business district. He was supposed to go *around* that part of town. Damn it! I'll call him. *You* tell him to take you around the downtown area. You should have known that yourself. Try it again tonight ... the *right* way. You both should have better sense."

He got up from the chair and began some coughing. He was too incensed at not having been obeyed to even try to continue a conversation with me. He reminded me to walk around the neighborhood as I made my frightened exit from the room.

* * *

His anger and swearing had diminished by the time he reached Martin on the phone. But he was emphatic and annoyed, and let Martin know that he was aggravated by not having his directions followed, and by Martin's insensitivity to the problem and his lack of support in corrective efforts.

His small amount of energy was spent when he finally finished his business at the main building and drove over to the Annex. He pulled up in front of the Annex, thinking about Thelma. He wished that Laurel could

give him information about *Thelma*, as she had before. But he knew that
Thelma was more suspicious of everyone now and was, most probably, not
confiding in Laurel. And, too, Laurel had seemed more frightened of him
and less trusting she probably would not tell all she knew.

When he met with *Thelma*, he saw that she was wearing her "clever"
smile that covered her devious thoughts, and he noted that she talked only
of casual subjects without her divulging any of her inner concerns. Not
only had *Thelma* not mentioned her boyfriend, Gary, for a number of visits
now, she said only pleasant things about her parents. He knew he needed to
break through her defenses, but he was so tired. When *Thelma* asked him
about her going out, he responded that it was fine with him if she left the
hospital but he needed to know where she was going. *Thelma* looked at him
suspiciously

"You're not having me watched, are you?" she asked, her eyes narrow-
ing.

"No. Why would I want to do that?" he questioned, watching her eyes
carefully.

"You know that my parents did that ... before I came in here." She was
frowning slightly.

Dr. Ashford muffled a cough. "Damn it," he thought, "these lungs are
giving out at the most inopportune times." His face was reddening.

"I haven't any reason to have you watched. And I have no way to do
it, even if I so desired," he said, a little hoarsely. "You and I need to trust
each other." He looked at her intently. He had meant to instill in her some
confidence in him, but he did not know about "red." She looked skeptical.

"Well, I do trust some people, but not the nurses or the orderlies here.
Not my parents. I hope that you are on my side. I need to trust somebody.
And I need to get out of here."

"Soon," he replied and shortened their session because of his pain. He
thought *Thelma* seemed calmed and much improved. She was smiling more
... and was friendly with Laurel. That had made him feel positive.

* * *

Thelma felt secretive. She had noticed the red, and red was bothering
her again. Her father did not visit anymore, but her mother had given

her a message from him, and it had seemed cryptic. She wanted to ask Dr. Ashford about the message ... but there was the red. She decided that it could wait. She would try to find out more from her mother. Maybe even see if Laurel knew something. Dr. Ashford and she walked to the center hall, where the doctor went out the exit, and Thelma looked about for Laurel.

* * *

"What do you think about the clothes my mother brought?" Thelma asked me.

"I think they are lovely. All of your clothes are nice. Don't you think that she is being very helpful to bring them?" I was curious about such a strange question. It sounded like the old Thelma, and this kind of talk and her "clever" eyes made me uneasy.

"Oh yes, she is very helpful. I just wondered if you saw anything strange about that one dress ... the yellow one?"

"I really didn't get a good look at it. Why? What did you think was wrong?"

"Oh, I just thought it might be *his* idea. My dad's I mean. Yellow ... and then his message ... oh, never mind. Do you ever go out to shop or anything?" Thelma carefully changed the subject, and I reminded her that I had problems with traveling about.

"It's all I can do to get my 'practices' in for walking and going on home trips. But I did hear several of the ladies talk about shopping, and I know of three who are going to a movie today ... if you're wanting some company," I offered.

"Maybe another day. It's really not that important," smiled Thelma.

Chapter Thirty-One
Losing Thelma Again

I noticed the "sly" smile was appearing more and more frequently on Thelma's face. That night I went up to Thelma's room a few minutes before dinner. We had become accustomed to going to the cafeteria together, and Thelma had not yet come to the main floor. Thelma's floor was almost empty of patient residents, except for Thelma and one lady at the other end of the hall. I heard stifled sobs and some rustling sounds, as I stepped from the elevator and started down the hall. Thelma's door was partially ajar, and I could see Thelma's arms flying about. I rushed in.

"Are you okay? ...What's wrong? ...Thelma, what are you doing?" I said on entering.

Thelma's eyes were red and wet from crying. The sly squint was gone. She stared frantically from bulging, crazed, and flashing eyes. She was sobbing and swearing, words that I could hardly believe were in Thelma's refined vocabulary. In her raised hand was a razor that she carried over to the closet. She slashed a dress still hanging on the hanger. Most of her clothes were thrown about the bed, and it was obvious that the razor had been used on them, too.

"Thelma! Stop!" I demanded loudly. I closed the door and tried to calm Thelma. "Don't do that! You'll only cause problems. Sit down! Talk to me! Put that razor down. We want to be able to get out of this place, remember?"

It was obvious that Thelma was completely out of control. She was not listening, and her violent slashing continued. The swearing intensified, and she ripped several more of her things from the closet. The closet was almost bare, and Thelma went to the bed, and began tearing at her things that were already destroyed. Unable to stop Thelma, and feeling threatened myself, I left the room and hurried down the elevator to the main floor. I was on the verge of hysteria myself, as I tried to report what was happening upstairs, to the nurse at the desk. My voice was shaky, as was my entire body. I felt that I was not making very good sense, as I tried to blurt out what was going on up in Thelma's room. Orderlies were called, and several nurses jumped on the elevator for Thelma's floor. I was too frightened to do anything but go to my own room and lie stiffly, face down on my bed, to avert a panic attack.

When Martin came to take me for the practice drive home, I was still in my room. I related Thelma's plight to Martin, and he seemed genuinely concerned. I had missed dinner but was afraid to ask Martin to stop anywhere, as I wanted this trip to go smoothly. Downstairs, snacks had already been set out for the evening. I grabbed a small carton of milk on our way out.

"We need to go around the downtown area. Dr. Ashford said..." I began, trying to sound assertive.

"I know, he called today and reamed me out," Martin interrupted, irritated. "How the hell was I to know?"

I looked at Martin's expression, trying to decide if he *knew* or not. Dr. Ashford said that he had told Martin before. I needed to trust at least one of them. There was no way to know who was telling the truth. I suspected that Martin had just forgotten since he had so much on his mind, trying to take care of the girls, and get back and forth to the hospital, and still try to do his job, and maybe worry about me, too.

The trip went fairly easily. It was longer than if he had gone the other way, but it was calmer for me. There were a few times when I felt anxious about the distance I had gone and how far it was *back* to the hospital, which I now felt was my "safe" place. We finally arrived and I walked rather hesitantly through the front door. The house looked smaller than I remembered it. I walked carefully about all the rooms trying to reacquaint myself with my own place. It seemed oddly vacant without the children. Everything was clean and neatly in place. Martin always liked things orderly and immaculate. I went to my closet to see if I wanted to take anything back with me. A blouse and pair of slacks was hanging there that were totally foreign to me. My heart seemed to skip, and I felt a sickening dread come over me.

"Martin!" I called, in alarm. He entered the room, a bit annoyed.

"Where did these come from? They're not mine." My voice sounded anxious.

"Yes, they are. You bought them a few weeks before you went to the hospital." He turned and walked out.

I didn't remember buying anything for months before going to the hospital. I had been too upset to shop. When I did have to purchase something, I was only able to shop near the entry and could never go above the ground level; elevators or escalators were out of the question. This made it necessary for me to only buy things that were right inside the doors of the larger stores, and often Martin would have to go to the cash registers to complete the purchase for me. I surely didn't remember putting *that* kind of effort into buying a dumb pair of slacks and a blouse, and I rarely purchased anything for myself. I would *try* to find some new clothes and then feel guilt ridden at my selfishness. I usually ended up finding something for the children instead. Those clothes, no. I didn't think that I would have allowed myself to be so self-indulgent. But then again, maybe I had forgotten more than I even dreamed.

"It doesn't matter," Martin called from the other room. "It'll come back ... probably just effects from your treatments. Don't worry about it."

I did worry about it all the way home ... and on into the night.

Martin had left almost immediately since he had work the next day, but I wanted to see Scott when I returned from my drive back to the hospital. When I saw him, I ran several stories past Scott to get his reaction. I told him about my fears regarding my memory of things at home. He reassured me that it would improve. Then I told him about Thelma's rampage. He had heard. Thelma was now back on Third North and in a locked room, again. She had been hysterical when the orderlies had taken her over, and they had had to administer a hypo. Scott said she was a pretty disturbed young lady, and treatment might take a while for her. I was glad that I hadn't waited to see them take Thelma away.

"They will give her more shock now, won't they?"

"Probably ... They need to calm her."

"How does frying someone's brain make patients better?" I asked. "It just makes them stupid and more pliable. Do the doctors know what it does to people's thinking? I've noticed that it just confuses the patients or makes them forgetful. It also makes them frightened and overly dependent. Do they just want Thelma to do as she is told?"

"Laurel, they just want her to be more rational. If she forgets her obsessions ... then they can talk with her ... and reason with her. You know how strange she gets. What else can they do?" he said.

"It just seems so primitive. Jarring their whole system with electric current, to get them to listen to reason. What happen to trust with this kind of punitive approach?" I responded.

"I guess they assume the patients will accept the treatment as being for their own good ... not as a punishment," Scott said defensively.

"Well ... from my experience ... I would say that is damned hard to do."

"Getting them to be dependent ... that's not bad ... under the circumstances. They are more apt to listen and try to change," Scott continued to give the psychiatric rationale.

"Right! Until they can think again. Then they realize that they're being controlled, and they get angry ... at least I *think* that's what's happening with Thelma," I said, shaking my head. "She's been saying things again that let me know that she's suspicious ... that people can't be trusted. If they keep shocking the hell out of her ... and she stops thinking ... then she gets better and is able to start thinking again ... Well! It will just never end. Is that why everyone keeps coming back here?"

"Just those like Thelma. She needs to work with her doctor, and find the errors in her thinking," Scott said.

"Hell, Scott, she has a right to feel paranoid. Her family *does* try to control her and people are doing things to her. If every time you did something that was not 'approved of' by your family, they plugged you up to the black box ... Well, you would get paranoid, too. She'll think she was shocked for ripping up her expensive clothes from her family rather than because she was irrational and out of control ... I say it's one vicious cycle," I said in frustration.

"Possibly ... for now ... but if the doctor can get her to understand that she has errors in her reasoning ... then they can break it ... the cycle, I mean. *You* don't think that you're being punished, do you? Do the other patients you've known? This is Thelma's confusion," Scott continued.

"I don't know about all of the others. Probably some of them do. How do we know what *they're* thinking? And we're only supposing what Thelma thinks. It just seems that this procedure for Thelma doesn't make sense," I reasoned

Scott shrugged. "You could be right. But it's all they have right now. I've seen a lot of patients improve, leave, and *never* come back. Thelma's case is difficult ... a lot depends on her doctor right now, and Dr. Ashford is one of the best in the business."

"What about Alice?" I countered. "She doesn't think everyone is out to punish her. She *knows* they're trying to stop her from contacting her surgeon. But she's rational enough to know that she's being a problem. Why do they risk her and the baby's health, with their need to zap current through all the patients? They even gave me one of the damned jolts! It seems to me that they're all 'shock happy,'" I said in frustration.

Scott replied, "I don't know why they're doing it to Alice. It's the current—" he paused, "—excuse the pun—accepted method of treatment. By the way, Alice is doing well. She's still on Second North ... and without clothes. But she is calmer and not wearing her Band-aid. Thought you would like to know."

"Any positive news around here is nice. How about visiting Thelma? Would they let me go over?" I asked.

Scott answered, "I'd wait a little while ... till she adjusts to being moved ... ask Dr. Ashford. You seem to be a good influence on her."

Scott seemed impressed that I had been able to make my trip after the previous failure. I was relieved that I hadn't had to tell him about the failure until after I had had some success. At this point, Scott was the only one I felt some trust. I asked about Dr. Ashford.

"Tell me honestly, Scott, is he a *good* doctor? I mean, very reliable ... not senile or anything?"

Scott smiled at my question. "He's fine, probably the best around. He has a great reputation. I think he is kind of a weird duck, but he is certainly competent. Why?"

"I don't know, just remarks that Martin makes. I think Martin doesn't really respect him. Yet he tells *me* to follow his advice. He acted like Ashford knew *everything* when he wanted me to go through 'shock.' Now he seems skeptical … and often hostile and demeaning about him. Said he was 'a senile old fogy.'"

"Maybe Dr. Ashford told Martin something he didn't want to hear," suggested Scott.

"Well, he does scold Martin. He treats us both like stupid little kids. He treats everyone as if they aren't too bright. At least not *his* equal."

"He is a little superior and self-assuming," acknowledged Scott.

Scott went on to me about the teenager with the "problem" who had been on the elevator with me. She had come from a small town several states away. She had severe epileptic seizures and rarely went more than an hour without having an episode. Two members of her family had brought her in a car all the way here, a two-day drive so that she could be seen by Dr. Barnes, who was one of the best known specialists in epilepsy in the *whole* country. He was trying her on some new medicine and giving her counseling. She had gone days, almost a week, without an episode. Scott felt that part of the success came just from removing her from her overbearing family.

Because Scott seemed in such an information-giving mood, I asked him about the large lady of the Scrabble game. We had to talk very softly, as Arlene was at the board in the center of the room with her buddies and, of course, winning the game as we spoke. She came from across the mountains the other side of the state. Her husband was a medical doctor, and she was addicted to drugs. That was why the nurses gave her shots instead of pills. I had noticed that they would call her back into the office when they told her it was time for her medication. Everyone else was just given a little cup with the pills and a small glass with water. I learned that Arlene came into town for treatment about every six months. Scott said she had a lot of difficulty withdrawing from the medicine and that her husband re-addicted her after she went home.

"He's in a lot of trouble now." Scott seemed pleased. "I've heard rumors that Arlene's doctor told her husband that this is the *last* time. If he gets her back on the substance again, her psychiatrist will report him for malpractice and illegal drug usage. See, Laurel, there's a lot of reasons why different patients keep returning. It's not that we never really help them here!"

We both looked up as Arlene had risen to go back with the nurse for her "shot," almost as timely proof of Scott's story.

"You know she always wins the stupid game," I commented.

"Let's go play with them and see how she does it," suggested Scott impishly.

The ladies were happy to have Scott join them and agreeable to teaching me, since I didn't know how to play. After two games the group broke up to retire for the night. Arlene had won both games.

"She's just very bright!" I said.

Scott agreed.

"But, I'm going to beat her ... I don't like to see how very self-satisfied she appears. It's a matter of principle," I vowed.

Chapter Thirty-Two
Final Words

The last few days of my hospitalization were occupied with walks to the Main Building. I visited Thelma and practiced moving about more. I spent most evenings making trips home.

The trips home were encouraging. My first failed attempt was followed by the successful one, which was taken after dark. It was easier to block out the reality of the experience at night. Since I made my initial success with the added assistance of darkness, it was time to move to the next step—daylight. Dr. Ashford had told Martin to come earlier, and Martin had reluctantly changed his routine to enable me to get several days of practices in during the earlier evening hours. Martin continued to skirt the downtown, at Dr. Ashford's insistence and to his own annoyance. The trips were getting easier—they even seemed shorter to me—and I was beginning to feel more confident about traveling in the daylight.

The second time I was home several of the neighbors dropped in for a very short visit, just to let me know they had missed me and were glad that I would be coming home in a few days. This acceptance and support helped me to feel more "normal"; they treated me as if nothing had changed, and I was still an ordinary member of their neighborhood. It felt good after feeling so crazy being in a mental hospital and needing a psychiatrist.

Even Martin was acting a little more positive. He was talking about things that would be happening—a neighborhood barbecue, a brother's birthday party, fixing the swing set for the kids, and acting as though our troubles were over. Martin was even talking to me a little more on the trips to and from the hospital. I told him little about my experiences at the Annex and about Thelma. I kept our time together focused on the days ahead. I covered any anxiety that I had during the drives so Martin would feel that everything was going very well.

I also started trying to separate myself from the hospital. I didn't want to continue to feel that this was my safe place. I talked less to all the patients, except for Thelma and the Scrabble Group.

Since I had vowed to beat Arlene at her own game, I had to make good on my threat. I got better each time I played, and my scores were gaining on Arlene's. I watched carefully and noticed the strategic placement of letters to get the maximum points; I saw that adding to others' words was even more important than a knowledge of vocabulary.

After a few days I won! It felt great but I noticed that Arlene was very distressed. This was Arlene's own private accomplishment, and she didn't want it taken from her. More than disappointed, though, she seemed mortified. Her whole well-being appeared to be tangled up with the winning of the Game. I began to feel that I had done a bad thing. That I had humiliated Arlene and struck her a fatal blow. There was no way to apologize, and besides, hadn't Arlene been almost cruel with her victories over the others?

I tried to put it out of my mind, but Arlene looked at me as if she felt betrayed. She avoided me at meals and didn't even try to hide her unfriendliness in the day room. Maybe this was her way of stopping me from playing again. Scott thought so.

I decided I had to beat her one more time just to prove to myself that it had really been a victory and not just a one-time fluke. Then, I thought, I can let her win again and regain her lost prestige. Scott was amused that I was so concerned about Arlene's confidence, when my own was suffering so.

I watched Arlene carefully to verify the drug stories that Scott had told. She did seem to get very uncomfortable, to sweat and get shaky just before disappearing into the nurses' station to get her shot. Even her eyes seemed to change. Once I was in the nursing area and witnessed the injection. The large otherwise overpowering woman seemed almost helpless and very dependent toward the nurse. The nurse was very supportive of Arlene and reassured her that she would be all right in a couple of minutes and just to "hang-on." Then, within a few moments, Arlene would be back at Her Game, where she was the paragon of power. I wondered about her relationship with her doctor husband. Husbands and their relationships seemed an unmistakable aspect of the women's incapacities in this place, and I pondered about Martha, Alice, Mickey, and the Elegant Ladies of Third South.

As soon as I could I went to the Main Building to visit Thelma. She was on Third North in the area just outside the locked rooms. She had been in the locked rooms for a day until she was under control. She didn't remember the hypo. She did know that she had destroyed her clothing. She had been told this, but she didn't know *why* she had done it. I was unable to tell her when she asked.

"I think you just were very upset and angry, and you 'fell apart.' We all do incomprehensible things when we are terribly distressed," I said.

Thelma agreed that she was very distressed but did not remember why. Now she was quite angry with Dr. Jennings because he told her she had to stay at the Main Hospital, and she wanted to go back over with me to the Annex.

"He also told me that I had to have more of those damned treatments!" she complained to me.

"I know, but you'll be back over at the Annex soon," I comforted her.

"Why is *he* deciding this? Where is that cute little red-faced doctor of ours? I'm going to ask him why he is allowing this," stormed Thelma. "You know what I feel like doing? I feel like throwing this ... right at his head."

Thelma indicated the ashtray that she was holding. It was a very heavy gold-colored glass ashtray of considerable size.

I laughed and said, "I don't blame you. Let him *know* you're really angry." I was only thinking to encourage Thelma to communicate more readily, with *one* of the doctors anyway. Scott had said that this had to happen for her to make progress. I also wondered why Dr. Jennings was taking on the role of the "punisher." Scott thought maybe this was part of a plan for getting Thelma to confide in Dr. Ashford. I wasn't sure that the doctors deserved that much credit for creative treatment.

My second visit to Thelma found her in the Elegant Ladies' former quarters at the back of Third South. Kaye had received a number of electroshocks and had been sent home. Helen's lawyer had come and obtained her release, with some legal threats to Helen's husband and her doctor. The executive suites had been empty until Thelma arrived. This place suited her. Thelma should have been surrounded with more class, even luxury. Her elegant demeanor and appearance were so congruent with these surroundings and so out of place in a mental hospital. Plus, she really valued her privacy. She didn't like to be around a lot of people and she disliked the nurses, who nevertheless checked on her regularly. Dr. Ashford had considered her social status, and he wanted her to be comfortable and not annoyed about her environment.

In her new quarters, Thelma and I visited about different things, but Thelma remained private about many of her thoughts. She did not want to discuss her parents, and she said she rarely thought about Gary, her lost love, anymore. He was in her history now. She supposed that she might never see him again, especially after having been in a mental hospital. It was too humiliating. He was so perfect. Once again her story impressed me as tragically romantic. Thelma's eyes were twinkly again, and she had a quiet smile that was not her slyly secretive one. She did mention that she still would like to break her ashtray over Dr. Jennings' head. She pointed out that she had brought it with her to her more graceful quarters. I looked at the yellow glass ashtray, raised one eyebrow, smilingly shook my head, and dismissed the conversation.

That night Martin brought me back to the hospital fairly early, so I went back to the Main Building to see Thelma again and found she was not in her room. A nurse from the Main Floor had let me up in the elevator and was unaware that Thelma had been moved. When I asked at the nursing station, I was told that Thelma was in another room, and could not have visitors. The whole floor seemed upset. The nurses were very tense and no one paused to acknowledge my visit.

As I looked about, I saw some significant changes. A card table had been set up between the elevator and the nursing station, at which a group of ladies were actually playing cards. I knew one of them, but the others all seemed to be new. Jeannie and Mickey were sitting in the day room and, when they saw me, motioned me over to talk. Jeannie announced that she would be going home soon. Mickey had only a few more treatments to go, and she would also be released before too long. Mickey was now insistent in wanting to exchange phone numbers with me, and she planned on visiting with me after we were both released. Mickey and I had discovered that we both lived in the same suburb on the northwest side of the city. I was not really interested in pursuing a friendship, but knew it would always remain a subject of curiosity if I were not to follow Mickey's recovery. If either of us didn't do well, it could also cause anxiety or stress. I needed to ponder a possible continued contact. Jeannie and Mickey had already planned a luncheon together, even though Jeannie lived some distance away. They had set a date and even designated a restaurant. I wondered if Mickey weren't ready to start class reunions, yearbooks, and the like.

I was smiling at this fantasy when Jeannie started speaking in a whisper. She told me that several of the patients had gotten angry with the nurses the night before. A nurse had ordered one of the new ladies to go to her room, and she refused. The nurse insisted and the patient became more irate, swore at her, and then threw a hot cup of coffee at the nurse, who tripped on the slippery floor and fell breaking her ankle. Now coffee was no longer given to them in the day room at night. Also, the nurses were not speaking much to the patients, as a number of the patients had laughed when the coffee was thrown and did not seem too distressed that a nurse had been injured.

Jeannie smiled. "We all thought that she deserved it. But no one said anything. I guess it will all blow over."

"What happen to Thelma?" I asked.

"I heard that they moved her to Third North. I don't know why. She had nothing to do with the coffee fiasco. She always stays to herself."

The lady at the card table, whom I knew, called over to me. "Laurel, come play my hand. I have to take a phone call."

This also seemed to be a change. Rarely had I observed anyone being given the privilege of having a phone call. I had felt very superior when I had my only call from Grandmother on that floor. I went over to the group and took the cards from the woman's hand.

"What are you playing?"

"Bridge" was the response.

I frowned a little, struggled with arranging the cards, and sat down. I didn't know how to play bridge. All that the Elegant Ladies had been able to get across to me was that you played your hand in sequence around the table, and that there was "bidding" to start. The bidding had been accomplished. All that I needed to do was to play the cards. I assumed that the highest card won. Everything pleased me, I looked around at my playmates. They had the usual "we-are-somewhat-here" look of Third Floor. If I didn't know maybe they wouldn't know. I played the hand and took most of the tricks some because I had the highest card and also because I wanted to see if anyone would object. Then I decided to take them each time, with any card, and see if anyone would notice. They didn't. I just smiled happily at each trick and repeated, "It's mine!" while gathering the other ladies' cards for myself. I was amused. Here they were going through the motions of a game, and not really knowing who was taking the cards, or why.

When the lady returned to play, I said, "You won. Good hand!" The group thanked me as I stood to leave. I felt someone standing at my shoulder, and turned to see Margaret.

"I thought you didn't play bridge," she said accusingly and without smiling.

"Well, I do now." I smiled. "And I probably will again. This is fun." Margaret seemed puzzled, and I didn't know how much Margaret had seen or if Margaret knew how to play the game herself.

I walked over to the elevator and asked if Margaret could let me downstairs.

"Maybe you should have to stay," Margaret answered tauntingly.

She must have observed the playing. I asked her about Thelma, and Margaret excused herself from the nursing staff to ride with me down the elevator and pick up something on the Main Floor. On the way down, Margaret told me that Thelma had become very agitated and had yelled at Dr. Jennings as he was doing the rounds.

"Then she picked up an extremely heavy ashtray and threw it at his head. Luckily it only grazed his scalp. She could have killed him! She was yelling and raving and they couldn't calm her. They had to put her back in the lockup rooms on Third North. Put her *out* with a hypo. I don't know how long she'll be there ... in the lockup."

I looked down at my feet. I was sure that I hadn't really told Thelma that it was a good idea to smack him, but I could see how my reaction to the idea might have seemed like approval, even encouragement, to Thelma. What I *had* wanted was for Thelma to express her anger *verbally*. Scott had said that this would be helpful. Nonetheless, I felt guilty. Margaret looked at me closely.

"What's the matter? Did you know she was that angry at the doctor?"

I shook my head. "I just knew that she was angry. I didn't know she would do anything." I didn't tell Margaret that she had threatened to do just that on several occasions.

The next day I tried again to visit Thelma. She was still in lockup. I played the strange bridge game again and won again, and none of the patients seemed the wiser. It was a very interesting, though odd game, a little different than Scrabble but easier to win. When the bizarre situation was beginning to overcome me, I left to go sort out my head at the Annex.

Chapter Thirty-Three
Last Day

The last day finally arrived. I had made numerous short walks back and forth down the street. On several occasions I, with several members of the Scrabble group, had walked the opposite direction from the Annex, away from the Main Hospital. One of the ladies had seen a vacant yard with an untended garden near the sidewalk about two blocks away. She had reported to the others that there were blueberries there for the taking. Three of us signed out on the roster sheet that our destination was "blueberry picking." This was the first walk where I had needed to go around a block. I was anxious but had two other ladies with me for support. I did tell them that I needed to take walks, but had not mentioned the anxiety factor. It had gone well.

Now, on this last day, I wanted to try an around-the-block excursion on my own. I walked up the street past the Main Hospital, and on to the next block. I planned to circle this block and to do it with relative ease. Anxiety built as I turned the corner and headed the next direction. I kept walking forward without looking back. I wanted to turn and see if I could see the corner where I had turned and determine if I were closer to that end of the block or the upcoming corner. But I picked up my steps and refused to look back.

At the next corner I began to worry intensely about being in unfamiliar territory and how terribly far away the hospital was. I began to walk more hurriedly and stumbled a little on the cracks in the irregular cement sidewalk. My breathing grew shallow and my arms and hands began to feel unreal. When my fingers began to have the old swelling feelings that I had almost forgotten, I started to breathe more quickly, and dizziness added to the symptoms that were trying to overcome me.

I hurried on and reached the middle of the block. This was the furthest point in my seemingly endless journey. From now on I would be on the return trip. I felt deep fear and my vision began to change on me. I could only see directly in front of me, and my sight was blurred. Peripheral vision was diminishing and a swirling, dark, cloudlike substance almost obliterated my remaining sight. I looked down at the cement walk and tried to focus on what was very near to me. The trees had started to feel threatening, and the sky was too bright. I held one hand in front of me and focused from it to the sidewalk and back, while still maintaining my rapid pace, with legs that almost felt nonexistent.

I tried to think about how Marilyn had probably gone this direction in her flight from the hospital. I was too jumpy and out of control to try to look for the daycare center that Marilyn had described. In thinking of Marilyn and how she wanted to be free, I built up my own terror about getting free. The panic hit!

I ran. My heart pounded frantically and my vision was minimal. I lost track of my arms and legs entirely; they had now gone numb. It was if my head, eyes, and heart were trying to get me back to safety, on their own, and my body was just not there with me; it had been blown off the face of the earth. I hardly remembered turning the last corner that allowed me to see Mountain View. I came panting up to the street crossing and stopped. There was my safety! I squinted my eyes to make sure that I had gotten back. I was not even in enough control to check the traffic before crossing onto my safe block.

I staggered up to the side entry near the OT shop and leaned on a railing near some steps. I heaved sighs of relief that I was still alive, then crumbled into a heap of stifled sobs. I remained only a few minutes fearing that a staff member would appear and report me, possibly causing me to lose my release. I wiped my eyes dry with the back of my hand and headed on around the corner to the front of the hospital and back to the Annex. Even though I was in familiar territory, I still had problems navigating my traumatized body on down the street and into the Annex. I hurried up the elevator, hoping that I would not see anyone before I could lie down, relax, and regain my composure.

In the elevator were a nurse and the young epileptic girl, who now had been here more than a week with no seizure. The girl looked pale and was obviously upset. The nurse was trying to explain to her that she needed to be more accepting, and not feel that her doctor was angry with her or that he liked his other patients better. She needed to understand that she must try to be more rational and grownup about things.

Next time he would see *her first* and the other patient second. He still liked her. He didn't have "favorites." The young girl kept repeating that she felt funny, and knew that a "fit" was coming on. I only wanted to get to my floor and get away by myself. What if I got stuck on the elevator while this spoiled teenager had a seizure? I was afraid I would have my own kind of "fit" of panic and someone would see me. I took several deep breaths and closed my eyes until the elevator stopped at my floor. I almost ran into my room, and dove onto my bed.

A short while later, I was called downstairs when Dr. Ashford came to see me for his last visit. I hurriedly put on lipstick and patted a cold washcloth on my face to hide any trace of tears and take away the redness. I managed to appear fairly calm for my doctor and was able to tell him, very evenly, that I had gotten "quite anxious"—even ran—when going for my longer walk. He did not seem very concerned. He only repeated that I needed to continue to extend my walks when I got home. He was very emphatic that I must make appointments with him and then *keep* them.

"Your husband *must* get you to my office!" he repeated several times.

I hoped that I could get there. It *was* downtown. It *was* on the sixth floor. I only smiled at him and agreed. He wished me good luck and said he would expect a call. I was dubious. My main goal was just to get out of here and get to my own home and perhaps have a hot bubble bath in my own tub at home and enjoy a very long cry.

I went back to my room and packed up my few belongings in the old worn suitcase that Martin and I had brought from home. I had several hours to wait, so I went downstairs to sit. I was a little sad, not because I was leaving Mountain View, but because I was so uncertain about my strengths to cope with what lay ahead. I sat on the ugly striped couch and picked up a magazine. Still worried, I pretended to read while listening to nearby conversations about the teenager having had a seizure and one about Arlene's husband coming to visit. I couldn't get interested. I looked up at the clock and noticed Scott coming in the front door. There was some relief! He smiled and walked over to me.

"Come for a walk with me!" he said cheerfully.

Another walk was the last thing that I wanted.

"A short one?" I pleaded. "I'm a little shook up."

"Sure," he agreed.

We started out the door as he remarked, "I was just over at the Main Building. Thelma is still in the locked area. Guess you won't see her before you leave. I wanted to come early ... before my shift ... and say goodbye. I hate goodbyes."

"So do I," I said quietly. I had almost hoped I wouldn't be having one with him. Outside Scott handed me a yellow rose that he had been holding out of my view.

"I picked it over in the garden. It's from the "impudent" bush. I remembered what you said about how it managed to be there ... almost perfect ... in spite of its location."

I smiled and nodded. I took it carefully because of its thorns and because its petals were so delicate. I touched an outer petal gently with my index finger. It was so smooth and soft. There was only one very tiny scar on the entire rose. A petal dimpled in at the center of its outer ridge. There was a small brown discoloration that was barely perceptible.

"It's beautiful," I said softly.

"It's sort of symbolic of our friendship," he said watching my face, "beautiful ... in spite of the surroundings ... like your 'impudent' bush."

I was afraid to look at him. My emotions were very tender today anyway. How could I deal with this sensitive moment? I moved my thumb along the rose stem until it found the thorn. I pressed the inside of my thumb onto the sharp point. The slight pain was enough to hold my focus and help me stop the tears that had begun to well up in my eyes.

"Thank you," I managed to say very slowly and evenly.

"Laurel, look at me. I want to tell you something. I want you to *really* listen."

Scott's voice was firm but gentle. I had to press harder against the thorn, but I looked at him.

"I want you to do whatever you need to do for *you*, for yourself. Do you understand?... Whatever, regardless of the support of others. You need to take care of *you!*"

248

I wondered if he meant that Martin was not supportive. He was, I wanted to say He *tried* to do everything that Ashford asked him to do. He just had trouble understanding. I looked away again ... and examined the rose.

"Laurel, look at me!" There was some impatience building in his voice. "I don't want you to come back. Hear me? Don't come back."

"Of course not," I said emphatically and smiled as I tried to lighten the conversation. "There is no way that I would let them bring me back here. They would have to put me in a straitjacket, use a hypo, and send the ambulance through the back alley entrance. *And* they would have to catch me first."

"I'm not joking, Laurel. I mean it. Do *not* let yourself get back here again. Do whatever Dr. Ashford tells you. Get some counseling. Don't let it build up again. I don't want to see you here ... *ever* again. "

He was almost pleading. I couldn't stand the intensity of my feelings and needed the physical pain I was self-inflicting from the thorn to stop myself from collapsing into a sobbing pile of anguish. I pushed even harder on the thorn's point, puncturing my thumb. As I flinched, Scott looked down and frowned.

"Be careful! What are you *doing*?"

I tried to act like it was an accident, but I knew Scott was hard to deceive. My tear-filled eyes were lowered as I stammered slowly, "I really appreciate how kind you have been, Scott. You have no idea ... how ... much it has meant to have somebody ... to ... to talk to ... and who ... treats you like a ... a ...real person."

"You *are* a real person! And you need to take care of that real person. Promise?"

I nodded as the tears started to spill over.

"I'll keep an eye on Thelma for you," he promised.

We had only gone to the end of the block, and we both had stopped and turned, without talking, to head back.

"Guess I'd better head over to the Main Building ... I go on duty soon."

"You're going to make a great psychiatrist. ... Please do keep an eye on Thelma. Thanks again for ... being my friend."

A few tears had found their way down my face, and Scott's usually brilliant and twinkling eyes had become cloudy and somber.

"Thanks for being *my* friend," he said almost in a whisper.

We reached the entry to the Annex and we both smiled at each other, a little embarrassed, and mumbled our goodbyes. I needed another trip to my room for another quick cry.

This time I stayed upstairs and ruminated over what my stay had garnered me. Panics were rare now. There had been only the one, recently, from my long walk in the neighborhood. I felt more calm, more relaxed. Was this from being away from my stress? Was it from the new medicine? Or was it a more positive, more lasting effect from the treatments? I wasn't so dizzy. I was able to think more clearly and less emotionally.

But I couldn't think clearly enough to know what had happened to me. Why had I become so frantic and unable to do ordinary things? Perhaps Dr. Ashford could help me with this. Scott seemed to feel that he could. But Martin ... I needed his help to get to my appointments with Dr. Ashford. Even then, I knew that it would be extremely difficult. And, too, I wasn't so sure that Martin wanted me to go. There was a question of money. Also, Martin wasn't very positive in his comments about my doctor. He didn't seem to like Dr. Ashford and the sentiments were returned.

If we were wealthy, I could come to the Annex, spend several weeks in consultation ... and go home again, as did several of the ladies that were so friendly with Arlene. However I could do it, I needed to get counseling or I would slip back to where I was at the beginning of the summer. Both Scott and Dr. Ashford had been emphatic about a follow-up. If only *Martin* would see how important it was.

This experience ... this month of extreme emotional trauma ... was it worth it? I knew that the things that I had witnessed would always be with me. It must be somewhat like stories I had read of returned war veterans and their memories of the horrors they had witnessed, less physically traumatic ... but emotionally as intense ... at least to *me*. I knew there was no way that I could share this ... and have it really understood. It was something that had to be lived, just as with a war. If you hadn't been there, the impact was not the same. Maybe that was what Mickey wanted my friendship for ... to be like a "war buddy" ... to share the memories and the pain. Yet, from observing all the others here at Mountain View, each patient's pain was different, each one's experience incomprehensible to any of the others, often not even noticed by the others. They were all too busy experiencing their own private war.

Actually, the war was not really the incarceration here ... it was the war within each of them. The hospitalization itself was minimal to the conflict that produced symptoms that drove them here. And saddest of all, to me, was the fact that I didn't know what that was for me. I did not know the cause of my distress. My focus and war had been the hospitalization and what I had seen about me ... the horrors of being in the mental wards. Was the *real* war an inner conflict that was more overwhelming yet? Underneath my new calm and resolve to improve my functioning was the *fear*. I was going home. Martin was coming for me and we would be going home. I was leaving with him ... and with the *fear*.

Very little was made of my departure. A few patients told me goodbye and went on back to the Scrabble Game. The nurse was polite and gave a few papers to Martin to sign. We walked undramatically to the car. The sun was going down. The air was remarkably cool for August. I could feel the faint tinge of early autumn. The locusts were singing. Martin didn't say much, and the ride was shorter than I remembered.

I was still alive, I marveled to myself. After all those units of insulin I was still alive ... I was alive though I was still scared.

Epilogue

I was not to receive therapy that the doctors advised. I grew worse and spent a year in an open hospital that was much like a halfway house. My father and stepmother kept my children. The hospital was funded by a Jewish charity and developed by two MDs. who were graduates of Menninger Clinic. It was an inspiration for a protocol that would be used later as a state facility for the emotionally disturbed. The concept was to provide the patients with constantly available personnel to help them talk about their problems. There was extensive use of psycho-therapy and appropriate medications. No shock treatment was given.

This more humane concept for treatment was of great help to a number of patients but then the facility was closed for lack of funds. The state hospital was formed shortly thereafter and was a model for mental health treatment throughout the country.

After the original hospital closed I, now much improved, moved into a room in the neighborhood where I lived by myself for a short time. I found a job as a receptionist at a motel on a busy nearby street. Within a few months I took my children and moved into a rental property that Martin and I had purchased in this suburb of the city. Martin and I were together on weekends as we tried to work out our differences.

After six months, I obtained a teaching job in the suburb where our rental house was located, and Martin moved in with his mother. Martin had received some counseling when I was at the "open hospital," but he discontinued his appointments, believing that all the problems were mine. As it turned out we both had severe adjustment problems stemming from our separate childhoods. I begged him to try to work out the problems *with* me. Instead he stopped paying for the water and electricity at the house. Since I was not yet receiving a full paycheck, the services were cut off. My therapist said I had no choice except for divorce because of the financial situation. I began divorce procedures. I kept the girls with me.

The separation was good for me although I spent many years trying to solve and mend my relationship with Martin. My therapist finally got me to see that Martin was destructive to me and that he had a lot of anger he could not deal with. I never remarried. Martin remarried but it only lasted five years. I finally realized that I didn't have to always try to please Martin.

I raised the girls alone with regular visits from their father although it is very difficult not to have any relationship with someone with whom you are co-parenting your children.

I continued teaching for many years and then went back to school myself, summers and evenings, to get my masters degree All this time I continued to paint and my art pieces were seen in important exhibits and galleries. After a number of years I obtained a sabbatical leave and went to work on my doctorate degree, teaching and working for the university. I went back to my school district for a year and then took a year leave of absence to finish my Ph.D. I returned to teaching and continued to teach for thirty more years.

My children seemed to adjust fairly well. My oldest daughter traveled extensively, receiving instruction in meditation in India and Switzerland. She married and is raising two children. My younger daughter studied theatre at prestigious schools in New York and London. She worked with an acting group off-Broadway for a number of years and then started her own acting company in a small town in the same state with me. She is now also a teacher.

I continued to have problems with anxiety and have spent much of my life in recurrent therapy and have continued to deal with varying degrees of agoraphobia. Nevertheless, I feel that I have been successful as a mother, artist, and teacher, all of which have given me great joy and satisfaction.